The Blasphemies
of Thomas Aikenhead

The Blasphemies of Thomas Aikenhead

Boundaries of Belief on the Eve of the Enlightenment

Michael F. Graham

EDINBURGH
University Press

For my mentors:
H. C. E. Midelfort
and the late Martin J. Havran

© Michael F. Graham, 2008, 2013

First published in hardback in 2008 by
Edinburgh University Press Ltd
22 George Square, Edinburgh EH8 9LF
www.euppublishing.com

This paperback edition 2013

Typeset in Sabon by
Carnegie Book Production, Lancaster

A CIP record for this book is available from the British Library

ISBN 978 0 7486 3426 2 (hardback)
ISBN 978 0 7486 8517 2 (paperback)
ISBN 978 0 7486 3427 9 (webready PDF)
ISBN 978 0 7486 8518 9 (epub)

The right of Michael F. Graham to be
identified as author of this work
has been asserted in accordance with
the Copyright, Designs and Patents Act 1988.

Contents

Abbreviations	vii
A Note on the Text	viii
Acknowledgements	ix
Introduction	1
1 Edinburgh and Scotland in the 1690s	10
1.1 The Capital City	10
1.2 The Legacy of the Covenants	17
1.3 Edinburgh and the Changes of 1688–90	25
2 The Politics of Blasphemy	33
2.1 'Profaneness' and Blasphemy	35
2.2 The Parliament of 1695	37
2.3 Political Changes and the General Assembly of 1695–6	43
3 'So unnaturall a seasone': The Dreadful Year 1696	53
3.1 Famine, the French, Fear and Fire	54
3.2 Edinburgh's Deism Scare	59
3.3 Dangerous Books and the War of Ideas	65
3.4 The Accusation of Thomas Aikenhead	72
4 The Making of a Blasphemer	79
4.1 Spiritual Crises and the Calvinist Mind	79
4.2 Who was Thomas Aikenhead?	83
4.3 Edinburgh's Town College and the Education of Thomas Aikenhead	87
4.4 The Attack by Mungo Craig	92
5 Trial and Execution	100
5.1 The Officials and the Prosecution	100
5.2 The Defence	104
5.3 The Witnesses	107
5.4 The Jury and the Verdict	111
5.5 Seeking Mercy	113
5.6 Last Words	117
5.7 Death and Remorse	121

6 The Aftermath: Public Opinion in Scotland and England	126
6.1 The Defence of Mungo Craig	126
6.2 More Blasphemy and the Revival of the Witch-Hunt	128
6.3 'A Noise' in England	134
6.4 The English Blasphemy Act	143
6.5 Aikenhead Remembered	147
Conclusion	155
Bibliography of Works Cited	163
Index	175

Abbreviations

APS	*Acts of the Parliaments of Scotland, 1124–1707*, 12 vols (London: HMSO, 1814–75)
BL	British Library, London
ECA	Edinburgh City Archives
EUL	Edinburgh University Library
Fasti	Hew Scott (ed.), *Fasti Ecclesiae Scoticanae*, 9 vols (Edinburgh: Oliver & Boyd, 1915–51)
HMC	Historical Manuscripts Commission
Home Diary	Helen Kelsall and Keith Kelsall (eds), *An Album of Scottish Families 1694–96, Being the First Installment of George Home's Diary* (Aberdeen: Aberdeen University Press, 1990)
MS	Manuscript
NAS	National Archives of Scotland, Register House, Edinburgh (main location)
NLS	National Library of Scotland, Edinburgh
NRH	New Register House
OPR	Old Parish Records
SHS	Scottish History Society
State Trials	William Cobbett and T. B. Howell (eds), *A Complete Collection of State Trials*, 34 vols (London: Hansard, 1809–26)
WRH	West Register House (auxiliary location of the NAS, Edinburgh)

A Note on the Text

In the 1690s Scotland and England had not yet adopted the Gregorian Calendar, which had been introduced in Catholic Europe in 1582, but was slow to win acceptance in Protestant countries and in Russia. As a result, dates in Britain were eleven days off those of most of continental Europe. But since the bulk of the action in this book took place in Britain, I have given dates according to the Julian Calendar, which still prevailed there, and would for another half-century. Nevertheless I have reckoned all years as beginning on 1 January, an innovation that was still not universal, but was coming to be the norm. On the rare occasions when money enters into this story, readers might find it helpful to know that one pound sterling was worth twelve pounds Scots. Because I like to let the past speak for itself, I have retained original spelling, capitalisation and italics when quoting from original sources, but have inserted bracketed material here and there to help the reader make sense of what is being quoted. While scholars often do not list publishers of books from the hand-press era (up to 1800) I have chosen to do so in the notes and bibliography in cases where the publisher could be determined, sacrificing consistency on the altar of increased information. For example, one of the jurors who decided Thomas Aikenhead's fate was himself a publisher and bookseller; readers might want to keep track of such details.

Acknowledgements

Despite the sad fate of its main protagonist, the research and writing of this book have been a great pleasure; perhaps the time it took to produce it can be taken as a measure of how much the author was enjoying himself. Among the things that made it so enjoyable were the kind assistance and sociability of many colleagues, and the helpful cooperation and generosity of several institutions. The book grew out of a paper delivered at the Sixteenth Century Studies Conference a decade ago, in which I sought to suggest distinctions between 'sin' and 'crime' in early modern Scotland. The Aikenhead case loomed large in that because of the severe response of the Scottish state to his 'sin'. The commentator for that panel was Benjamin Kaplan, and his perceptive comments steered me off on the tangent that became this book. The project received generous financial support from the Sally A. Miller Humanities Center and the Faculty Research Committee at the University of Akron, as well as the Reformation Studies Institute at the University of St Andrews, where I was fortunate to spend the first half of 2003 as the James Cameron Faculty Fellow. I would like to extend particular thanks to Professor Andrew Pettegree, who was then director of the institute, and his wife, Jane, for their help and hospitality in St Andrews. The community of scholars at St Andrews is a lively and supportive group, and I should also thank Dr Bridget Heal, Andrew's successor as institute director, Dr Roger Mason of the Scottish History Department there, and Robert Crawford of the School of English, who not only took an interest in my project, but has given kind permission to use a wee bit of his poem 'Burns Ayont Auld Reekie' as an epigraph. Ted Cowan invited me to Glasgow to give a talk in May 2003, and I am grateful to him and members of the Scottish History Department at the University of Glasgow, aided and abetted by Alexander Broadie, for their helpful comments on part of what was to become Chapter 6 of this book. Michael Lynch welcomed me into the circle of Scottish historians in Edinburgh when I was a complete neophyte at the beginning of the 1990s, and he was generous with his time in discussing this project also, as were his colleagues Julian Goodare and Jenny Wormald. Among the select group that pursues the Scottish past from the New World, Elizabeth Ewan, David

Mullan and Daniel Szechi have my gratitude for their assistance, although the last of them has crossed over to the Old World again.

Here in Akron, my colleagues Michael Levin and Constance Bouchard carefully read over my manuscript and in the process made it better, even if I have been stubborn in not taking all their advice. I am also grateful to Walter Hixson, interim chair of the Department of History, who gave me a reduced teaching load in the autumn of 2007 to enable me to complete the writing of this book. Wade Wilcox, administrative assistant, and Nicolette Silvestro, student assistant, also provided technical help at critical times. I was fortunate to spend much of the summer of 2007 in Oxford and Antwerp in the company of the 'Reformation of the Book, 1450–1700' seminar, supported by the National Endowment for the Humanities and directed by John King and James Bracken of the Ohio State University. I thank them and all the 'seminarians' for the synergy produced by our various projects together, all centred on the first three centuries of print, which certainly improved this book. Special additional thanks are due to the Ohio State University Libraries and James Bracken, in his capacity as their assistant director, for supplying me with a reproduction of the drawing of the tollbooth, which comes out of the library collection. It is used in this book with their kind permission, as well as the permission of the *Book of the Old Edinburgh Club*, in which it originally appeared. The maps that appear in the introduction and Chapter 1 were expertly prepared by Ann Donkin, archaeogeophysical surveyor in the Department of Classical Studies, Anthropology and Archaeology at the University of Akron.

Historians could not reconstruct the past without the help of the archivists and librarians who are its keepers. In Edinburgh, the staffs of the National Archives of Scotland, the National Library of Scotland, the Edinburgh University Library and the Edinburgh City Archives were unfailingly helpful, providing access and their expert knowledge to scholars (such as this one) free of charge, thus exemplifying a fundamental value of open enquiry that is under attack in some quarters. I owe similar thanks to the staff of the British Library in London. The librarians at the Bodleian Library in Oxford were also patient and helpful, and I could not have got much done on this project when in Ohio were it not for the staff of Bierce Library at the University of Akron, and the OhioLink network, for which all researchers in the state should be grateful.

I also thank Esmé Watson and John Watson, my editors at Edinburgh University Press, for their interest in taking on this book, and for suffering patiently its author's questions and concerns. It seemed appropriate to me that Aikenhead's story be told through the press that graces the university he attended. But nobody bears the burdens of authorship as much as those who live with authors, so my deepest thanks go to Elizabeth Armstrong, who not only shares my life but is an excellent editor, and has cleared up many ambiguities and infelicities in the text of this book. Our children David, Katharine and Sean have been hearing about Thomas Aikenhead for a long time. Thanks to him, they got to go to school in Scotland for a term; I hope this book will remind them of our collective adventures, and repay their patience with an occasionally distracted father.

Introduction

>Daft rammishes an gowks
>Witter oan an oan as if thi nemm wiz Tam
>Aikenheid, no Tam o Shantir, as if aw
>Wir ramskerie leid wiz jist ane dour stane baa.
>Muck-wreistlin Scoatlaun, durt's yir histoarie,
>Naishunlet aye oabsessed wi kickin baas –
>Yi scum yir makars oar cute-gralloch thaim – Ach!
>
>(Robert Crawford, 'Burns Ayont Auld Reekie'[1])

Let us start with a hanging, to focus the mind. Early in the afternoon of Friday, 8 January 1697, Thomas Aikenhead, a twenty-year-old sometime student at the town college (now University) of Edinburgh, was taken out of the condemned prisoners' cell in Edinburgh's tolbooth to be hanged for blasphemy, having been convicted of that crime about two weeks earlier. Coming out of the tolbooth, he paused near the mercat cross and handed over two documents (possibly reading from them) – one an intellectual autobiography that was both a justification for his religious scepticism and an expression of regret, and the other a covering letter addressed to his 'friends', pleading his true remorse. He then asked the two ministers attending him, James Webster of the Tolbooth parish, where Aikenhead had offered repentance the previous Sunday, and George Meldrum of the Tron parish, where he had probably lived before taking up residence in the tolbooth, to pray for him, which they did, publicly. Following that, Aikenhead offered prayers himself, specifically invoking the Trinity, one of the aspects of Christian doctrine that he had been accused of ridiculing. Then, clutching a Bible, Aikenhead began what must have been a chilly and terrifying walk to the scaffold. At least it was mostly downhill.

A public execution such as this one was in large measure a religious ritual – hence the prayers, the symbolic use of the Bible and the plentiful opportunities for the condemned to warn others to avoid his miserable fate and assure them that he accepted the justice of what was about to happen. But the act itself was the result of a process controlled by the state, and its agents were present in force. Aikenhead was flanked by two columns of troops, which suggests that the authorities feared some kind of disturbance. From the mercat cross they filed down the High Street, past the Tron Kirk, in front of which Aikenhead had uttered one of his alleged blasphemies on a cool evening the previous August. After passing through the Netherbow Port, which led into the top of the Canongate (a neighbourhood recently devastated by a severe fire), they turned left, and headed down Leith Wynd, passing between Trinity Hospital and Kirk on the left, and the Correction House and the Paul's Work orphanage on the right, with Calton Hill looming behind. Past the hill they turned to the north-east, and marched down the road towards the port of Leith, roughly following the Leith Walk of today. At this point they would have left the built-up area of Edinburgh. At the formal boundary between Edinburgh and Leith (not terribly significant any more, since Edinburgh had gained jurisdiction over Leith more than a hundred years earlier), they stopped and turned left. Here was the Gallowlee, the execution site reserved for those guilty of the most heinous crimes. For common thieves, murderers and even many witches, the Grassmarket below Edinburgh Castle would do. But this execution was far from typical. On the contrary, it was a smokeless *auto-de-fé* aimed at placating an obviously angry God, invoking new laws against blasphemy that would never be used with such force again. At the Gallowlee, still holding the Bible, Aikenhead seemed 'surprised & terrified for death', according to the devout Sir John Clerk of Penicuik, an eyewitness who certainly approved of the proceedings. Aikenhead again confessed his crimes and sang part of the Fifty-First Psalm:

> Have mercy on me, O God, according to thy steadfast love;
> according to thy abundant mercy blot out my transgressions.
> Wash me thoroughly from my iniquity, and cleanse me from my
>   sin!
> For I know my transgressions and my sin is ever before me.
> Against thee, thee only have I sinned, and done that which is evil
>   in thy sight,
> so that thou art justified in thy sentence and blameless in thy
>   judgment ...

The doomed man then prayed some more 'but w[i]t[h] great disorder (as is said) of speech', giving 'but little evidence of his sincere repentance', Clerk of Penicuik reported. A hood was placed upon him, and he was hanged. Those hanged rarely died instantly, so onlookers probably would

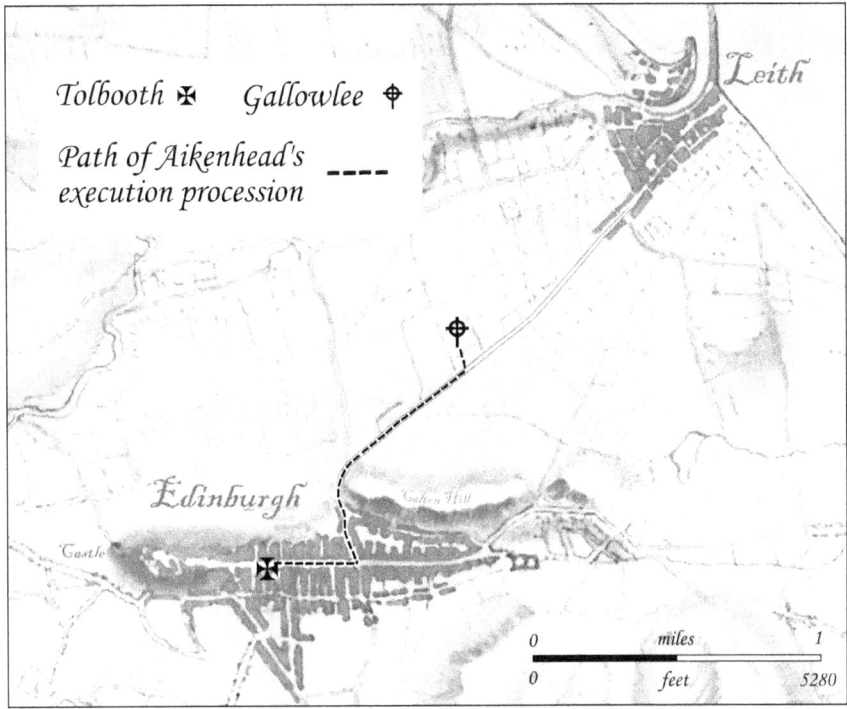

Figure I.1 Thomas Aikenhead's final journey.
(Map prepared by Ann Donkin.)

have watched him shudder for several minutes as he twisted in the chilly January breeze and gathering darkness, fists clenched, nose and mouth oozing bloody mucus, gradually suffocating. The moment of death was often marked by the appearance of stains as the victim's bladder and bowels released their contents.[2] Later, Aikenhead's corpse was buried at the foot of the gallows.

Clerk of Penicuik, like many of those present, clearly got the message intended by the authorities. Indeed, he was one of them, having represented the shire of Edinburgh at the parliament that had passed a new blasphemy statute in 1695.[3] As he wrote in his diary: 'ye sanctified use of this be given to me and all p[ersons] for [Christ's] sake O L[ord] my heart atheism & unbeliefe be rooted out O L[ord] in my soul for thy [Christ's] sake.' He searched for signs of Aikenhead's true repentance, because such remorse was an essential element in execution as a public performance. Some onlookers thought Aikenhead was truly penitent, while others did not, and this would be an ongoing subject of debate in the aftermath.[4] There was a third group that did not believe the hanging should have taken place at all, whether or not the victim was remorseful; this group is hardest to identify at the hanging itself, and had good reasons to keep silent. But its presence is suggested by the large guard and the report of one contemporary that Aikenhead had received encouragement from people who gathered under his cell window in the tolbooth at night.[5] Aikenhead's execution was the final scene in a drama that had been building for more than a year, and would be a defining moment in the providential story of Scotland as God's Covenanted Kingdom. It would create embarrassment abroad and a mixture of righteous justification and soul-searching at home. Not surprisingly, historians have been more unanimous in their verdict.

Thomas Babington Macaulay probably echoed the feelings of many of his nineteenth-century Anglo-American contemporaries when he condemned the execution as a vestige of Scottish superstition and intolerance in his *History of England* (1849–55): 'the preachers who were the boy's murderers crowded round him at the gallows, and, while he was struggling in the last agony, insulted Heaven with prayers more blasphemous than anything he ever uttered.'[6] More recent scholars, while displaying less anti-clerical fervour and less poetic licence, have nevertheless placed blame solely on the shoulders of the ministers, interpreting the Aikenhead case as a sign of a Presbyterian Kirk determined to assert its coercive authority.[7] The case receives passing mention in surveys of Scottish history or British heterodoxy during the period, sometimes with mistakes as to the year, location or method of execution, or the victim's name.[8] Aikenhead has even inspired poetry and a forgotten historical novel.[9] But it took until 1992 for any historian in the modern era to offer a fresh analysis of the evidence in the case. Michael Hunter, in an essay titled ' "Aikenhead the Atheist": The Context and Consequences of Articulate Irreligion in the Late Seventeenth Century', cited some previously unknown evidence, particularly a long letter from the minister Robert Wylie, to offer an intellectual history of Aikenhead's crimes, seeing him as a serious (if unrefined) critic of conventional Christianity who could have gathered some of his ideas from books in circulation at the time, cobbling them together into his own peculiarly heterodox cosmology.[10]

Unfortunately, Hunter, concerned more with the history of ideas than social and political factors, did not really consider the context of the case: the bustling capital of a kingdom in growing economic and political crisis, governed by a regime struggling to keep alive a revolutionary legacy in the face of conflicting currents, many of them coming from England, its southern neighbour and more powerful partner in the union of crowns. A government that bases its authority on a particular ideology and that feels itself threatened will often prosecute an individual dissident to demonstrate that it still holds power (witness the death sentence for blasphemy imposed in 2002 by Iranian judges against the historian Hashem Aghajari, for his suggestion that the Qur'ān is subject to modern interpretation, a sentence later commuted to a prison term after widespread protests). This is not to deny Macaulay's claim that the ministers were critical players in this story, or Hunter's assertion of the importance of Aikenhead's ideas and their genealogy. But neither Macaulay nor Hunter really explained why Scotland's magistrates, who alone held the power to impose physical punishment, chose to use it in such a dramatic way. This question is further highlighted by the fact that not only was Thomas Aikenhead the last person executed in Britain for the crime of blasphemy; he was probably the first so treated in Scotland, a kingdom that hardly had a reputation for toleration. Two recent studies of the decline of witch-hunting also make passing reference to Aikenhead's case, exploring the conjunction, first noted among historians by Macaulay, between it and one of the last revivals of the Scottish witch-hunt; like the witches of Renfrewshire, Aikenhead was an 'enemy of God', albeit of a less traditional type.[11]

The Aikenhead case seems ripe for the microhistorical approach pioneered by Natalie Zemon Davis and Carlo Ginzburg, but thus far little used in the field of Scottish history.[12] As with the peasant imposter Arnauld du Tilh and the eclectically-minded miller Mennochio, Aikenhead's travails left a paper trail in the courts, and the trial records, many of which were published early in the nineteenth century, provide the central documentation for the story.[13] But, while the trial (and execution) may comprise the main drama here, they make little sense if divorced from their historical context. A full exploration of that context is critical for any microhistorical study of Thomas Aikenhead. It will help us comprehend what to modern eyes seems incomprehensible – the imposition of capital punishment for a crime of belief at the end of the era of confessionalisation, even after the alleged British watershed of 1688–9, and on the eve of the Enlightenment – and in so doing will help to elucidate the historical relationship between 'sin' and 'crime'. Certainly, witches were still occasionally burned at the stake in late seventeenth-century Scotland, and would be, in sporadic revivals of the witch-hunt, for three more decades.[14] But witchcraft accusations by this time were always founded on *maleficia* – alleged evil deeds towards others. Aikenhead's crime, in contrast, had no human victim. Further, while denunciations of religious dissent, coupled with threats of severe punishments for dissenters, had been standard Scottish (and indeed west European) fare for centuries, few such threats had actually been carried out in Scotland. In fact, the 136 years since the Reformation Parliament of 1560, for all their politico-religious upheaval, had been remarkably free of martyrs for belief (or unbelief). Many had died for causes related to religion, particularly in the period of highly politicised covenants after 1638, but these victims had found themselves on the wrong side of political struggles, and were more likely to meet their ends on the battlefield than the scaffold. There was no such obviously political element in Aikenhead's demise.

Then why did the authorities choose to make such a dramatic example out of one relatively obscure student? There is no single answer to this question, but a series of historical convergences made a victim like Aikenhead seem almost necessary in 1696–7. This study will piece those convergences together, reconstructing the atmosphere of crisis and uncertainty in which critical decisions were made. But almost as significant as the case itself was its afterlife. It was covered in London newspapers and debated – both inside and outside Scottish and English political and clerical circles – in its aftermath, casting a shadow into the early decades of the eighteenth century. Thus it provides an Anglo-Scottish chapter in the early history of 'public opinion' as well. And, finally, we must not forget that the case arose in a city that would become one of the leading centres of the Enlightenment. Many of the statements allegedly uttered by Aikenhead – about the origins of Scripture, the historicity of figures like Moses and Jesus, and the logical consistency of the idea of the Trinity – while not exactly mainstream by 1750, would not at that later date have earned a Scottish critic anything worse than public ridicule or the denial of professional advancement. But the Aikenhead case was born in the initial collision between Covenanted Presbyterianism and the countercurrents of deism, biblical criticism and religious scepticism. As the historian of philosophy Noel Malcolm has recently put it: 'Among the faithless, Aikenhead's joke about "Ezra's fables" had become, so to speak, an article of faith' by 1750. David Hume got to die in his bed, while his devout friends, such as the Edinburgh minister Hugh Blair, worried about his eternal fate.[15] Thomas Aikenhead had a much less comfortable send-off.

NOTES

1. Robert Crawford and W. N. Herbert, *Sharawaggi: Poems in Scots* (Edinburgh: Polygon, 1990), p. 50.
2. This account of Aikenhead's execution is based on National Archives of Scotland (hereafter NAS) MS GD18/2092/1, Sir John Clerk of Penicuik's Spiritual Journal, entry for 8 January 1697; *The Post Man*, 265 (16 January 1697); Robert Paul (ed.), 'The Diary of George Turnbull, Minister of Alloa and Tyningham, 1657–1704', *Scottish History Society Miscellany*, 1 (Edinburgh: Scottish History Society, 1893), pp. 295–445,

at p. 370. I am grateful to Professor Daniel Szechi for pointing me in the direction of Clerk's spiritual journal. Geographical details come from *The Early Views and Maps of Edinburgh, 1544–1852* (Edinburgh: Royal Scottish Geographical Society, 1919), maps 1 and 2; Helen Dingwall, *Late Seventeenth-Century Edinburgh: A Demographic Study* (Aldershot: Scholar, 1994), pp. 14–15. Aikenhead's final two letters are in William Cobbett and T. B. Howell (eds), *A Complete Collection of State Trials*, 34 vols (London: Hansard, 1809–26) (hereafter *State Trials*), xiii, pp. 930–4. This translation of the first two stanzas of the psalm comes from *The New Oxford Annotated Bible* (New York: Oxford University Press, 1973), p. 694. For the physiology of hanging, see V. A. C. Gatrell, *The Hanging Tree: Execution and the English People, 1770–1868* (Oxford: Oxford University Press, 1994), pp. 45–50.
3. *Acts of the Parliaments of Scotland, 1124–1707*, 12 vols (hereafter *APS*) (London: HMSO, 1814–75), ix, p. 347.
4. Claiming he was truly repentant: NAS MS GD 406/1/4204 (David Crawford to the Earl of Arran, 9 January 1697); NLS MS Wodrow Quarto XXX, fos 244r–245r (Alexander Findlater to Robert Wylie, 8 January 1697); Paul (ed.), 'Diary of George Turnbull', p. 370; *The Post Boy*, 266 (16 January 1697); *The Flying Post*, 267 (26 January 1697); William Lorimer, *Two Discourses: The One Setting forth The True and only way of Attaining Salvation. The Other shewing why and How all ought to Reverence Jesus Christ, the Son of God and Saviour of Men* (London: John Lawrence, 1713), p. vi. Claiming he was not: Mungo Craig, *A Lye Is No Scandal, Or a Vindication of Mr Mungo Craig from a Ridiculous Calumny Cast Upon Him by T. A. Who was Executed for Apostacy at Edinburgh, the 8 of January, 1697* (Edinburgh[?], 1697), p. 9; Thomas Halyburton, *Natural Religion Insufficient and Reveal'd Necessary to Man's Happiness In His Present State* (Edinburgh: Heirs of Andrew Anderson, 1714), p. 123.
5. Lorimer, *Two Discourses*, p. v.
6. Thomas Babington Macaulay, *The History of England from the Accession of James II*, 3 vols [1849–55] (London: J. M. Dent, 1905), iii, p. 510.
7. James Cameron, 'Theological Controversy: A Factor in the Origins of the Scottish Enlightenment', in R. H. Campbell and Andrew S. Skinner (eds), *The Origins and Nature of the Scottish Enlightenment* (Edinburgh: John Donald, 1982), pp. 116–30, at p. 117; James Cameron, 'Scottish Calvinism and the Principle of Intolerance', in B. A. Gerrish and Robert Benedetto (eds), *Reformatio Perennis* (Pittsburgh: Pickwick Press, 1981), pp. 113–28, at pp. 123–5; Andrew Drummond and James Bulloch, *The Scottish Church 1688–1843: The Age of the Moderates* (Edinburgh: Saint Andrew Press, 1973), pp. 13–15; George Davie, *The Scottish Enlightenment* (London: Historical Association, 1981), pp. 9–10; Arthur

Herman, *The Scottish Enlightenment: The Scots' Invention of the Modern World* (London: Fourth Estate, 2002), p. 7; Alexander Broadie, *The Scottish Enlightenment* (Edinburgh: Birlinn, 2001), pp. 33–4; Richard Sher, *Church and University in the Scottish Enlightenment* (Princeton: Princeton University Press, 1985), p. 152.

8. Rosalind Mitchison, *Lordship to Patronage: Scotland, 1603–1745* (Edinburgh: Edinburgh University Press, 1990), p. 152; William Ferguson, *Scotland: 1689 to the Present* (Edinburgh: Oliver & Boyd, 1968), p. 114; Leonard Levy, *Blasphemy: Verbal Offense against the Sacred from Moses to Salman Rushdie* (New York: Knopf, 1993), pp. 232–3; Robert E. Sullivan, *John Toland and the Deist Controversy* (Cambridge, MA: Harvard University Press, 1982), pp. 10–11, 44, where Aikenhead is said to have been 'an adolescent medical student' who was burned at the stake; Roger Lund, 'Irony as Subversion: Thomas Woolston and the Crime of Wit', in Roger Lund (ed.), *The Margins of Orthodoxy: Heterodox Writing and Cultural Response, 1660–1750* (Cambridge: Cambridge University Press, 1995), pp. 170–94, at pp. 174–5, where the year of the execution is given as 1698; Keith Brown, *Kingdom or Province? Scotland and the Regal Union, 1603–1715* (London: Macmillan, 1992), pp. 73–4, where it is moved back to 1696; David Allan, *Scotland in the Eighteenth Century: Union and Enlightenment* (Harlow: Longman, 2002), p. 47, where the location is given as the Grassmarket and the year as 1696; Neil Davidson, *Discovering the Scottish Revolution, 1692–1746* (London: Pluto Press, 2003), pp. 102–3, where Thomas Aikenhead is called Alexander Aitkenhead; David Nash, *Blasphemy in the Christian World: A History* (Oxford: Oxford University Press, 2007), p. 164, where the execution is dated 1698.

9. Crawford and Herbert, 'Burns Ayont Auld Reekie', in *Sharawaggi*, pp. 48–55, at pp. 50–1; Henry Bogle, *Who Murdered Aikenhead?* (Detroit: Harlo, 1973).

10. Michael Hunter, '"Aikenhead the Atheist": The Context and Consequences of Articulate Irreligion in the Late Seventeenth Century', in Michael Hunter and David Wootton (eds), *Atheism from the Reformation to the Enlightenment* (Oxford: Clarendon Press, 1992), pp. 221–54, later reprinted in Michael Hunter, *Science and the Shape of Orthodoxy: Intellectual Change in Late Seventeenth-Century Britain* (Woodbridge and Rochester, NY: Boydell, 1995), pp. 308–32, which will be the version cited in this study.

11. Ian Bostridge, *Witchcraft and its Transformations, c. 1650–c. 1750* (Oxford: Clarendon Press, 1997), pp. 24–6; Michael Wasser, 'The Western Witch-Hunt of 1697–1700: The Last Major Witch-Hunt in Scotland', in Julian Goodare (ed.), *The Scottish Witch-Hunt in Context* (Manchester: Manchester University Press, 2002), pp. 146–65, at p. 151.

12. Natalie Zemon Davis, *The Return of Martin Guerre* (Cambridge, MA:

Harvard University Press, 1983); Carlo Ginzburg, *The Cheese and the Worms* (Baltimore: Johns Hopkins University Press, 1979).
13. The published trial records are in *State Trials*, xiii, pp. 917–40. I have augmented these with the High Court of Judiciary's process papers on the case, which are NAS MS JC26/78/1/1–14. Hunter also makes the comparison between Aikenhead and the Mennochio case, examined by Ginzburg. See Hunter, 'Aikenhead the Atheist', p. 309.
14. The last Scottish execution for witchcraft, which took place under irregular judicial procedures, occurred in 1737. See Bostridge, *Witchcraft*, p. 36.
15. Noel Malcolm, *Aspects of Hobbes* (Oxford: Clarendon Press, 2002), pp. 383–6; Broadie, *Scottish Enlightenment*, pp. 139–40, 149–50; Sher, *Church and University*, pp. 65–6.

1

Edinburgh and Scotland in the 1690s

1.1 THE CAPITAL CITY

Thomas Aikenhead's trial and execution took place in a city that, while vastly changed since then, still retains some elements that Aikenhead and his contemporaries would recognise, thanks to the combination of Edinburgh's dramatic topography and the preservation of several buildings in the central city that were standing during Aikenhead's lifetime. The Old Town of today, which then comprised the bulk of the city, still straddles the ridge that rises from Holyrood Palace, at the foot of its eastern end, to Edinburgh Castle, perched on an ancient lava flow, which surveys the surrounding landscape from its commanding position at the western end. The tolbooth where Aikenhead spent his last days – memorialised by Sir Walter Scott as the 'Heart of Midlothian' – is gone, its location marked for posterity in the paving stones of Parliament Square. But the High Kirk of St Giles still stands adjacent, a third of the way down the High Street from castle to palace. A bit further down is the Tron Kirk, built in the seventeenth century to feed the increased spiritual needs of a growing population, but which has recently served growing swarms of tourists in various guises, including that of the Old Town Information Centre. The Netherbow, through which Aikenhead made his final formal departure from his native burgh, is gone, but nearby is a house old enough to have provided short-term lodgings for John Knox, who preached in St Giles' more than a century before Aikenhead's birth.[1]

North of today's Old Town one finds the greenery of the Princes Street Gardens and then, once past the ever-changing retail façades of Princes Street itself, the quiet order of Edinburgh's New Town, developed in the eighteenth century as a residential haven removed from the squalor of the medieval burgh and its narrow alleys and closes. None of this sophisticated architectural urbanity existed in the 1690s. Today's gardens were then a public sewer – the Nor' Loch, which still limited the burgh's northward expansion – and today's new town was still a collection of farms and fields. To the north-east, on the Firth of Forth and down a long fertile hill, was (and still is) the port of Leith, over which Edinburgh held jurisdiction, and which provided trading connections to the eastern seaboards of Scotland and England as well as northern Europe.[2] What growth Edinburgh was then experiencing was to the south; Greyfriars Kirk had been built in the early seventeenth century, and the 'town college' (now University) of Edinburgh had been founded in 1583 to give young men from the burgh and surrounding areas an alternative to the older universities of St Andrews, Glasgow and Aberdeen.

Visitors were impressed with Edinburgh's High Street. The Englishman Thomas Morer described it in 1702 as 'wide and well paved … it swells in the middle, the kennels [gutters] being made on *each side*, so that 'tis commonly very clean'. He found many new buildings 'made of stone, with good windows modishly framed and Glazed, and so lofty that *Five* or *Six* Stories is an ordinary height; and one Row of Buildings there is near the *Parliament-close* with no less than *Fourteen*. The reason of it is, their scantiness of room …'[3] Older buildings were often made of timber, but the burgh council began encouraging the conversion of the town to the stone that so characterises it today in 1674, when, reacting to a serious fire, it began offering a seventeen-year tax abatement for any stone-fronted building constructed in place of a wooden one. Robert Mylne, developer and master mason to the Scottish Crown, then began buying decrepit properties, tearing them down and building new stone structures around central courtyards. He built Mylne's Square, opposite the Tron Kirk, in the 1680s, and Mylne's Court, on the north side of the Lawnmarket in the higher reaches of the High Street, around 1690. The amenities of the town centre were further improved by the provision of water, pumped in from the nearby village of Colinton to a series of fountains in the High Street, beginning in 1681.[4]

But in the alleys, closes and wynds that ran north and south, down from the central spine of the High Street, the picture was not so pretty. Describing the area between the High Street and the Cowgate (which ran parallel to the south, but at a significantly lower elevation, eventually opening into the Grassmarket under the south-eastern flank of the castle), Morer wrote of 'many *little lanes* of communication, but very steepy and troublesome, and withal so nasty (for want of *Bog-Houses*, which they very rarely have) that *Edinburgh* is by some liken'd to an *Ivory Comb*, whose Teeth *on both sides* are very foul, though the space between them is clean and sightly'.[5] A bit further south was the college, 'consisting of one small Quadrangle, and some other Lodgings, without Uniformity or

Order'. Morer praised the college library, however: 'a large and convenient Room made about 60 years ago for that purpose. The roof is covered with Lead, and is neatly kept within; well furnish'd with Books.'[6] Gilbert Rule, the college's principal, told him he had hopes for the college becoming a university, and that the institution 'wants only peace and Quietness to perfect the Design'.[7] But, given the growth Edinburgh was experiencing, peace and quietness were in short supply.

Greater Edinburgh's population in the 1690s was between 40,000 and 47,000, making it the second-largest city in Britain; only London was larger. It had nearly quadrupled in size in the previous century and a half. All but about 10,000 of its residents were living in the 'inner ring' of Edinburgh and the Canongate (the suburb under Edinburgh's jurisdiction that straddled the lower end of the High Street, east of the Netherbow), and most of them were poor.[8] The tall buildings noted by Morer and other visitors were the result of strong population growth, coupled with a topography that encouraged people to build up rather than out. This concentration of people living literally on top of each other, with workshops on the street level, increased the danger of building collapses and fire. Morer complained of exterior stairs that had to reach such heights that they extended well into public thoroughfares, impeding traffic.[9] Even by early modern standards, this was a very crowded city, and it had the reputation of being one of Europe's filthiest. Raw sewage was often tossed out of upper-storey windows onto the narrow passageways below with scant warning, or else privy closets jutted out over the alleys and closes. The total area covered by the burgh was a mere 160 acres.[10]

Edinburgh was also a very professional city. As the kingdom's capital, it hosted central law courts, parliaments, general assemblies of the Reformed Kirk of Scotland, Privy Council meetings, treasury commissions and other meetings of officials of the absentee Crown. This meant that it had more than its fair share of advocates, writers to the signet, simple 'writers' (among the humblest of literate professionals, but often with some training in the law), ministers and factors (essentially accountants), as well as college regents, doctors (the Royal College of Physicians was established in 1681), surgeons (their meeting house would be completed in 1697) and others who would today be regarded as 'white-collar' professionals. The city was also a mecca for aristocrats and lairds attending to legal affairs, or merely seeking urban sociability. They could find the latter in lodgings or in a wide array of taverns, coffee houses (which would have English newspapers available) and bookshops, these supported by a book trade that employed between fifty and sixty of the burgh's residents.[11] The minor border laird George Home was a regular visitor to Edinburgh, recounting

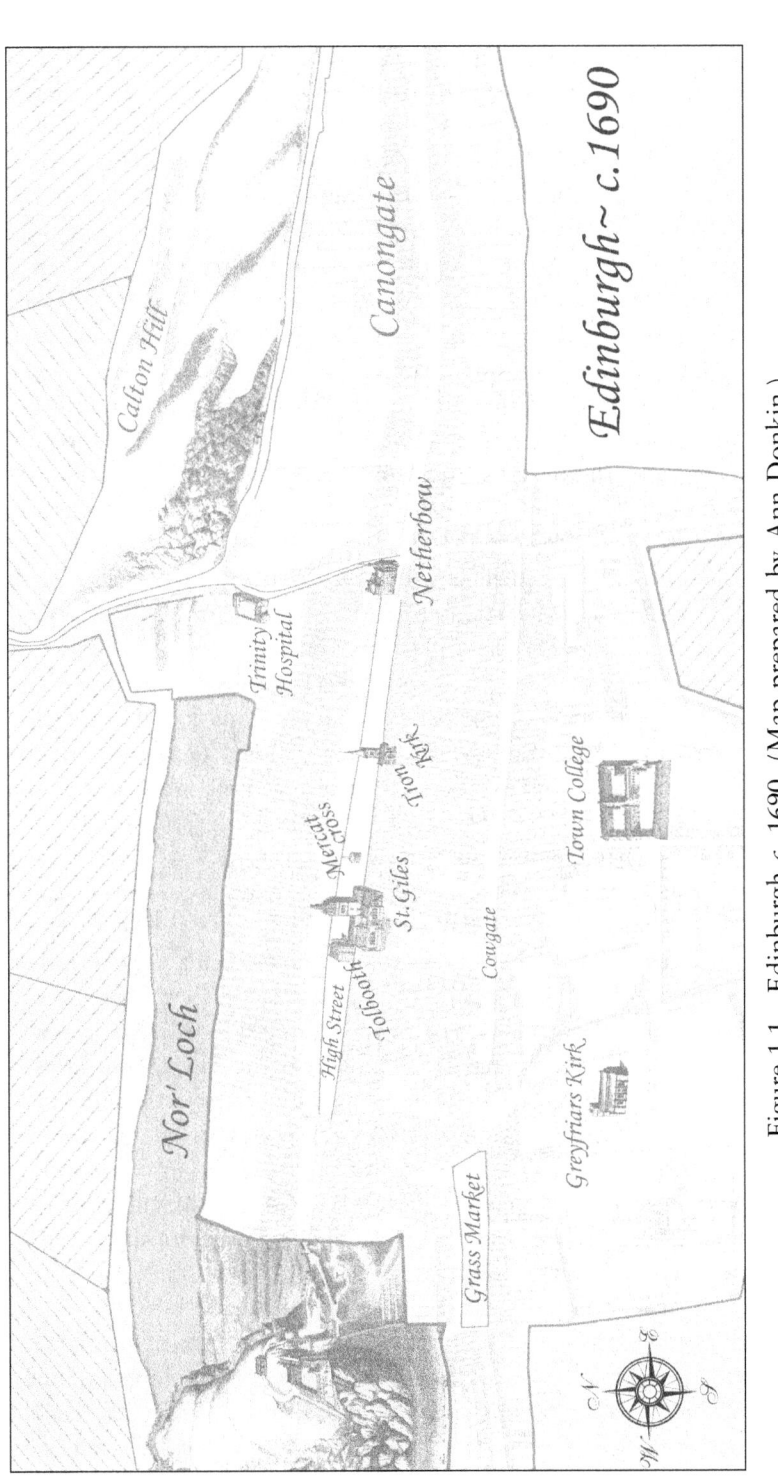

Figure 1.1 Edinburgh c. 1690. (Map prepared by Ann Donkin.)

in his journal that he stopped into a coffee house to read international news after going to church at the Tron one Sunday in March 1695. Eleven months later, in another Edinburgh coffee house, he read about a battle between Spaniards and 'Moores' in North Africa in the *Flying Post*, a semi-weekly paper from London. He listened enthusiastically to the political gossip he picked up during his Edinburgh sojourns, but enjoyed other forms of conversation there also, as when he stepped into George Mosman's bookshop (he was a regular customer there) one day in June 1695 and became involved in a lengthy conversation about gardening with the Earl of Crawford.[12] The town's rhythms were marked in part by the bells of St Giles', ringing at one in the afternoon to broadcast the closing of shops for lunch, at ten in the evening to warn taverns to close for the night, and whenever the High Court of Justiciary was called into session.[13] Thus Thomas Aikenhead's travails, in which literacy and the discussion of books and ideas were essential elements, took place in an exceedingly busy, crowded, literate and sociable urban environment. Scotland's capital was full of reading and conversation.

But the city's government was in the hands of its merchant-dominated burgh council. Indeed, both ministers and lawyers were exempt from burghal taxation but also excluded from formal participation in its politics. The merchants controlled politics, and only a member of the merchants' guild could attain the highest burgh office of provost or serve as one of the town's four bailies. The merchants, along with the burgh's (less powerful) craftsmen, also controlled commerce in the traditional way – by limiting entry into their ranks, and using the burgh council's legal authority to enforce the privileges of their guild members. The *de jure* control of commerce did not lead to the *de facto* control of wealth, however. The seventeenth century had been a good time for Scotland's legal profession, and by the 1690s the combined wealth of Edinburgh's 380 lawyers was greater than that of its 600 merchants. Indeed, the lawyers controlled more wealth than all the city's merchants and craftsmen combined.[14] Like the city's other occupational groups, the lawyers had their own corporate organisation: the Faculty of Advocates, which, in conventional guild fashion, sought to limit entry into its ranks and safeguard professional standings as well as provide collegial fellowship. Its membership included some of the most powerful men in the kingdom, and it also boasted of its own library.[15]

Merchants and craftsmen were not immune to the charms of scholarship either, although they saw it as the handmaiden more of godliness than of justice. The need to supply suitable candidates for the ministry had been a primary reason for founding the town's college, and this was still seen as its main purpose. James Wallace, an Edinburgh baxter and burgess, reflected the prevailing view when he donated 200 books to the college in 1688 out of 'the zeal and Affection I have to the Advancement of true Piety & Learning, and considering that universities & colledges are the seminaries both of Church and State'.[16] Indeed, the founding core of the college's library in 1583 had been a collection of 268 theological books donated by the pious and Reformed lawyer Clement Little.[17] The first professorial chair established at the institution had been that of divinity in 1620, followed by one in Hebrew (an aid to biblical studies) in 1642. Only late in the seventeenth century had it added chairs in mathematics, 'physic' and medicine.[18] The college library, housed in a building completed in 1644, was adorned with pictures of the reformers Martin Luther, Philip Melanchthon, Ulrich Zwingli, John Calvin and, for additional inspiration, the skull of George Buchanan, Scotland's pre-eminent Calvinist humanist. The academic term ran from mid-October until mid-July, and the poorer sons of the city's burgesses would receive special bursaries of £10 Scots annually from the burgh council to help with their expenses.[19] For example, John Potter, who would later testify against his fellow student Thomas Aikenhead, was given a bursary in April 1692, his father having died 'through the violence of the late tymes', leaving his son in a 'very mean conditione ... haveing nothing for his support and encouradgement in following his studies'.[20] The typical student started around age 14, and there were 300–400 of them in the 1690s, with perhaps 50 receiving bursaries. Like many college or university students before and since, these aspiring scholars could be violent and unruly, and town–gown relations were not always smooth; in 1681 a group of them torched the provost of Edinburgh's house.[21] Most of the teaching was still done by regents, often young men themselves, who would take an entire class through its four-year arts curriculum. After that, a student might choose to enter one of the higher faculties of theology or medicine.[22] So the town college was a small community, under the patronage of the burgh council, within the larger community. That larger community was also broken geographically into smaller units for the purposes of worship and taxation: its seven inner parishes, plus one for the Canongate and another for Edinburgh's inner suburbs.[23]

Some parishes, such as the Tron and Greyfriars, had their own church buildings. Others, such as Tolbooth Kirk, New Kirk and Old Kirk, had to share; they worshipped in different parts of the interior of St Giles'. Even those parishes that had their own buildings were close together, so that, while a person might belong to a particular parish for the purposes of taxation or poor relief, they could easily attend sermons with a different congregation. The English lawyer Joseph Taylor, having recently visited

Edinburgh, wrote in 1705 that 'the Nobility generally resort to the Trone Church, which is the principall, and the Lord High Commissioner [the king's representative in the General Assembly] has a Throne erected in it', alongside places for the provost of Edinburgh and the Lord High Chancellor, who represented the king in parliament.[24] The minister at the Tron was the academically inclined (and mature – he was born in 1634) Aberdeen native George Meldrum, who had been appointed to that post by the burgh council in June 1692. Meldrum won praise from the minister/historian Robert Wodrow for his charity and from the Glasgow minister James Stirling for having 'a most sweet, plain, pathetick way of preaching'.[25]

But the Tolbooth congregation, convening in the north-west corner of St Giles', also had its prominent members, such as Sir John Lauder of Fountainhall, a senator of the college of justice and member of the Privy Council, who was confirmed in his possession of a prime pew there, also by the burgh council, in 1692. In the middle of the following year the council placed James Webster in the pulpit of the Tolbooth. Born around 1660, and described by one devout Presbyterian as 'so turbulent a man', and by another as 'rash, imprudent [and] fiery', the Fife native Webster did not share Meldrum's penchant for moderation, and the Tolbooth became Edinburgh's leading evangelical parish under his leadership.[26] Its elders included many of the capital's more prominent merchants, one of whom in particular stood to profit from any religious revival: he was George Mosman, a leading publisher and book merchant specialising in Presbyterian works. One of his main clients was the Reformed Kirk of Scotland, whose General Assembly had appointed him official printer to the Kirk. Mosman would be part of the assize jury that sent Thomas Aikenhead to the gallows.[27]

Elders in parishes such as Tolbooth Kirk took seriously their responsibilities to uphold standards of 'godly' behaviour among their parishioners. The construction of a Calvinist-style disciplinary system, with the kirk session (ministers, elders and deacons) as its local enforcement unit, had been one of the hallmarks of Scotland's reformation in the sixteenth century, and the system was functioning throughout the lowlands by around 1600, making its ministers and elders leading agents in a cultural revolution.[28] Their ultimate sanction was excommunication, which carried the implication of social, legal and even commercial ostracism, but far more common were public warnings and the performance of public repentance, or public humiliation. In the latter rituals, parishioners guilty of sins such as fornication, adultery, slander, assault, sabbath breach and the like would be forced to sit on a 'stool of repentance', prominently placed in the congregation, during one or more sermons. To enhance the educational value of the spectacle, they might also be made to wear special clothing or a paper crown emblazoned with words describing their particular offences. In a society that placed great value on honour and reputation, such punishments could be particularly stinging, and the level of neighbourly oversight in a crowded urban centre like Edinburgh left little room for privacy. Strangers were both startled and bemused at the apparent rigor of Scottish Presbyterian preaching and discipline, as well as the homely simplicity of its religious services. Taylor and his companions visited one of Edinburgh's kirks, where one of them made the mistake of sitting on the stool of repentance, thinking that it was an empty seat 'but was prevented by an Old Man, who perceiv'd him to be a stranger. The Minister made such a prodigious noise in broad Scotch, and beat his pulpit so violently, that he seem'd better qualified for a Drummer than a Parson.'[29] While Taylor did not identify the preacher in question, it could well have been James Webster.

But, while the kirk's ministers and elders may have seen themselves as primarily concerned with reforming the behaviour within their parishes, Edinburgh's burgh council, many of whose members sometimes served as parish elders as well, saw this as a civic responsibility also. In August 1693, concerned that the Sabbath was being abused by drunkenness, 'prophane swearing & cursing', the council ordered that its bailies apprehend the guilty and fine them, place them in the jougs (an iron collar attached by a chain near the mercat cross), or jail them, depending on their ability to pay.[30] Similar orders were common from the early days of the Scottish Reformation onwards. But there were newer, more licentious currents flowing through the capital in the 1690s. In November 1692 the council had granted a licence to William McLean, the king's master of revels, to erect a public stage in the city, with the proviso that performances there be 'free of all offence, cursing, profanity or anything contrare to piety'.[31] This was yet another local manifestation of a broader, long-term conflict. The clash between piety (usually defined by its adherents) and its adversaries – religious, social, political and cultural – had shaken Scotland to its very foundations in the seventeenth century, pulling all Britain into its vortex. And for many, that struggle was not over yet.

1.2 THE LEGACY OF THE COVENANTS

Just as the nature of Scotland's religious reform gave its rituals a distinct flavour, so it had provided many Scots with a sense of national identity and even destiny. Uneasy cooperation between the Scottish Crown and the

Kirk in the wake of the Reformation had started to break down in the late 1590s, and James VI's removal to England, whose throne he inherited in 1603, had exacerbated the sense of some ministers that the Reformed Kirk was a rare beauty that must be protected from all innovations, particularly those coming from the Crown, now increasingly anglicised.[32] James's growing distrust of the independence of the General Assembly, and that body's reluctance to censure the more politicised preaching of some of its members, led the king to ignore it – not even calling it into session for many years – and to govern the Kirk through royally appointed bishops instead. While some of these bishops were themselves quite thoroughgoing Calvinists,[33] they were in a bad position after the accession of Charles I in 1625. Unlike his father, this king had no experience of his northern kingdom, and he expected his bishops to be the point men for royal ecclesiastical policies that now sought to push beyond the ritual reforms of James VI (private baptism, kneeling at Communion, confirmation by bishops) towards a more thorough anglicisation of religious services. The bishops were resented by more doctrinaire Calvinist ministers, who saw them as representing an alien and perhaps even 'popish' reformatting of rituals, and by noblemen, who saw them as wielding too much political power. Meanwhile, the government of Charles I sought to examine all grants of ecclesiastical lands made since 1540, a scheme that obviously threatened noblemen and lairds (roughly equivalent to the English gentry) in possession of such lands. This 'revocation' was intended to regularise land tenure and ensure salaries for ministers, but it did little to improve relations between the Crown and the Presbyterian clergy.[34]

All these antagonisms came to a head in July 1637, when the forced introduction of an English-style prayer book, the brainchild of Charles I and William Laud, his archbishop of Canterbury, led to an orchestrated riot in Edinburgh. Within months, an unusual coalition of noblemen and disaffected ministers was leading the country into a rebellion, or even a revolution, sealed by the National Covenant of 1638. Covenants had figured in Scotland's movements for religious reform since 1557, drawing on the tradition of bonds (contracts promising mutual support and protection) between noblemen and their followers, but the National Covenant had an explicit political agenda well beyond anything contained in its forebears.[35] It was linked with the revival of the General Assembly as a legislature for the Kirk including lay as well as clerical leadership. Charles's refusal to back down brought on a crisis that ultimately led to wars in all three of his kingdoms – Scotland, Ireland and England. The costs, in terms of blood, money and stability, would be huge, and Scotland would taste a particularly bitter fruit.

The National Covenant had (disingenuously, in the king's eyes) linked the security of the Presbyterian Kirk with the security of the monarchy, suggesting that the latter was just as threatened by 'innovations' in religion as the former. Its logic was extended to Britain as a whole through an alliance with the English parliament, sealed with the Solemn League and Covenant in 1643.[36] But this would break down when 'Independents' in the English parliament and army decided that officially sanctioned Presbyterianism was nearly as bad as the officially sanctioned episcopacy they had just overthrown, and refused to impose Presbyterianism on England for a three-year trial period, as agreed. Nevertheless many Scots who adhered to the covenants would continue to view themselves as bound to this wider British Presbyterian vision. In January 1649, England's parliament and army executed Charles I without consulting his Scottish subjects. Then, after a failed attempt to revive the Stewart royal house in the person of Charles II, which ended with Oliver Cromwell's English army defeating the bedraggled Scots army at Worcester in 1651, Scotland faced English conquest and occupation. While the heritage of the covenants appeared to have been political disaster, adherence to their ideals had become a litmus test in Scottish politics, used to purge leadership (as in the 1649 Act of Classes), define factions (as when the movement split over Charles II's apparent adherence to the cause in 1650–1) or to question the commitment of ambitious men. As one recent commentator has summed it up, 'the religious covenant was a tripartite compact between the king, the people and God to uphold religious purity in which the Israelites were replaced by the Scots in the role of chosen people'.[37] Cromwell's death in 1658 paved the way for a restoration of the monarchy in all three kingdoms, but when Charles II returned from exile to accept this inheritance in 1660, it soon became clear to his Scots subjects that he had only signed the Covenant to win their alliance – indeed, many had realised this back in 1650. His preferences in church government resembled those of his father, and the bishops were restored in Scotland in 1661, although never given the positions of political importance that Charles I had given them.

But, in addition to bloodshed on an unprecedented scale, the seventeenth century produced long memories, which divided the nation. As David Stevenson has written, 'the Scottish Revolution had failed, but the fact that it had taken place meant that things could never be the same again'.[38] Many clergy and elites conformed to the episcopal settlement of 1661, but others refused, gathering in outdoor conventicles that occasionally became recruiting grounds for regional rebellions.[39] A group of covenanters in the south-west seized a government commander in 1666 and marched towards Edinburgh before turning back because of lack of support, and were then defeated at Rullion Green. Some of the religiously disaffected started experiencing visions like those of the schoolmistress Katherine Ross:

> In the year 1667, in the Summer, one Afternoon bring taken up about the Publick, the Lord was pleased to make Intimation to my Soul, that he was risen again in *Scotland*, and laid the Foundation of a Work in the Blood of his Witnesses, that all the Devils in Hell, nor Men on Earth should not prevail against.[40]

A dissident minister tried to assassinate James Sharp, Archbishop of St Andrews, during a visit to Edinburgh in 1668. He failed, but another attempt, by another group, which happened upon the archbishop's coach in open country near St Andrews eleven years later, was successful when the attackers dragged Sharp out of his coach and slaughtered him, despite his terrified daughter's pleas for mercy on his behalf. An exasperated government and ecclesiastical establishment mixed policies of conciliation and repression, winning over some covenanter ministers, which it 'indulged', but a hard core remained outside the orbit of the established Episcopal Kirk. By the mid-1670s, Edinburgh itself was home to several indoor conventicles, at which city officials winked. The Privy Council, which represented the Crown, was less indulgent, however.[41]

Sharp's murder set off a chain of events that culminated in the largest uprising of the period. After defeating a government force early in June 1679, a covenanter army burned and looted part of Glasgow. It took an English force of 10,000 troops, led by the Duke of Monmouth (an illegitimate son of Charles II), to quash the rebellion at Bothwell Bridge near Hamilton, where the rebels had spent three weeks debating the extent to which they could have dealings with 'indulged' Presbyterian ministers, rather than preparing for the onslaught. Between 200 and 400 covenanters were killed, and many others brought to Edinburgh, where they spent the summer confined in Greyfriars kirkyard. In the end, only a handful were prosecuted for treason (and hanged at the site of Sharp's assassination), although many others died in a shipwreck while being transported to America.[42] By the end of the year James, duke of York, the king's Catholic brother and heir apparent, was ensconced in Holyrood Palace as royal commissioner, charged with bringing order to a kingdom that clearly had not yet made peace with its recent past.

Neither repression nor conciliation, nor a combination of the two, seemed capable of pacifying Scotland's turbulent religious politics. Several different groups claimed to be the true heirs of the Covenant. Some were willing to compromise with the episcopal establishment while others refused any cooperation, taking their persecution as proof of the truth of their cause. Charles II and his brother saw the bishops as essential pillars of their authority, and the bishops, royalist to the core, returned the favour. For Crown and bishops, the Covenant was anathema, tied as it was to the overthrow of both between 1637 and 1649. The Duke of York's overt Catholicism (unlike his brother's closet Catholicism) added another layer of complication. Meanwhile, the Low Countries, with which Scotland enjoyed trade contacts of long standing, beckoned as a haven for political and religious exiles. There, and in London, dissident Scots rubbed shoulders with Englishmen opposed to the policies of Charles II or to the succession of his brother. It was as a result of associations like these that several prominent Scots faced legal prosecution in the wake of the discovery of the Rye House Plot, a supposed plan to assassinate Charles and James, in 1683. The best-known executions were those of the English Whigs William Lord Russell and Algernon Sidney, but the elderly Scot Robert Baillie of Jerviswood, so ill that he had to be carried to the gallows, received the same treatment in Edinburgh. His kinsman by marriage, Patrick Hume of Polwarth, went into hiding, holing himself up in his family's burial vault under Polwarth kirk for a month, supposedly strengthening himself through the recitation of psalms, before fleeing, disguised as a surgeon, to the Low Countries via London and Bordeaux. Many of his family's lands were then confiscated by the government.[43] A similar journey was undertaken by William Carstares, a minister from a covenanting family who had graduated from Edinburgh's town college in 1667. Having spent time in London and Holland, he was imprisoned in London and Edinburgh in 1675–9 for plotting with other Scots exiles against Charles II's government. Back in England, he was arrested again following the discovery of the Rye House Plot, shipped to Edinburgh, tortured with thumbscrews (in part to gather evidence against Baillie of Jerviswood) and eventually released. He returned to exile, joining those advising the Dutch Stadholder William of Orange, who was gathering a large circle of disaffected English Whigs and Scots covenanters, often called Whigs themselves. Carstares became one of William's chaplains.[44]

In many ways, the outlook for the Presbyterian cause improved after the accession of James, duke of York, to the thrones of Scotland and England in 1685. Catholicism was unpopular in all but a few regions, and the bishops and aristocratic supporters of the established Episcopal Church had reason to worry about the direction in which policies were pointing, particularly once the new king extended toleration to Catholics and (even worse in conservative eyes) Quakers in 1686. The following year he made the same offer to Presbyterians, despite their association with the covenants. This latter problem was mitigated in government eyes by several years of policies that had effectively debarred those who would not disavow the covenants from holding offices in burghs or other corporations. Thus this new toleration would extend to Presbyterian religion but not covenanter politics. Nevertheless, one covenanter exile who took advantage of this indulgence managed to gain appointment to the Privy Council. This was the advocate Sir James Stewart of Goodtrees, son of a former provost of Edinburgh. His political rehabilitation was particularly remarkable considering that he was the author of *Napthali, or the Wrestlings of the Church of Scotland* (published in Amsterdam in 1667), a work so harshly critical of government-sponsored episcopacy that the Privy Council had ordered it burned by the public hangman in Edinburgh in the year of its publication. Even worse, he had been sentenced to death *in absentia* for his involvement in an invasion of Scotland under the Whig ninth Duke of Argyll after the accession of James VII. Stewart of Goodtrees, part of the circle of exiles in the Low Countries that included Hume of Polwarth and Carstares, had written the declaration Argyll issued in justification of his rebellion. He neglected to join Argyll on that fatal expedition, however, and would survive, as would Hume of Polwarth, to play a critical role in the prosecution and execution of Thomas Aikenhead.[45] Others suffered closer to home, continuing to see the covenants as defining the true body politic. Janet Hamilton, wife of the covenanter Alexander Gordon of Earlston, shared his imprisonment in Blackness Castle, and while there at the end of 1687 renewed her own personal covenant with God, linked to the larger covenants with the clause:

> I desire to adhere to all the articles of the Covenants, National and Solemn League, to which I stand engaged, only I disown the King's [i.e. Charles II's] part of it, he having unkinged himself by the breach of covenants, and by making our land a land of graven images, that was so solemnly given up to God.[46]

Ultimately, Scottish Presbyterians did not support King James any more enthusiastically than English Whigs did. Few of them trusted his apparent commitment to toleration, a virtue valued by few in that confessional age anyway, particularly among those who regarded themselves as bound to the covenants. The king's religious policies only alienated his most likely supporters: the bishops and Episcopalian noblemen. While Scotland played no active part in the events that led to his flight into exile in 1688, prominent Scots exiles such as Carstares and Hume of Polwarth accompanied William of Orange in his ship, the *Brill*, in the invasion of England that spurred James's departure.[47] This 'Glorious Revolution', carried out at the behest, and in the interests, of England's political elite, was bloodier and therefore less 'glorious' in Scotland than in England (and even worse in Ireland, where the result was civil war).[48] In the short term, a power vacuum left Scotland in political limbo. Supporters of the exiled king rallied behind John Graham of Claverhouse, Viscount Dundee, and, although they defeated a Williamite force at the pass of Killiecrankie in July 1689, Dundee's death in the battle left this first Jacobite movement leaderless. There was sporadic fighting until the Battle of Cromdale in May 1690, but most of Scotland's political leaders had by then fallen in behind the succession of William and Mary.[49]

But many things remained uncertain, particularly the nature of the religious settlement that the new monarchs would favour. They were solidly Protestant, but seem to have preferred an episcopalian approach in Scotland, since that would keep Scotland in a kind of religious conjunction with England, and facilitate the maintenance of some royal control over church affairs. Scotland was, after all, already working within an episcopalian system, so existing clergy could keep their jobs if it were to continue. In addition, the presence of bishops in parliament had strengthened the Crown's hand there since 1661. But local Presbyterian gangs, particularly in areas of the south and west where the legacy of the Covenant was strong, took matters into their own hands by forcibly ejecting Episcopal clergy from their parishes. Furthermore, the Scottish bishops failed to respond to any of William's overtures in 1689, thus seeming to confirm the suspicion that they were Jacobites. The 'Convention Parliament', which gathered in March that year, sealed the situation by abolishing episcopacy in July, an approach made much easier by the fact that Dundee and other supporters of the exiled king had stormed out early in the session. Additional pressure was supplied by gangs of Cameronians – radical covenanters from the south-west – roaming the streets of the capital city. In the past, Scots parliaments had been managed by the Crown through the appointment of a group known as the Lords of the Articles, a kind of executive committee that would shepherd royal business through the unicameral legislature. But the Convention Parliament eliminated the Lords of the Articles, making the Scots parliament henceforth much more difficult to direct from above.[50] If the moderate Protestant William wanted to foster toleration like that favoured by the Catholic James, he would encounter opposition.

When the tenth Earl of Argyll presented William with the Scots Coronation Oath at Whitehall (he never visited his northern kingdom) in May 1689, the new king raised questions about the article that obliged him to 'root out Hereticks and Enemies to the true Worship of God, that shall be convicted by the true Kirk of God of the foresaid Crimes, out of our Lands and empire of Scotland'. Wary of the covenanter agenda behind such a requirement, William said he would not interpret this as meaning he had 'to become a persecutor', but he took the oath anyway.[51] In the following year's parliamentary session, William made it clear that he at least wanted toleration for Scottish Episcopalians, but he did not get it, because of his dependence on a Presbyterian party to get the taxation he needed to continue his campaigns against Louis XIV's France. The final religious settlement passed in 1690 was strictly Presbyterian, based on the Westminster Confession, which had been developed as part of the Solemn League and Covenant of 1643, including, characteristically, the abolition of any 'yule vacance'.[52] Those who had found themselves cast out of politics in the latter years of Charles II's reign and during that of his brother were now back with a vengeance.

In fact, however, it would prove impossible to stamp out a version of Christianity that had been officially endorsed for the previous twenty-eight years. Episcopal religious practices were outlawed, but strictures against them would be only sporadically enforced. With the king refusing to endorse any crackdown, and public opinion in England strongly pro-episcopal, Scotland's Presbyterian authorities would find, much to their disgust, that they would have to follow a more politic course than their covenanted consciences would prefer. About 140 Episcopal clergy would be turned out of their jobs (including twenty-five of the twenty-six ministers in the Edinburgh Presbytery), often replaced by Presbyterians, who had been purged as early as 1662, but Scotland would in fact be a religiously pluralist society from this point forward. The turbulent seventeenth century had produced other forms of dissent as well, most notably Quakerism, briefly given legs by the toleration extended to it under James VII. It, too, would survive after the settlement of 1690, as would the slender strand of Scots Catholicism. While Episcopalians would be the largest group of dissenters in Edinburgh in the 1690s, there were also Catholics, particularly in the Canongate, and Quakers meeting in a house by the West Port.[53] This would be profoundly unsettling for champions of Presbyterianism, who looked to 1689–90 as ushering in the age when the covenants could finally be fulfilled. When Janet Hamilton, now (along with her husband) free from imprisonment, renewed her personal covenant in January 1691, she lamented the laxity of the revolution settlement:

> Oh what did I see next? The work of God betrayed not by enemies, nor by that party only that had sat at their ease, but by those ministers and people that had joined their lives in the high places of the fields, taking cheerfully the spoiling of their goods. These are they that have buried the work of the Lord, ladened the hearts of their poor afflicted brethren,

buried the Covenant and the work of Reformation, which was the glory of our land.⁵⁴

In a similar vein, the Presbyterian minister James Hogg noted that:

> We are a people in Covenant with the Lord, and in a suitableness to these covenants, during the course and long tract of persecution we had endured, their inviolable obligation had been owned with all possible solemnity for many years.

But despite that, after the revolution of 1689–90

> Men of a leading influence, in church and state [did] by a kind of strange concert agree to suppress the testimony of the former times, not to mention our covenants, at least in any solemn way, and with the honour due to them; and to manage in church matters, as much to the mind of the rulers, as could consist in any manner with our known principles.

To Hogg, the most suitable comparison seemed to be the behaviour of the Hebrews (another chosen, covenanted people) after the Babylonian Captivity.⁵⁵

Clearly, some felt that the crowning works of Reformation had been betrayed at the moment of triumph. Scotland's government was in one sense revolutionary, but to maintain legitimacy in the eyes of some it would have to demonstrate its willingness to uphold the principles of 1638 and 1643. Those principles did not include toleration of heterodoxy. As the exemplar of heterodoxy in late seventeenth-century Scotland, Thomas Aikenhead would provide authorities the chance to prove that the covenants still mattered.

1.3 EDINBURGH AND THE CHANGES OF 1688–90

As the seat of parliament, Edinburgh played host to much of the regime change of 1688–90 in Scotland. Residents also participated in these changes, and then felt their impact on local institutions. The Convention Parliament gathered downhill from the threatening guns of Edinburgh Castle, still held for James VII by the Duke of Gordon in the spring of 1689. Students at the town college had celebrated the apparent *coup d'état* as early as December 1688 by burning an effigy of the pope, allegedly in front of an audience of 16,000 supporters.⁵⁶ But some of their teachers would be viewed as partisans of the old regime, and they would pay for it with their jobs.

In fact, a 1690 parliamentary visitation of the college by a committee that included Patrick Hume of Polwarth would instigate staff changes from the top down. The college principal, Dr Alexander Monro, was already a marked man, having refused to offer public prayers for William and Mary from the pulpit of St Giles' in April 1689. At the visitation, he was fired from the principalship for his episcopalian beliefs, as was the divinity professor Dr John Strachan.[57] Monro was replaced by Gilbert Rule, one of the visitors, an elderly covenanting minister who had spent time as an exile in Dublin as well as the Netherlands. The prominent professor of mathematics David Gregory, who had brought the natural philosophy of Isaac Newton into the college's curriculum, was charged with 'atheism', and was alleged to be out of the habit of taking communion, and far too much in the habit of drinking excessively with the college regents Herbert Kennedy and Alexander Cunningham, as well as the local free-thinking (and Jacobite) physician Archibald Pitcairne.[58] Having seen the writing on the wall, Gregory left for the more tolerant atmosphere of Oxford, where he was given the Savilian Chair of Astronomy, in part through Newton's influence. The visitors were keen to return the town's college to its strictly Presbyterian theological roots; they took a dim view of the cutting-edge philosophical training, particularly that involving the ideas of Descartes and Newton, for which it had become known in the previous decade.

But the shops, taverns, coffee houses and private rooms of Edinburgh had plenty of room for the sort of chatter that Rule and Hume of Polwarth were trying to quash; the world of 1638–51 could not be wholly re-created in the 1690s. One of the best-known local conversationalists (and drinking partner of Gregory, Kennedy and Cunningham) was Pitcairne, educated in the town college and then overseas, who was one of the founding members of the Royal College of Physicians. His Jacobitism made him anathema to the new regime, and spurred him to spend a year (1692–3) in a chaired professorship at the University of Leiden, but otherwise he passed the 1690s in Edinburgh, living near the Tron Kirk. In 1694 the burgh council agreed to let him treat the sickly poor of the town who lacked relatives for free, provided that he could use their bodies for dissection after they died. Recalling him at his death in 1713, the devout Robert Wodrow wrote of Pitcairne:

> He was the most celebrated physitian in Scotland this age ... I am told he still spent three or four hours evry morning in reading and writing; and some people talk, that evry day he did read a portion of the Scripture though, it seems, he made ill use of it. He was a professed Deist, and by many alledged to be ane Atheist, though he has frequently professed his belife of a God, and said he could not deny a Providence. However, he was a great mocker at religion, and ridiculer of it. He keeped noe publick society for worship; on the Sabbath [he] had his sett meetings for ridiculing of the Scripture and sermons. He was a good humanist, and very curiouse

in his choice of books and library. He gote a vast income, but spent it upon drinking, and was twice drunk evry day. He was a sort of a poet.

Among his poetic offerings was a brief Latin dialogue verse wondering why Scots Presbyterians would celebrate the nativity of George Heriot, jeweller and benefactor of a local school, but not the nativity of Jesus.[59] Pitcairne would be a continuing thorn in the side of Edinburgh's neo-covenanters, but his talents, wealth and connections would protect him from serious repercussions.

Another intellectual dissident passing through Edinburgh in the wake of the revolution of 1688–9 was the Irishman John Toland, who had studied at Glasgow, but in June 1690 was awarded a master of arts in Edinburgh's college, under Kennedy's tutelage, with his diploma signed by Monro, Strachan, Gregory and Kennedy, among others.[60] Later, when English ecclesiastical authorities were trying to connect the dots in Toland's background (he burned a copy of the *Book of Common Prayer* in an Oxford tavern in 1694, and would publish the controversial *Christianity not Mysterious* late in 1695), the Oxford academic and future bishop of Lincoln and then London Edmund Gibson would write that, after leading a student riot at Glasgow, Toland

> removed to *Edenburrow*, and set up there for a *Rosicrucian;* gave them the new name of *Sages*, and printed a book in French and English with this title, The Sage of the Time. He had contriv'd that there should be some appearance of a flame in a closet next [to] the street and noe harm done. When all was safe and the House not burnt down or injur'd as the neighbours expected, his reputation grew upon it quickly, but whether under the name of Conjurer or what other title, I know not.

Gibson's terminology may have been imprecise; the Protestantism of Rosicrucian thought and symbolism might have appealed to Toland in the wake of the revolution of 1688–9, and some Scots had shown interest in Rosicrucianism in the first half of the seventeenth century, but the equally secretive social movement of Freemasonry was more widespread than Rosicrucianism by 1690. Either would have aroused the suspicion of an aspiring establishment churchman like Gibson. *The Sage of the Time*, if printed, does not appear to have survived. Another hostile writer later claimed that Toland had thrown away his Greek New Testament while in Scotland 'and in a great Rage cried *Damn the Galatians*, which was the Place where he was then reading'. He seems to have sought notoriety through public displays of heterodoxy and esoteric learning. Toland would soon leave for England, but it seems likely that his exploits would be remembered, particularly among the students at the town's college.[61] His brief sojourn in Edinburgh, as well as the ongoing presence of a figure like Pitcairne, reminds us that the city remained an eclectic place, despite the authorities' best efforts to revive the public culture of the covenants. The intellectual flowering of its eighteenth-century Enlightenment did not grow out of nothing.

Another challenge facing the post-1689 regime was how to deal with those generally regarded as being on the side of the covenants but who had made compromises in the previous decades. Stewart of Goodtrees, appointed lord advocate – the Crown's highest legal representative – in 1692, was one. Another was Meldrum, appointed minister at the Tron that same year. The former, as mentioned earlier, had accepted indulgence and served on James VII's Privy Council. Meldrum had reconciled himself to the established Episcopal Kirk in the 1660s, serving in the pulpits of Aberdeen, but had lost his posts when he refused to take the Test Act (forcing him to recognise the royal supremacy over the Kirk and renounce the covenants) in 1681. The fact that he was appointed to important posts in the Reformed Kirk after 1690 – preaching at the Tron Kirk and moderating two general assemblies – without demonstrating some sort of repentance for his earlier trimming rankled some of the more enthusiastic preservers of the legacy of the covenants.[62] Of course, such potential cleavages in the new regime could be papered over if the parties involved could find causes to rally around. The fears of 'atheism' raised by the case of Thomas Aikenhead would prove to be such a cause.

NOTES

1. The earliest surviving map of Edinburgh to provide much detail is that of James Gordon, parson of Rothiemay, drawn up in 1647. It was republished, with minor alterations to reflect burgh improvements, as an engraving by Andrew Johnston completed between 1708 and 1714. See William Cowan and Charles Watson, *The Maps of Edinburgh: 1544–1929* (Edinburgh: Edinburgh Public Libraries, 1932), pp. 11, 28–9.
2. Walter Makey, 'Edinburgh in Mid-Seventeenth Century', in Michael Lynch (ed.), *The Early Modern Town in Scotland* (London: Croom Helm, 1987), pp. 192–218, at pp. 193–4.
3. [Thomas Morer], *A Short Account of Scotland* (London, 1702), p. 71. The tall building near the Parliament Close (called Robertson's Land) also impressed the English lawyer Joseph Taylor, who visited in 1705. See William Cowan (ed.), *A Journey to Edinburgh in Scotland by Joseph Taylor, Late of the Inner Temple* (Edinburgh: William Brown, 1903), p. 107.
4. Dingwall, *Late Seventeenth-Century Edinburgh*, p. 12.

5. [Morer], *Short Account*, pp. 72–3.
6. Ibid. p. 77.
7. Ibid. p. 84. In fact, the term 'university' was sometimes used to describe the institution as early as the 1680s. See Robert Anderson, Michael Lynch and Nicholas Phillipson, *The University of Edinburgh: An Illustrated History* (Edinburgh: Edinburgh University Press, 2003), pp. 41–2.
8. Dingwall, *Late Seventeenth-Century Edinburgh*, p. 20; R. A. Houston, *Social Change in the Age of the Enlightenment: Edinburgh, 1660–1760* (Oxford: Clarendon Press, 1994), p. 3. Michael Lynch has estimated the town's population in 1560 as 12,000 – see Michael Lynch, *Edinburgh and the Reformation* (Edinburgh: John Donald, 1981), p. 3.
9. [Morer], *Short Account*, p. 72.
10. Houston, *Social Change*, p. 141; T. C. Smout, *A History of the Scottish People, 1560–1830* (Glasgow: William Collins, 1969), pp. 150–1; Makey, 'Edinburgh', p. 197.
11. Alastair Mann, *The Scottish Book Trade, 1500–1720: Print Commerce and Print Control in Early Modern Scotland* (East Linton: Tuckwell, 2000), p. 220. The provision of newspapers in Edinburgh coffee houses would have provided critical access to an otherwise expensive media, given that the 2*d*. sterling price of a London paper would have been equivalent to 2*s*. Scots. See Karin Bowie, *Scottish Public Opinion and the Anglo-Scottish Union, 1699–1707* (Woodbridge: Boydell Press, 2007), pp. 21–2.
12. Helen Kelsall and Keith Kelsall (eds), *An Album of Scottish Families 1694–96, Being the First Installment of George Home's Diary* (Aberdeen: Aberdeen University Press, 1990) (hereafter referred to as *Home Diary*), pp. 47, 71, 75, 108, 113.
13. Houston, *Social Change*, p. 45.
14. Michael Lynch, *Scotland: A New History* (London: Pimlico, 1992), p. 254.
15. This was the nucleus of what was to become the National Library of Scotland. For its early holdings, see Maureen Townley (ed.), *The Best and Fynest Lawers and Other Raire Bookes: A Facsimile of the Earliest List of Books in the Advocates' Library, Edinburgh* (Edinburgh: Edinburgh Bibliographical Society, 1990); and *Catalogus Librorum Bibliothecae Iuris Utruisque, tam Civilis quam Canonici Publici quam Privati ... A Facultate Advocatorum* (Edinburgh: Mosman, 1692).
16. Edinburgh University Library [hereafter EUL] MS Da.1.30/5.
17. Anderson, Lynch and Phillipson, *University of Edinburgh*, pp. 11, 38.
18. Ronald G. Cant, 'Origins of Enlightenment in Scotland: The Universities', in R. H. Campbell and Andrew S. Skinner (eds), *The Origins and Nature of the Scottish Enlightenment* (Edinburgh: John Donald, 1982), pp. 42–64, at pp. 44–5, 53, 60.
19. [Morer], *Short Account*, pp. 78, 85–6.

20. Edinburgh Council Archives [hereafter ECA] MS SL1/1/34, fo. 39r.
21. [George Ridpath], *The Scots Episcopal Innocence* (London, 1694), pp. 54–6.
22. [Morer], *Short Account*, p. 85; Dingwall, *Late Seventeenth-Century Edinburgh*, p. 227; Christine Shepherd, 'University Life in the Seventeenth Century', in Gordon Donaldson (ed.), *Four Centuries: Edinburgh University Life, 1583–1983* (Edinburgh: Edinburgh University Press, 1983), pp. 1–15, at p. 4; Cant, 'Origins of Enlightenment', pp. 44–5.
23. For a map of the parishes, see Dingwall, *Late Seventeenth-Century Edinburgh*, fig. 1.
24. Cowan (ed.), *A Journey to Edinburgh*, p. 106.
25. ECA MS SL1/1/34, fo. 64r–v; *To the Memory of the very Reverend and Truly Pious Mr George Meldrum* (Edinburgh, 1709); *Fasti*, p. 139; Robert Wodrow, *Analecta: Or Materials for a History of Remarkable Providences*, 4 vols (Edinburgh: Maitland Club, 1842–3), i, pp. 175–7, iii, p. 123.
26. ECA MS SL1/1/34, fos 83r, 188v; *Fasti*, i, p. 123; A. Ian Dunlop, *The Kirks of Edinburgh* (Edinburgh: Scottish Record Society, 1988), pp. 94, 97; [James Erskine, Lord Grange], *Extracts from the Diary of a Senator of the College of Justice* (Edinburgh: Thomas Stevenson, 1843), p. 10; Wodrow, *Analecta*, iii, p. 307.
27. NAS MSS CH2/140/2, fo. 3; JC26/78/1/8; Mann, *Scottish Book Trade*, p. 152.
28. Michael F. Graham, *The Uses of Reform: 'Godly Discipline' and Popular Behavior in Scotland and Beyond, 1560–1610* (Leiden and New York: E. J. Brill, 1996); Margo Todd, *The Culture of Protestantism in Early Modern Scotland* (New Haven: Yale University Press, 2002).
29. Cowan (ed.), *A Journey to Edinburgh*, p. 137. Taylor also complained that women dressed so modestly in this kirk that he and his fellows were given 'but little opportunity of passing our Judgment on the Scotch beautyes'.
30. ECA MS SL1/1/34, fo. 225r–v.
31. ECA MS SL1/1/34, fos 106v–107r.
32. The best recent survey of ecclesiastical politics in the reign of James VI (and one that suggests that the level of opposition to the Crown's ecclesiastical policies has been exaggerated) is Alan MacDonald, *The Jacobean Kirk, 1567–1625: Sovereignty, Polity, and Liturgy* (Aldershot: Ashgate, 1998).
33. A point made by David Mullan in *Scottish Puritanism, 1590–1638* (Oxford: Oxford University Press, 2000).
34. Walter R. Foster, *The Church before the Covenants: The Church of Scotland, 1596–1638* (Edinburgh: Scottish Academic Press, 1975), pp. 165–7.
35. David Stevenson, *The Scottish Revolution, 1637–1644: The Triumph of the Covenanters* (Newton Abbot: David & Charles, 1973), pp. 13–126;

Mullan, *Scottish Puritanism*, pp. 285–90; Arthur Williamson, *Scottish National Consciousness in the Age of James VI* (Edinburgh: John Donald, 1979), pp. 140–6.
36. The texts of both documents can be found in Gordon Donaldson (ed.), *Scottish Historical Documents* (Edinburgh: Scottish Academic Press, 1970), pp. 194–201, 208–10.
37. Allan MacInnes, *The British Revolution, 1629–1660* (New York: Palgrave Macmillan, 2005), p. 115. For a political narrative of the period, see David Stevenson, *Revolution and Counter-Revolution in Scotland, 1644–1651* (London: Royal Historical Society, 1977).
38. Stevenson, *Revolution and Counter-Revolution*, p. 240.
39. Ian Cowan, *The Scottish Covenanters, 1660–1688* (London: Gollancz, 1976), pp. 50–63.
40. *Memoirs or Spiritual Exercises of Mistress Ross* (Edinburgh, 1735), p. 26.
41. Cowan, *Scottish Covenanters*, pp. 83–4.
42. Ibid. pp. 95–102.
43. Robert Scott-Moncrieff (ed.), *The Household Book of Lady Grisell Baillie, 1692–1733* (Edinburgh: Scottish History Society, 1911), pp. xv–xvii.
44. A. Ian Dunlop, *William Carstares and the Kirk by Law Established* (Edinburgh: Saint Andrew Press, 1967), pp. 18–21, 35–53.
45. E. Calvin Beisner, 'His Majesty's Advocate: Sir James Stewart of Goodtrees (1635–1713) and Covenanter Resistance Theory under the Restoration Monarchy' (Ph.D. thesis, University of St Andrews, 2002), fos 304–15; Mann, *Scottish Book Trade*, p. 181; George Omond, *The Lord Advocates of Scotland*, 2 vols (Edinburgh: David Douglas, 1883), i, pp. 243–80.
46. W. K. Tweedie (ed.), *Select Biographies*, 2 vols (Edinburgh: Wodrow Society, 1845–7), i, pp. 500–1.
47. Dunlop, *William Carstares*, pp. 59–60.
48. Brown, *Kingdom or Province?*, pp. 170–4.
49. Paul Hopkins, *Glencoe and the End of the Highland War* (Edinburgh: John Donald, 1986), pp. 120–231.
50. P. W. J. Riley, *King William and the Scottish Politicians* (Edinburgh: John Donald, 1979), p. 4; Hopkins, *Glencoe*, pp. 126–7.
51. E. W. M. Balfour-Melville (ed.), *An Account of the Proceedings of the Estates of Scotland, 1689–90*, 2 vols (Edinburgh: Scottish History Society, 1954–5), i, pp. 88–9.
52. Riley, *King William and the Scottish Politicians*, p. 39; Brown, *Kingdom or Province?*, pp. 176–7; *APS*, ix, p. 196.
53. Houston, *Social Change*, pp. 69–70.
54. Tweedie (ed.), *Select Biographies*, i, p. 503.
55. *Memoirs of the Public Life of Mr James Hogg* (Edinburgh, 1798), p. 27.

56. NAS MS GD158/1036, Thomas Stewart to Sir Patrick Hume of Polwarth, 25 December 1688, cited in Derek J. Patrick, 'People and Parliament in Scotland, 1689–1702' (Ph.D. Thesis, University of St Andrews, 2002), fo. 96; Anderson, Lynch and Phillipson, *University of Edinburgh*, p. 48.
57. R. K. Hannay, 'The Visitation of the College of Edinburgh in 1690', *Book of the Old Edinburgh Club*, 8 (1915), pp. 79–100, at pp. 79–81, 86; William K. Dickson (ed.), 'Letters to John MacKenzie of Delvine from the Rev. Alexander Monro, 1690–1698', *Miscellany V* (Edinburgh: Scottish History Society, 1933), pp. 193–290, at pp. 198–200.
58. Hannay, 'Visitation of the College of Edinburgh', pp. 82–4.
59. W. T. Johnston (ed.), *The Best of Our Owne: Letters of Archibald Pitcairne, 1652–1713* (Edinburgh: Saorsa, 1979), p. 5; Wodrow, *Analecta*, ii, p. 255; NLS MS H.23.a.16, item 63; NAS MS E70/4/7, fo. 8.
60. *A Catalogue of the Graduates of the Faculties of Arts, Divinity, and Law, of the University of Edinburgh* (Edinburgh: Neill & Co., 1858), p. 138; John Toland, *A Collection of Several Pieces of Mr John Toland*, 2 vols (London: J. Peele, 1726), i, pp. vii–viii.
61. Bodleian Library MS Ballard V, fo. 48r (Gibson to Arthur Charlett, 21 June 1694); *Remarks on the Life of Mr Milton, as Published by J.T.* (London, 1699), p. 59; David Stevenson, *The Origins of Freemasonry: Scotland's Century, 1590–1710* (Cambridge: Cambridge University Press, 1988), pp. 96–104, 227; Sullivan, *John Toland and the Deist Controversy*, pp. 5–7.
62. *To the Memory of … Mr George Meldrum*, p. 3; John Warrick, *The Moderators of the Church of Scotland, 1690–1740* (Edinburgh: Oliphant, Anderson & Ferrer, 1913), pp. 94–5; Dunlop, *Kirks of Edinburgh*, p. 295.

2

The Politics of Blasphemy

By 1695 the honeymoon period for the new Presbyterian regime that came to power with the Revolution of 1689 (if, indeed, there had even been such a period) was certainly over.[1] Having thrown off the yoke of Restoration episcopacy, thus achieving a fundamental goal of the covenanting ideology to which so many of them subscribed, those who now comprised the political nation faced several related questions. First and foremost, how far should they push their victory? At what point (if ever) should those who had been involved in the government of Scotland under Charles II and (particularly) James VII and II be brought back into any positions of authority? Could distinctions related to degrees of implication in those now discredited governments be made? A parallel and inextricably linked debate was going on within the Presbyterian Kirk, which now once again dominated national religious life, but which would face a serious manpower shortage if, as many of its leaders insisted it should, it were to refuse the services of parish ministers who had conformed under episcopacy. The issue of the Episcopal clergy was complicated by relations with England, whose Anglican religious establishment viewed the Scots Episcopal clergy as co-religionists who ought at least to be tolerated, and preferably employed as well, north of the border. The ongoing hard-core Presbyterian refusal to make concessions to Episcopalians was answered by Englishmen of High Church inclinations with a refusal to countenance Protestant dissent in England (as English Protestant dissenters included Presbyterians).[2] For most Scots Presbyterian clergy, episcopacy was danger enough. But in addition, there was the threat of underground Catholicism and the relatively new scourge of Scottish Quakerism. Unless – as few would have suggested at the time – religious pluralism were to be accepted, such threats had to be identified and confronted.

These political and religious challenges were exacerbated by Scotland's position as the weaker partner in a union of Crowns whose head (now William III – or William II in Scotland – alone after the death of the popular

Mary in 1694) was a foreigner both to Scotland and England who needed to make use of the resources of both kingdoms in his ongoing military struggles against the France of Louis XIV. William would have preferred an episcopal religious settlement in both his kingdoms, but this was made impossible in Scotland by the apparent Jacobitism of the bishops in 1689, and the opposition to episcopacy expressed by the Convention Parliament of 1689–90. Beyond any religious considerations (and the king was pragmatic enough to lay these aside), William needed a Scottish kingdom that would not provide a foothold for his deposed uncle or the latter's French patron, and that would provide supply for troops. This ensured frequent meetings of parliament, necessary for the voting of taxation, but these parliaments were managed on the king's behalf by others, and they were at times difficult to control, particularly since one of the changes of 1689–90 had been the abolition of the Lords of the Articles, a committee traditionally used by the Scottish Crown to manage parliamentary business.[3] As a result, the discussions held at the gathering of the political nation could not always be orchestrated according to the script written in Whitehall. This would be demonstrated dramatically in 1695.

At the beginning of 1695 the management of Scottish affairs was in the hands of a group centred around John Hay, marquis of Tweeddale, a religious and political moderate who was well connected with leading political figures in England.[4] Tweeddale was Lord High Chancellor of Scotland, giving him an important voice on the Privy Council and the critical ceremonial position of representing the king at the Scottish parliament, which William never attended. The firmly Presbyterian Earl of Melville was Lord Privy Seal, while the key legal positions of Lord Justice Clerk and Lord Advocate were filled by Adam Cockburn of Ormiston and Sir James Stewart of Goodtrees, respectively. Both had strong Presbyterian credentials, but the latter, who would play a critical role in the fate of Thomas Aikenhead, had earned a black mark in the eyes of some by accepting a pardon from, and then serving in the government of, James VII. From exile in Holland, he had written the declaration that justified the Earl of Argyll's 1685 landing and uprising against James VII, but he had neglected to join the invasion himself. In 1687 he was pardoned and returned to Scotland, two to three years ahead of many of his convenanting colleagues. He had a reputation as an able lawyer, but his political machinations had garnered him the nickname 'Wily Jamie'.[5]

Those were the leading officials on the ground in Edinburgh. At court, Scottish affairs were nominally under the direction of Willem de Bentinck, earl of Portland, but he, like the king, was hampered by the fact that he was Dutch. So the king's (and Portland's) real advisers on Scotland were

William Carstares, the king's Scottish chaplain, and the two Scottish secretaries, James Johnston and Sir John Dalrymple, master of Stair. Carstares was a minister of covenanting heritage – his father had been forfeited after the Pentland Rising of 1666, and Carstares himself had been tortured with thumbscrews in 1684 for his suspected knowledge of the Rye House Plot. Freed thereafter, he had joined William's court in Holland, and sailed with him to England in 1688 on William's own ship, the *Brill*.[6] Johnston was the son of the lawyer and leading covenanter Archibald Johnston of Wariston, and had grown up in exile in Holland, giving him impeccable Presbyterian/revolutionary credentials, although, as will be seen, he was moving in a more moderate direction, and would later be a leading critic of Thomas Aikenhead's execution. Since taking office he had shown a willingness to scold the clergy for their excessive zeal and presumption, and in March 1694 he had written of the need for Scotland's governors 'to be quit out of the dread of the high church party'.[7] Dalrymple of Stair was a counterweight to the 'high presbyterians' who dominated the Scottish administration – he had served in the government of James VII while his own father was in exile in Holland – but he would be forced out of office early in 1696, ostensibly because of his bureaucratic role in the slaughter of the MacDonalds of Glencoe in 1692.[8]

2.1 'PROPHANENESS' AND BLASPHEMY

Since the General Assembly of the Kirk was not a source of revenue, the king did not give it permission to meet as often, or for as long, as parliament. William was frustrated (and the bishops of England offended) by the General Assembly's reluctance to make peace with clergy who had conformed under episcopacy and, if the Presbyterian ministry were not going to cooperate on that point, he preferred that their meetings be brief and infrequent. An assembly in early 1692 had been cut short, and a subsequent assembly had been postponed twice before it was finally allowed to convene at the end of March 1694.[9] This assembly at least appointed a committee to review applications from former Episcopal clergy north of the Tay, but the king would have preferred much more. It also passed an Act 'against Profaneness' that lamented the dishonouring of God 'by the impiety and profaneness that aboundeth in this nation'. As manifestations of these, the ministers listed many of the ills that had been denounced in General Assembly pronouncements dating back to the sixteenth century: swearing, cursing, Sabbath breach, fornication, adultery and drunkenness. But there were some new elements as well, such as the 'mocking of piety and religious exercises' and 'blasphemy'. The Act urged ministers to 'preach plainly and faithfully against these vices' and warn listeners of the judgements threatened by God against their practitioners. Church courts were told to take action against offenders and urge magistrates to enforce relevant Acts of Parliament.[10]

This was far from being the first mention of blasphemy, either in the records of the General Assembly or, for that matter, in parliamentary legislation. It had occasionally come up, in the sense of 'swearing' or 'cursing', in both, dating back to the sixteenth century, and parliamentary statutes had mandated fines for the offence.[11] These drew on medieval Christian thinking about blasphemy, which saw it primarily as what David Nash has called 'a public-order problem', with the typical offender being someone who 'uttered curses belittling the power of God or denying his divinity as part of impetuous outbursts', often under the influence of alcohol, anger or both.[12] But in the latter seventeenth century the word had taken on a more specific – and more sinister – meaning. Rather than indicating a looseness of speech that might suggest an overly casual or disrespectful attitude towards the sacred, it now meant a conscious attack on fundamental tenets of Christianity. This was clear in an Act of Parliament passed in 1661, which stated:

> Considering that hitherto ther hath been no law in this Kingdom against the horrible cryme of blasphemy ... whosoever heirafter not being distracted in his wits shall raill upon or curse God or any of the persones of the blessed Trinity, shall be processed befor the Chieff Justice; and being fund guilty shall be punished with death.

The same was to hold for anyone who 'shall deny God or any of the persones of the blessed Trinity and obstinately continew therin'.[13] This law was made retroactive to February 1649 (and indeed was a restatement of an Act passed by the radical covenanter parliament meeting then, but which was not regarded as legitimate after the Restoration). It was little used, however. A woman in Dumfries who reportedly drank to the Devil's health was acquitted of blasphemy (although fined 500 merks) in 1671.[14] Three years after noting that case in his *Laws and Customs of Scotland*, in which he defined blasphemy as *'divine lese Majesty, or Treason'*,[15] the Lord Advocate Sir George MacKenzie of Rosehaugh took time out from prosecuting the rebels of Bothwell Bridge to pursue a blasphemy charge against Francis Borthwick, the younger son of a laird who converted to Judaism and underwent circumcision while abroad. Borthwick had then returned to Edinburgh where he allegedly

> did raile against our Lord and Saviour Jesus Christ denying him to be God and affirming him to be meir man and a false prophet and outrageouslie

revileing him by such other horrid blasphemies as are not fitt to be uttered, renouncing and curseing ye holy sacrament and rite of his baptizme and he did wish great & horrid execrations with all maner of judgement to befall him if ever he should returne to ye Christian Religion.

Perhaps sensing the legal judgment that might befall him if he stuck around, Borthwick fled rather than appearing for trial, and was declared an outlaw in June 1681.[16] The law then fell into disuse. So, when the General Assembly of 1694 called for ministers and magistrates to take action against (among other things) blasphemy, this was presumably the sort of blasphemy, and the parliamentary statute, that members had in mind.

2.2 THE PARLIAMENT OF 1695

King William was not unsympathetic. While he had a reputation for tolerance, and had explicitly disavowed being a 'persecutor' when taking the Scots Coronation Oath in 1689, neither he nor any other ruler, then or now, really wanted to appear to be a *defender* of blasphemy.[17] It also seems likely that a minister like Carstares would have suggested to him that the General Assembly would be more sympathetic to his goals regarding the displaced Episcopal ministers if the King seemed willing to take a more aggressive line with other ills perceived by the 'high presbyterians'. Even Johnston, though he later was to claim that the 1695 blasphemy statute was 'obtained by trick and surprise', wanted to get concessions from the Presbyterian ministry, since he had promised Thomas Tenison, the Archbishop of Canterbury, that he would do something to ease the lot of the unemployed Episcopalians.[18] These considerations were incorporated into the instructions sent from the king, via Johnston, to Tweeddale on what was wanted from the parliament scheduled to convene in May 1695, the fifth session of the Convention Parliament.[19] First and foremost, Tweeddale was to obtain all necessary supplies for standing forces, and get additional money to buy and maintain frigates for as long as the war against France lasted. After this, he could turn to the issue of the displaced Episcopalians, 'to get such Acts past, as shall tend to the composing [of] differences about Church matters and amongst Church men', setting a new deadline for the ousted ministers to take oaths of allegiance. Then he was to shepherd the passage of an Act establishing a Scots company for trading with Africa and the Americas (this was the genesis of the Darien fiasco, which would end with the loss of 2,000 colonists' lives and over £1.8 million – much of the nation's liquid wealth – when a poorly situated colony on the Isthmus of Panama failed in 1698–1700). After these four top items came a long list of Acts the king wanted passed – twenty-five in all

– presumably in descending order of importance, including various legal reforms and the founding of a post office. Twenty-first on the list was the instruction 'to pass an Act for Reviving old lawes and to consent to new ones for Punishing and discouraging all Prophaneness and irreligion'.

Certainly, 'prophaneness and irreligion' could run the gamut from dancing or playing golf on the Sabbath to apostasy or philosophical atheism. Johnston may have envisioned a legislative crackdown on items at the former end of the scale, which would result in stricter enforcement of fines and more people inhabiting the 'stools of repentance' in their churches; this would explain his 'trick and surprise' comment. Tweeddale was given additional 'secret instructions', and these, perhaps more reflective of the king's true priorities, did not mention any legislation relating to religious issues at all.[20] Meanwhile, rumours were circulating in Edinburgh that parliament would gather and then swiftly be dissolved to allow new elections that might yield a majority in favour of episcopacy. While there is no evidence in official correspondence of such a plan, the rumour, which the devout Presbyterian George Home noted in his diary, suggests the extent to which those who remained committed to the covenanting legacy still felt embattled. The Convention Parliament itself had been elected in the spring of 1689 under a franchise that had barred Catholics from voting but had allowed participation of all Protestants who met property qualifications, and the result was a legislature that favoured Presbyterianism in its covenanted form. Home and many others wanted to keep it that way.[21]

As the parliament convened in 1695, the Presbyterian ministers did their best to organise a lobbying campaign, even though they had not had the advantage of a recent General Assembly to plot it out. The first sitting of the parliament was on 9 May. Johnston himself had come from Whitehall to assist Tweeddale with parliamentary management, and even William Carstares, the king's Presbyterian chaplain, was in Edinburgh for a while in May, but he headed south shortly thereafter.[22] On 14 May the parliament, as had become customary in the 1690s, established four committees: one for the address to the king, one for the 'Security of the Kingdom', one for trade and one for contested elections.[23] Reflecting its heavy responsibilities, the Security Committee was the largest, with seven members from each estate of peers, barons and burgh representatives.[24] Meanwhile, a small group of ministers from all over the kingdom, but dominated by those from Edinburgh, began meeting, sending delegations to visit Tweeddale, Johnston, the Lord Advocate James Stewart, and the Justice Clerk Adam Cockburn of Ormiston.[25] The ministers were also preparing their own address to parliament, and apparently sharing drafts of this document with the officials they met. Johnston for one thought the ministers' list of concerns was too long. They tried several times to get him to comment and he put them off; he finally told the ministers George Meldrum, William Crichton and George Hamilton on 27 May that the list 'should be contracted as much as possible, y[ai]r being laws already for many of yese things in ye paper'.[26] The grievances were distilled into seven items in the next three days and then published.[27] All but one of the items warned of the dangers posed by Episcopal clergy, seen as a threat to doctrine, discipline and the patrimony of the kirk. Only the first item seems independent of this fixation on the dangers of incorporating the outed ministers. It warned that

> notwithstanding of many good and excellent laws made against Prophanity of all sorts, yet all kind of Wickedness doth exceedingly abound, especially cursing, and swearing, Sabbath breaking, Drunkenness, Uncleaness, &c. And in all appearance will more and more encrease, unless some method be fallen on for a vigorous Execution of those Laws.

Given what we know of Johnston's goals, it is not hard to see why he had been unimpressed with this address. More significantly for our purposes, 'blasphemy' seems to have dropped out of the catalogue of dangers since the General Assembly of 1694. Perhaps it had been taken out in response to Johnston's concern for brevity; there was, after all, already a law against it in the books. But sometime in the next few weeks it would return to the catalogue. The ministers' address was referred to the Security Committee, a legislative shunting that might surprise modern readers, but that surely made sense to contemporaries, many of whom regarded staving off God's wrath as one of the most critical issues in public security.

The ministers also employed sermons, one of the leading weapons in the marketplace of Scottish public opinion, in their campaign. Published sermons would often note the audience, so as to inform future readers who did, and who did not, pay attention. David Williamson, minister of Edinburgh's West Kirk, preached one on 9 June before Tweeddale and other high officials, using as his text Isaiah 38:3, in which Hezekiah wept in fear of his impending death.[28] Williamson warned that all people, even powerful men such as those in his audience, would eventually face death, and they must prepare themselves by glorifying God, studying Scripture, taking account of their own behaviour and carrying out their public responsibilities.

> How many of all Ranks, walks in Drunkenness, Lying, Swearing, whordom [sic], sabbath-breaking, Living a Prayerless Life bringing forth the Fruits of Atheism, which excludes People out of Heaven and brings on the Wrath

of GOD ... I am afraid there is a storm of Wrath and Vengeance coming on the land, if matters mend not.[29]

Later, Williamson seemed to echo the address of the ministers and their fears of the Episcopal clergy, but linking those with the old covenanter scourge of innovation and the new fear of atheism. Here perhaps we see a fuller, unedited version of the address:

> Many of them [Episcopal clergy] who refuse to own the Government of Kirk and State, take on them[selves] to preach Irregularly, Baptize Children, and even of scandalous persons, without regard to the removing of the Scandal; and marry persons clandestinely without Knowledge or consent of Parents. Who are secure of their Children at this rate? ... Some of them have likeways brought in *innovations* in Worship, never used under any Government of Protestants in Scotland ... from all which flows and abounds Prophaness, Irreligion and Atheism, notwithstanding of all the excellent Laws made against them.[30]

Admittedly, 'atheism' was a term used rather indiscriminately in the seventeenth century.[31] Like 'blasphemy', it could cover a multitude of sins or unacceptable beliefs or declarations. But the two would be linked in the Aikenhead case, as was the relatively new term 'deism'.[32] Whether or not Johnston's concerns led to the omission of any of these terms from the ministers' address, they were now creeping back onto the agenda. But in the meantime the interests of the political nation had been distracted elsewhere.

Soon after the 1695 parliament had got down to business, and even before it had voted the supply the king had listed at the top of Tweeddale's instructions, it became fixated on a scandal that had not figured in any of William's instructions to this parliament, secret or otherwise. This was the matter of Glencoe – the slaughter of members of a sept of the MacDonald clan by government troops quartered on them in February 1692, ostensibly because MacDonald of Glencoe had missed (barely) a deadline for swearing allegiance to William and Mary. This incident of state-sponsored terrorism aroused an indignation that caught the government by surprise. Ironically (given that the slain MacDonalds had been Episcopal in religion), the outrage was fuelled in part by Presbyterian apprehensions about the government's plans. As Gilbert Burnet, Johnston's cousin who had emigrated southwards and become an English bishop, analysed it: 'a great party came to be formed in this session [of parliament], of a very odd mixture: the High Presbyterians and the Jacobites, joined together to oppose every thing ...' At his home in the Borders, George Home had already heard by 22 May that 'the parlia[ment] was designing to look into the affairs of the M[a]cDonalds of Glenco who were murthered by a party of Argiles regim[en]t ... they say ther was ane order for it from the King, but I hear not how it was procured'.[33] Among the officials most implicated in Glencoe was Sir John Dalrymple, master of Stair, Johnston's colleague as Scottish secretary. There was no love lost between the two, and Stair's opponents, who included much of the political nation, milked this issue for all it was worth.[34] The Security Commission made a motion to investigate the matter on 21 May, only to be put off by Tweeddale, who said it was being investigated by a separate royal commission. By June, parliament was passing repeated motions that it wanted to hear the commission's report, and Tweeddale was forced repeatedly to make excuses, reluctant to have the matter discussed openly.[35] When he sought the king's advice, Tweeddale did not get much – William was campaigning in Flanders, spending much more time with generals than Scottish undersecretaries such as Robert Pringle, Tweeddale's intermediary.[36] The marquis was forced to follow his own instincts. Meanwhile, parliament voted supply and approved the establishment of the African Company, while public interest focused on the political circus that the Glencoe scandal had become. Gentleman visitors to the capital like George Home sat in on meetings through much of June, hoping to hear juicy details of ministerial malfeasance.[37] Finally, on 27 June, Stair's enemies were promised what they were seeking: a discussion of the Glencoe affair the next day. But first, in the morning, the Security Committee was to bring in for consideration all legislation relating to the address from the ministers. Only after those items were considered would business turn to Glencoe.[38]

Thus, when the Security Committee presented several Acts on the morning of 28 June, the minds of many members would have been focused elsewhere, eager to discuss the biggest political scandal since the Revolution. In fact the committee, probably urged by Johnston, had sidestepped many of the condemnations of the outed ministers contained in the ministers' address. Where the ministers had argued that the Episcopal clergy themselves were the problem, the committee chose to attack symptoms, so that another bill could take on the 'problem', in a way more to the government's liking, later in the parliamentary session. What parliament hurriedly passed that morning were four Acts – one against blasphemy, one against irregular baptisms and marriages by outed clergy, one against 'profaneness' (which, as described in the Act, amounted to public scandal) and one allowing magistrates to reschedule Saturday or Monday markets so that travel to them did not encourage Sabbath breach.[39] Of most interest here is the fact that 'blasphemy' was clearly removed from the general category of 'profaneness', where it had resided at the 1694 General Assembly, and restored to a separate place, in keeping with the statute of 1661. Thus parliament was unequivocally affirming that 'blasphemy' was a sin of a very different, and more serious, order, worthy of renewed public attention. Tweeddale could say that he was acting within the king's instructions, and the 'high presbyterians' were granted a major concession, to sweeten the bitter pill that would follow when the agenda turned to the outed ministers themselves. Of the three London newspapers with dispatches from Edinburgh covering that day's sitting, one of them, the Tory-leaning *Post Boy*, did not even mention the blasphemy statute. It devoted the bulk of its report to Glencoe and added as an afterthought that the parliament passed 'an Act discharging all prophane Cursing and Swearing, and other Debaucheries', suggesting that its correspondent saw all the religious Acts as one. But the *Flying Post*, whose newswriter was the Scot and committed Presbyterian George Ridpath, kicked off its coverage with the religious acts – specifically mentioning blasphemy – and then went on to Glencoe, albeit devoting many more column inches to the latter. Interestingly, the government-sponsored *London Gazette* began its report with the blasphemy statute, although its coverage of that day's meeting was on the whole the briefest of the three. Several issues later, the *Flying Post* even published the texts of the Acts against blasphemy and profaneness, because of their 'being much taken notice of here' – that is, in Edinburgh.[40]

The blasphemy Act itself stipulated that the 1661 Act AGAINST Blasphemy was 'to be put to due and punctual execution', thus recognising its near desuetude. But it also expanded on that earlier statute, adding to the category of blasphemers those who might question the authority of Scripture or 'the providence of God in the government of the world'. First offenders were to be imprisoned, pending their public repentance, second offenders to be heavily fined, with a portion of the fine going to any informer in the case, and the penalty for a third offence was death.[41] With these graduated punishments, the statute was a bit milder (and thus more likely to be invoked) than that of 1661. Parliament had softened the penalties as it refined the definition of blasphemy. There is no record of any debate on, or opposition to, this bill, or any of the other four bills passed that morning, and it seems doubtful that anyone would have tried to block it. First of all, members wanted to move on to the Glencoe business, and, secondly, nobody would have spoken up in the Scottish parliament for a person's right to blaspheme. Tweeddale himself would have been in a hurry, as the king's deadline for ending the session was approaching, and he had not yet received an extension.[42] So the statutory framework that would eventually lead Thomas Aikenhead to the gallows had been erected while attention was focused elsewhere, as a way of placating a Presbyterian party into acceptance of something else.

That something else would come on 16 July, when parliament passed an Act allowing former Episcopal clergy to keep their benefices and practise their calling provided they took the Oath of Allegiance to the king.[43] This was the Church compromise that Johnston and the king had been seeking, since it offered the possibility of healing the rift that had split Scottish Protestantism. Johnston then travelled north of the Tay, lobbying with the outed ministers to take the oath, and, by October, 116 of them had done so, one of them writing a personal thank-you note to Tweeddale, commending his 'fatherlie tenderness and seasonable compassion towards the poor remains of a broken and languishing societie'.[44] On the other side, the Presbyterian minister David Blair, writing to William Carstares, consoled himself that this Act did not mean the Episcopalians would have to be accepted 'in to ministerial communion' with the Presbyterians, but he could not help noting that its passage had coincided with another postponement of a General Assembly, this postponement coming so late that many clergy had already arrived in Edinburgh: 'it was a pity to see the ministers flocking in from all parts; and, in the mean time, their adversaries flouting at them for having lost their labour.'[45] After these twin blows to Presbyterian prestige, the magistrates would have to show some commitment to godliness.

2.3 POLITICAL CHANGES AND THE GENERAL ASSEMBLY OF 1695–6

Carstares, who managed to remain in the king's good graces until the end, may have decided that Johnston's own commitment to godliness, despite the latter's covenanting exile past and illustrious parentage, was now in question. In the spring and summer of 1695 a rift developed between the two that has never been fully understood.[46] It may have originated in Johnston's bid, staved off by Carstares, to force the Oath of Allegiance on Presbyterian clergy attending the General Assembly of 1694.[47] One observer had commented on the frostiness between the two in April 1695, and in November wrote that they clearly were not getting along. Even worse for Johnston's position was that he by then had 'a great deal of the nobility against him'.[48] This would have included the Earl of Melville, the Duke of Queensberry and John, Lord Murray, who would become Earl of Tullibardine in 1696 and later succeed his father as Marquis of Atholl. Murray was a very recent convert to the Presbyterian cause, and could still be tarred as a Jacobite by critics.[49] The king was generally angry about the way the parliamentary session had turned out – first the forcing of the Glencoe matter and then the passage of the Darien Act, which was now causing controversy in the English parliament. His adviser Portland blamed Johnston for the 'republican' extension of parliament without royal warrant.[50] Writing to Tweeddale from London, Johnston privately admitted that he had never even read the 'East India Act' – the legislation that had set up the Scots trading company – until after the Scots parliamentary session was over, but that he thought Sir James Stewart of Goodtrees, as king's advocate, had exceeded the limits of his instructions in drafting it, perhaps because of bribery from Scots merchants.[51] By November he was lamenting that 'all our affairs were right in the King's mind as I certainly know, but now the Trade-Act undoes all. It proves a popular handle for all bad designs both with respect to the King and us.' This would have been particularly frustrating for Johnston, given the apparent success of his longstanding efforts to heal (at least in the legislative sense) the rift within the Scots Protestant clergy. He suggested to Tweeddale that the fallout from the 'Trade-Act' might force him and Tweeddale from office, just as Dalrymple of Stair was expected to be sacked over Glencoe: 'My l[or]d Stairs is to go out which he knows but ads that you and I go with him.' By early January 1696, Stewart of Goodtrees was in London, allegedly plotting Scots ministerial changes with Carstares, and rumours soon reached Edinburgh that he had managed to place the blame for the Trade Act on Johnston. Johnston told Tweeddale he was willing to resign, but he wanted to make clear to all that he had no financial interest in the Scots trading company.[52] However unholy the alliance that opposed him, Johnston's position became too precarious. Hard-core Presbyterians, unhappy with his moderate tendencies, joined with aristocrats, some of whose loyalty to the settlement of 1689 could be questioned. The twin fiascos they exploited – the 'Trade-Act' and the Glencoe inquiry – could hardly be laid on Johnston's doorstep. But politics is never fair. From Edinburgh, George Home reported: 'Ther is a great noise in toune that one of the secretaries are turned out ... they say Stair would be content to goe out provided the other [Johnston] went off also.' The English parliament was up in arms over the Trade Act, and

> the K[ing]'s answer was that he was ill used in Scotland but that he hoped some remedy would be found out for these inconveniences. We are here very angry the English should meddle w[i]t[h] us as if we depended on them. Mr Johnstons trouble is all from this and they say the Lo[rd] Stair foments it.[53]

The Politics of Blasphemy   45

Early in 1696, both Scottish secretaries were replaced, first Dalrymple by Murray and then Johnston by Sir James Ogilvy, a younger son of the Earl of Findlater. Johnston had to vacate his Whitehall lodgings in late February.[54] The new Scots administration in Whitehall would have a more aristocratic face. By turning against his former ally Johnston, Stewart of Goodtrees managed to hang onto his position as Lord Advocate in Edinburgh, as did Cockburn of Ormiston as Justice Clerk, leaving two firm Presbyterians in control of the legal apparatus of the state. The ambitious Stewart would be among those vying for the post of Lord President of the Court of Session, left vacant by the death of James Dalrymple of Stair, the erstwhile secretary's father, in November 1695.[55] In May, Tweeddale was replaced as Chancellor by Sir Patrick Hume of Polwarth, another ex-Johnston ally and covenanting exile of 1684–8, whose mandate was to hold the government together without offending any of the magnates – an unenviable task, which would leave him perpetually uncertain of his standing.[56] Stewart of Goodtrees' successful machiavellian machinations made him a figure of whom his fellow officers of state would have to be wary. Johnston would remain in England, cultivating friends there such as John Locke, and keeping a weather eye on Scottish affairs.[57] The combination of bitterness at losing his position and his association with broad-minded English *literati* would lead to his being perhaps the leading Scottish critic of the Aikenhead execution a year later.

Meanwhile, the king felt confident enough of the state of Scottish Church affairs to allow the General Assembly to meet again. It convened in mid-December 1695. Perhaps the moderating influence of John, Lord Carmichael, the king's commissioner, prevented any overt complaints about the Episcopal clergy from creeping into the resolutions passed.[58] But there were plenty of other enemies to true religion around, about whom there was a greater consensus in Church and State. The assembly passed an Act against itinerant Catholic priests, and expressed concern about the education of young noblemen whose parents were popish.[59] Quakers were another target: ministers and church courts were to try and 'reclaim' them, but 'in case of their obstinancy, to proceed against them with the censures of the Church, and especially against the ringleaders, that are traffickers and seducing [sic] of others'.[60]

Even more dangerous was another kind of seducer. This would be reflected in the Act 'against the Atheistical Opinions of the Deists' passed on the morning of 4 January 1696:

> The General Assembly of this National Church, taking into their serious consideration that, in many places, not a few of Atheistical principles, who go under the name of Deists, and for the time refuse the odious character

of Atheist, maintain and disseminate pernicious principles tending to Scepticism and Atheism; and that there is no small ground to fear the spreading of that gangrene through this land, where (as it is credibly informed) there are not wanting active factors for Satan, and his kingdom of darkness, who make it their great business to overturn and ridicule true and pure religion ...

In response to this clear and present danger, the assembly told ministers

to warn and guard the Lord's people against that infernal course, and to detect the abominableness of the tenets of those men, such as the denying of all revealed religion, the grand mysteries of the Gospel, viz The Doctrine of the Trinity – the incarnation of the Messiah – His satisfaction to justice – salvation through Him – justification by His imputed righteousness to them who believe on His name – the resurrection of the dead – and, in a word, the certainty and authority of scripture revelation; as also, their asserting that there must be a mathematical evidence for each purpose, before we can be obliged to assent to any proposition thereanent, and that natural light is sufficient to salvation.

Authors who made such claims were to 'be named to the people'. Ministers were advised to 'deal seriously with the seduced ... but especially with seducers and imposters, that, after sufficient instruction and admonition, these be proceeded against as scandalous and heretical apostates used to be'.[61]

Those who drew up this Act were doubtless aware that it paralleled the Blasphemy Act of the previous summer, but offered more detail. In fact, the way in which this Act listed specific challenges to Christian orthodoxy – it could almost be taken as an update on the Nicene Creed – suggests that its authors had at least a passing familiarity with some of the more notorious deist authors of the late seventeenth century, such as Charles Blount, who in his *Oracles of Reason* (1693) had praised deism by name, had ridiculed the plausibility of the Genesis account of the fall of Adam and Eve and who had offered an alternative history of the Arian/Trinitarian debate in which the Trinitarians were presented as 'enemies to all human learning'.[62] Blount questioned the Mosaic authorship of the first five books of the Jewish Scriptures, asked how Noah could have fit two of every animal as well as food for forty days on an ark 'within the Extent of Three Hundred Cubits', argued that the world had to be more than six thousand years old, and that the Universe was probably eternal.[63] Blount's book was circulating in Edinburgh, as will be seen, and there are other, hostile reports of deism in the capital at the time. William Lorimer, an English non-conformist clergyman who was to visit Edinburgh in 1696, wrote that 'some were said to come from London, or from beyond Sea, or from both, and to have brought with them to Edinburgh the Plague of blasphemous Deism ...'⁶⁴ One who, although native to the city, had recently come from beyond sea was the physician Archibald Pitcairne, who has been suggested by James Cameron as the inspiration behind the General Assembly's act.⁶⁵ The continentally-educated Pitcairne was a founding member of the Royal College of Physicians, and had been appointed professor of medicine at the College/University of Edinburgh in 1685. But his Jacobite sympathies made Edinburgh less hospitable to him after 1689, so in 1692 he had accepted a post at the University of Leiden. He did not stay there long, however, returning to Edinburgh in 1693 to practise medicine again, and to participate in pamphlet wars against both his professional rivals – at least one of whom accused him in 1695 of drunkenness, atheism and 'bantering the Scripture' – and the High Presbyterians. Robert Wodrow's (very mixed) views on Pitcairne were noted in the previous chapter.⁶⁶ Among Pitcairne's activities that winter was writing a comedy entitled 'The Assemblie, or, the Scottish Reformation', although this would circulate only in manuscript until 1722.⁶⁷ He lived near the Tron Kirk, a neighbourhood also inhabited by Thomas Aikenhead, to whose deceased mother he was related by marriage.

But these anti-orthodox currents were not restricted to Edinburgh. The minister Alexander Telfair wrote at the end of 1695 a pamphlet describing the haunting of a house in his Kircudbrightshire parish that year, offering as his primary reason for publishing it 'the conviction and confutation of that prevailing spirit of Atheism, and Infidelity in our time, denying both in Opinion and Practice the Existence of Spirits, either of God or Devils; and consequently a Heaven and Hell'.⁶⁸ Thomas Halyburton, who had been a classmate of Aikenhead's at the College in Edinburgh before transferring to St Andrews for health reasons, and who later became a Presbyterian minister, recalled in his rather Augustinian memoirs how, when living in a noble household in Wemyss in the late summer of 1696, he was frequently 'engag'd in Debates about the Truth of Religion, the Divinity of the Scriptures and the most important doctrines delivered in them, whereby I was drawn to read the writing of Deists, and other Enemies of Religion'.⁶⁹ Halyburton's retrospective view presented this as a close shave; he nearly joined their ranks himself. What is more, he had first been assailed by these doubts when he had been a student in Edinburgh, sitting in lectures alongside Thomas Aikenhead.

We should be wary of reading too much into the literature of Reformed ministerial complaint, a genre with a long history in Scots Presbyterianism as well as English Puritanism. Such jeremiads tended always to warn that sin was at an all-time high. What is significant here is how the nature of the threat to godly society seems to have changed. The old dangers of drunkenness, fornication, adultery and popery were still there, but they had now been joined by a particularly sinister form of irreligion. This was not the generalised 'atheism' of the sixteenth and early seventeenth centuries, which could mean any form of incorrect belief. Rather, as identified by the blasphemy statute and the General Assembly's act against deism, this was the refusal to accept certain particular aspects of the Nicene Creed, the basic blueprint of Christianity. Francis Borthwick had questioned these back in 1681, but from the perspective of Judaism – an older, known threat. These deists, or atheists (and the two terms would still be used interchangeably), were something new. They also reflected a pollution from outside – primarily, it would seem, from that source of so many other threats to the Covenanted State: England. But by 1696 it had taken root in Scotland, and now both the Kirk and the magistrates, as represented by parliament, had pledged to root it out. Doubtless many of the ministers who voted for the Act against deism were sceptical of the magistrates' commitment – Scottish authorities had always seemed more godly in passing Acts of Parliament concerning religion and the agenda of Reform than in enforcing them.[70] We cannot know how many deists there were in Scotland at the beginning of 1696. But there was clearly a heightened awareness of the danger of this sinister conspiracy against the Godly. It would also be reflected in an increased number of Scottish pamphlets on the subject, in sermons, and in the books purchased by the library of the College of Edinburgh. This state of alert, coupled with the manifold stresses of the year that was to come, would inspire the ministers and magistrates to go out and find a couple deists in order to placate an obviously angry God. Thomas Aikenhead would be the least fortunate of them.

NOTES

1. The standard guide to the Scottish politics of the era is Riley, *King William and the Scottish Politicians*.
2. Craig Rose, *England in the 1690s: Revolution, Religion and War* (Oxford: Blackwell, 1999), pp. 214–15.
3. Riley, *King William and the Scottish Politicians*, pp. 4, 39; Patrick, 'People and Parliament in Scotland', ch. 8.
4. Riley, *King William and the Scottish Politicians*, p. 54.
5. Omond, *Lord Advocates*, i, pp. 243–80; Beisner, 'His Majesty's Advocate', fos 304, 313–15.
6. Dunlop, *William Carstares*, pp. 18–21, 35–6, 42–7, 59–60.
7. Riley, *King William and the Scottish Politicians*, pp. 60–1; James Johnston

to Mr Robert Crichton, 24 November 1692, NAS MS SP3/1, fo. 56v; Johnston to the Earl of Annandale, 22 March 1694, *HMC, Fifteenth Report, Appendix, Part IX: The Manuscripts of J. J. Hope Johnstone, esq. Of Annandale* (London: HMSO, 1897), p. 96.
8. Riley, *King William and the Scottish Politicians*, pp. 75, 94–7.
9. Thomas Pitcairn (ed.), *Acts of the General Assembly of the Church of Scotland, 1638–1842*, 2 vols (Edinburgh: Ritchie, 1843), i, p. 235.
10. Ibid. i, p. 241.
11. e.g. in 1551 (*APS*, ii, p. 485), 1581 (under which a fourth-time utterer of 'abhominabill aithis' might be warded for a year, *APS*, iii, p. 212), 1645 (*APS*, vi, part i, p. 458).
12. David Nash, *Blasphemy in the Christian World: A History* (Oxford: Oxford University Press, 2007), pp. 3, 109–10.
13. *APS*, vii, pp. 202–3.
14. George MacKenzie, *The Laws and Customs of Scotland in Matters Criminal* (Edinburgh: Thomas Brown, 1678), p. 28. For the parliament that met early in 1649, dominated by the Marquis of Argyll and his supporters, see John J. Scally, 'The Rise and Fall of the Covenanter Parliaments, 1639–51', in Keith M. Brown and Alastair J. Mann (eds), *Parliament and Politics in Scotland, 1567–1707* (Edinburgh: Edinburgh University Press, 2005), pp. 138–62, at pp. 156–8.
15. MacKenzie, *Laws and Customs*, p. 25.
16. NAS MSS JC2/15, fos 339v–340r, JC6/10, fo. 314r; Hugo Arnot, *A Collection and Abridgement of Celebrated Criminal Trials in Scotland, 1536–1784* (Glasgow: Napier, [1785] 1812), pp. 363–4.
17. Balfour-Melville (ed.), *Proceedings of the Estates*, i, pp. 88–9.
18. James Johnston to John Locke, 27 February 1697, in E. S. De Beer (ed.), *The Correspondence of John Locke*, 8 vols (Oxford: Clarendon Press, 1976–89), vi, pp. 17–19; Riley, *King William and the Scottish Politicians*, p. 82.
19. NAS MS SP4/18, fos 11–14.
20. NAS MS SP4/18, fos 15–16.
21. *Home Diary*, p. 56; Derek Patrick, 'Unconventional Procedure: Scottish Electoral Politics after the Revolution', in Keith Brown and Alastair Mann (eds), *Parliament and Politics in Scotland, 1567–1707* (Edinburgh: Edinburgh University Press, 2005), pp. 208–44, at pp. 212–14.
22. Tweeddale to James Johnston, 7 May 1695, NLS MS 7029, fos 27v–28r; Tweeddale to Alexander Johnston, 11 May 1695, ibid. fo. 30v.
23. The committee system evolved as an alternative to the abolished Lords of the Articles, and the particular committee structure of 1695 had first been employed in the 1693 parliamentary session. See Patrick, 'People and Parliament in Scotland', fo. 368.
24. *APS*, ix, pp. 347, 351.
25. NAS MS CH1/2/2a, fos 1–5; NLS MS 9251, fo. 107.

26. NAS MS CH1/2/2a, fo. 2v.
27. *The Humble Representation of the Ministers from the Synods and Presbytries of this Church, Met at Edinburgh, May 30 1695 Years* (Edinburgh, 1695).
28. David Williamson, *A Sermon Preached in the High Church of Edinburgh, June 9th 1695* (Edinburgh: George Mosman, 1696).
29. Ibid. p. 35.
30. Ibid. pp. 50–1.
31. Michael Hunter, 'The Problem of "Atheism" in Early Modern England', *Transactions of the Royal Historical Society* (5th series), 35 (1985), pp. 135–57, at p. 142; David Wooton, 'New Histories of Atheism', in Michael Hunter and David Wooton (eds), *Atheism from the Reformation to the Enlightenment* (Oxford: Oxford University Press, 1992), pp. 13–53, at pp. 24–6.
32. While Hunter has traced the first use of the word 'deist' to the 1590s, it was not much in use until the late seventeenth century. See Hunter, 'Problem of "Atheism"', p. 156.
33. Gilbert Burnet, *History of his own Time*, 2 vols (London: Thomas Ward, 1724–34), ii, pp. 156–7; *Home Diary*, p. 65. For a highly detailed account of the inquiry into Glencoe, see Hopkins, *Glencoe*, pp. 395–435.
34. Riley, *King William and the Scottish Politicians*, p. 94–7.
35. *APS*, ix, pp. 354, 366, 371, 376.
36. Robert Pringle to Tweeddale, 27 May, 10 and 24 June 1695, NLS MS 7018, fos 84r–85r, 96r–v, 102r–103r.
37. *Home Diary*, pp. 70, 72.
38. *APS*, ix, p. 381.
39. *APS*, ix, pp. 386–8.
40. *Post Boy*, 25 (4–6 July 1695); *Flying Post*, 22 (4–6 July 1695) and 25 (11–13 July 1695); *London Gazette*, 3094 (4–8 July 1695). Details on political leanings of papers from E. S. De Beer, 'The English Newspapers from 1695 to 1702', in Ragnhild Hatton and J. S. Bromley (eds), *William III and Louis XIV* (Liverpool: Liverpool University Press, 1968), pp. 117–29.
41. *APS*, ix, pp. 386–7.
42. Pringle to Tweeddale, no date but in July 1695, NLS MS 7018, fo. 120r. Apparently an extension was sent, but it was lost when the French captured the packet boat carrying it. See Hopkins, *Glencoe*, p. 410.
43. *APS*, ix, pp. 449–50; Burnet, *History*, ii, pp. 156–7.
44. George Seton to Tweeddale, 30 October 1695, NLS MS 7019, fo. 113r–v; Sir James Ogilvy to Carstares, 26 October 1695, in Joseph McCormick (ed.), *State Papers and Letters Addressed to William Carstares* (Edinburgh: John Balfour, 1774), p. 263; Riley, *King William and the Scottish Politicians*, p. 95.
45. David Blair to William Carstares, 18 July 1695, in McCormick (ed.), *State Papers and Letters*, p. 255.

46. Riley, *King William and the Scottish Politicians*, pp. 93, 107; Dunlop, *William Carstares*, pp. 91–2.
47. Wodrow, *Analecta*, ii, pp. 2–3.
48. Walter Stewart to William Hamilton, 23 April 1695 and 27 November 1695, in *Selections from the Family Papers Preserved at Caldwell*, 3 vols (Glasgow: Maitland Club, 1854), i, pp. 190, 193.
49. James Johnston to the Earl of Annandale, 9 April and 13 April 1695, *HMC, Johnstone*, pp. 75–6; Riley, *King William and the Scottish Politicians*, pp. 108, 121.
50. Annandale to Tweeddale, 3, 9 and 14 December 1695, NLS MS 7019, fos 145r–146r, 153r–154r, 157r–158r; Hopkins, *Glencoe*, p. 414.
51. Johnston to Tweeddale, 10, 12 and 17 October 1695, NLS MS 14408, fos 402r–409v.
52. Johnston to Tweeddale, 12 December 1695, 10, 28 and 30 January 1696, NLS MS 14408, fos 433r–434r, 444r, 453r, 456r; *Home Diary*, p. 121.
53. *Home Diary*, p. 108.
54. John, Lord Murray to Tweeddale, 14 January 1696 and 6 February 1696, NLS MS 7020, fos 4r–v, 14r–v; *Post Boy*, 122 (Saturday 15–Tuesday 18 February 1696).
55. A successor would not be named until 1698, when the position went to Dalrymple of Stair's third son Hew. Riley, *King William and the Scottish Politicians*, pp. 120, 122.
56. NAS MS SP4/18, fos 218–21; Riley, *King William and the Scottish Politicians*, pp. 108–9, 112–14, 122.
57. e.g. James Johnston to the Earl of Annandale, 18 May 1696, *HMC, Johnstone*, pp. 99–100; several letters from Johnston to Locke in 1697–8, in De Beer (ed.), *Correspondence of John Locke*, vi, pp. 17–19, 56–7, 311–13.
58. Riley, *King William and the Scottish Politicians*, p. 62, where he is described as 'an undoubted presbyterian but no zealot'.
59. Pitcairn (ed.), *Acts of the General Assembly*, p. 247.
60. Ibid. p. 248.
61. Ibid. p. 253.
62. Charles Blount, *The Miscellaneous Works of Charles Blount, esq.* ([London?], 1695), pp. 23–51, 92, 97–105.
63. Ibid. pp. 5, 16–7, 182–6, 217.
64. Lorimer, *Two Discourses*, p. iv.
65. Cameron, 'Theological Controversy', p. 128.
66. [Archibald Pitcairne], *A Modest Examination of a Late Pamphlet Entituled Apollo Mathematicus* ([Edinburgh?]: [Watson?], 1696), pp. 14–16; Wodrow, *Analecta*, ii, p. 255; Johnston (ed.), *The Best of Our Owne*.
67. NAS MS CH12/16/25 is one copy, dated 6 March 1696.
68. Alexander Telfair, *A True Relation of an Apparition, Expressions and*

Actings of a Spirit, Which Infested the House of Andrew MacKie in Ring-croft of Stocking (Edinburgh: George Mosman, 1696), p. 3.
69. *Memoirs of the Life of the Reverend Mr Thomas Halyburton*, 2nd edn (Edinburgh: Heirs of Andrew Anderson, 1715), p. 52.
70. Michael F. Graham, 'The Civil Sword and the Scottish Kirk, 1560–1600', in W. Fred Graham (ed.), *Later Calvinism: An International Perspective* (Kirksville, MO: Thomas Jefferson University Press, 1994), pp. 237–48.

3

'So *unnaturall* a *seasone*': The Dreadful Year 1696

On 26 January 1696, George Home, visiting Edinburgh from his border estate, as he often did, attended religious services at the 'Old Church' – one of the four sub-congregations into which the High Kirk of St Giles had been divided. While Home often recalled details of his church attendance in his diary – noting who preached at services or what scriptural texts provided the basis for sermons or who his worshipping companions were – on this day he failed to record any of these. Instead, he opted to recall something that must have seemed more unusual: 'ther was a mad man came into the Church and made some disturbance but he went out befor the sermon begun.'[1] We have no way of telling today who this 'mad man' was, or what he said or did to cause a disturbance, or even whether we would regard him as mad (as opposed to merely rude, awkward or openly critical of religious dogma) today. But the incident provides a fitting opening to the story of what would prove to be one of the bleakest and most troubled years in Edinburgh's long history. It was a year of famine, the fifth of what came to be called 'the seven ill years'. The harvest of 1695 was particularly thin, and that of 1696 would be even worse, with high food prices, unemployment and starvation. The people of Scotland would live much of the year under a French invasion scare, with frequent musters, mobilisations and restrictions on travel. Parts of the kingdom (although not Edinburgh) were hit by epidemic disease; even the washing-ashore of large numbers of 'sea-calves' near Edinburgh in November was taken to portend 'some unhappy event'. This came on the heels of a fire in the Canongate that left up to fifty families homeless.[2] It was also a year in which loose philosophical talk in Edinburgh would inspire the authorities to take a close look at what books were available in local shops. Britain in general would be seized by panic over an alleged plot to assassinate King William. The strains caused by these pressures, coupled with the fragile balance of Scottish factional politics, would create an atmosphere in which the authorities of Church and State had to find scapegoats to unify a society fractured by stress. By the end of the year they would find some. The apparent bewitchment of an eleven-year-old girl near Paisley would lead to a revival of Scotland's witch-hunt. But, more significantly for our purposes, 1696 would end with Thomas Aikenhead, perhaps a 'mad man' of another sort, facing execution for things he allegedly said about God.

3.1 FAMINE, THE FRENCH, FEAR AND FIRE

While the economy of late seventeenth-century Britain was fairly diverse and well developed compared to those of other European states and regions, Scotland lagged well behind England within the British framework. It was overwhelmingly rural, and its only significant exports were sheep and cattle (or their hides) and cloth. In this last category was the linen industry, which had grown tremendously over the course of the seventeenth century. While there was some trade with continental Europe and even North America, most of those exports went to England, and Scotland's other industries, particularly coal and salt, were by the 1690s largely consumed by the domestic market. In what was primarily a subsistence economy, there was little demand for domestic manufactured goods, and little cash available to import them from elsewhere. The war against France, which had been going on since 1689 (known to history as the Nine Years War or King William's War), strangled what little trade there was between Scotland and continental Europe. In 1692, only twenty-nine vessels traded out of Leith, the kingdom's leading port, and most of those probably traded with England. Even export to England was limited by English tariffs; the 1603 Union of Crowns had not led to a union of economies.[3] Indeed, it was these poor trade conditions that would soon lead so many Scots to embrace the Darien colonial scheme – aimed at giving Scotland its own overseas trading empire – despite the opposition of English merchants and the non-cooperation of William II and III's government. With few exports to offer, Scotland was dependent on its own food production to feed its population and fire its domestic economy, and that food production failed disastrously in the mid-1690s.

The gloomy mood is reflected widely in letters, diaries and newspapers from the period. In early July, foreseeing disaster, Edinburgh's authorities began buying up grain and other foodstuffs that came into the port of Leith 'for the use of the poor in this place who are like to starve'. In the months that followed, the Privy Council took steps to encourage the import of grain, not only suspending tariffs on imports, but even offering a bonus payment out of the treasury of 20 shillings for every boll of victual imported.⁴ By November, with the failure of the autumn harvest obvious, things had only got worse. James Hamilton of Pencaitland, writing to the Earl of Arran from Edinburgh on 10 November, reported that the Privy Council was not even handling much business owing to 'the country being extreamly impoverished with the want of both of money and victuall'. (Ironically, that was the day Thomas Aikenhead was first brought before the council.) Eleven days later, Pencaitland informed Arran that the army in Scotland could not be provisioned because taxes had fallen short, in large measure because of the fact that the Scots had spent £100,000 sterling (or £1.2 million Scots) on grain imported from England in the previous year. What little cash was left was 'in the bank bot more in the African (i.e., Darien) offices and so does not circulat'. Two weeks later he reported that many tenants could not even pay half of their rents.⁵ Other correspondents painted a similar picture, and all the often-garrulous Edinburgh merchant James Nimmo recorded in his diary for 1696 was the scarcity of gold and silver owing to famine. Writing a couple decades later, Gilbert Burnet recalled that, in 1696, 'Scotland was falling under great misery, by reason of two [sic] successive bad harvests, which exhausted the nation, and drove away many of their people; the greatest number sent over to Ireland'.⁶

The kingdom's ongoing inability to feed itself left it ill-prepared to face the threat that most concerned its king: the possibility of a French invasion. At the end of February John, Lord Murray, one of the new Scottish secretaries in Whitehall, wrote to Tweeddale, then still Chancellor and thus nominal head of the Scottish Privy Council, of the king's belief that French ships were headed for Scotland. Murray urged Tweeddale to put the kingdom on a defensive footing: 'take the best measures thats [sic] possible both to secure the coasts & keep the country in quiett where there are any disaffected.' William first wrote to the Privy Council warning of this danger in March, and urging that all regiments be brought up to full strength and militias placed under 'persons of undoubted loyalty', but by then the council had already issued a proclamation 'for securing the Kingdom Against An Invasione from France', followed a week later by another calling up the militia and all fencible men. Meanwhile, Edinburgh's burgh council ordered that an inventory be taken of all horses in the burgh worth more than 100 merks, that officers search the town for arms and ammunition, and that constables compile lists of all lodgers. On 12 March, the town's militia mustered on the Bruntsfield Links. Many Episcopal clergymen who had not taken the Oath of Allegiance were jailed and then released only upon promises that they would leave the kingdom, or at least depart from Edinburgh and its suburbs.⁷ Despite these early preparations, it appears that little was actually done to secure the kingdom, and the deepening subsistence crisis over the summer and autumn only increased the difficulty.

Not surprisingly, in an era when wars were still fought over successions to thrones, the legitimacy of the Williamite coup of 1688–9 in the British kingdoms was challenged by France, which gave succour to the exiled James II and VII and his court. Many Scots Episcopalians were suspected (in some cases rightly) of Jacobite sympathies, and attacks on kingdoms could be personalised as attacks on kings, launched either from within or without. Assassination had been a common political tool since the late sixteenth century, and it was feared that King William might meet a French-backed assassin's bullet, just as his ancestor William I of Orange had died at the hands of a Spanish agent in 1584. Indeed, the invasion scare of February and March was tied to such a fear. On 24 February, the king informed the English parliament that a Jacobite plot to assassinate him as he rode through Richmond Park had been foiled when one of the plotters informed the authorities.[8] Murray wrote to the Scottish Privy Council with this news the next day, and just over a month later the king himself gave his Scots councillors notice of 'that wicked and horrid design of Assassinating our Royall person and Invading our Dominions'.[9]

The reaction to this came in three forms – military, political and spiritual. The military response in Scotland has already been described, and the political response spanned both British kingdoms, with the drawing-up of an 'oath of association' in which subjects would swear loyalty to William as the 'rightful and lawful' monarch. Many of these efforts were local and apparently spontaneous, although there was certainly some encouragement from Whitehall. The idea was to smoke out Jacobites, who could not take the oath, and the king's letter of 4 April told Scottish privy councillors to proceed with the the Association. In England, eighty-nine Tory Members of Parliament and nineteen Tory peers initially refused to swear, although most of them were later pressured into doing so. In the short run, English Whigs even succeeded in using the oath to purge Tories from commissions of the peace and town corporations, although this only lasted a few months.[10] Among the Scots, Murray, a fairly recent convert to Presbyterianism whom James Johnston had even suspected of Jacobite leanings, was probably happy to use the Association to demonstrate loyalty, and much of the regime on the ground in Edinburgh shared that enthusiasm. In mid-April, the Privy Council approved the Association.[11] The Justice Clerk Cockburn of Ormiston, as was typical of many ultra-Presbyterians, viewed events through a manichean, covenanted lens in which godliness and loyalty to the Williamite regime were one and the same, as were – on the flip side – religious dissent, political disloyalty and reprobation. He wrote to Carstares, the king's Presbyterian chaplain and adviser on Scottish religious matters, on 31 March, telling him about security preparations in the light of the assassination and invasion plot. With satisfaction, he reported progress in moving the Association forward, and that most dissenting ministers in Edinburgh had been rounded up by order of the Privy Council. 'I assure you, the conventicles now in Edinburgh are "the nests of disaffection". And therefore, as far as law will go, I wish them all banished out of town.' He got his way; the Edinburgh correspondent of London's *Protestant Mercury* wrote on that same day: 'We have no more Episcopal preaching in our city, all the Episcopal Ministers being imprisoned, and their Meeting-Houses shut up.' By May, the council was moving to shut down dissenting meeting houses in nearby Tranent and Dalkeith as well.[12]

Such efforts at political purgation needed spiritual equivalents. Responding to entreaties from the commissioners of the General Assembly, the Privy Council proclaimed a 'day of Humiliatione' to be observed on 15 March in and around Edinburgh, on 22 March elsewhere south of the Tay, and on 29 March north of the Tay (all Sundays). These were required 'forasmuch as we and our people have just reason to apprehend the severest judgements of almighty God whose clemency and goodnes we have abused to his dishonor'. The council urged people to give thanks for the king's narrow escape from assassination and 'implore [God's] assistance Against all forraign Invasions and Intestine commotione'.[13] Similar efforts continued through the summer, with a two-stage fast called in June to pray for success in the war. In its proclamation, the Privy Council reminded the population that the nation deserved punishment 'for our great unthankfulnes and manifold provocationes' of God. Another two-stage fast was called for late August and early September in recognition of God's obvious anger, seen through the likely shortfall in the harvest and the continuing bad weather – 'so unnaturall a seasone'. In addition, the burgh's magistrates cracked down on vice and illegitimacy in May, instigating a round-up of 'Lewd Women', who were put on an English ship anchored at Leith and shipped to Virginia.[14]

These efforts to propitiate a vengeful God reflected the widespread attitude that the Almighty would punish the whole society for the sins of some of its members. Representatives of the Kirk's General Assembly even asked the Privy Council to make sure these fasts were observed on pain of civil punishment.[15] While belief in predestination meant that every human's eternal fate was already fixed and could not be altered by any person's action, this did not preclude the possibility, or even the likelihood, of God intervening in this world to make His feelings known.[16] Public sinfulness mocked Him, and thus could not be tolerated. This belief justified Calvinist efforts at social discipline, and it would soon inspire the foundation of 'societies for the reformation of manners' in England and Scotland. The residents of greater Edinburgh would get another reminder of God's power and anger on 7 November, when a large fire broke out in the Canongate.

Details vary as to the exact severity of the Canongate fire, but it was certainly very serious, and the plight of the victims inspired an outpouring of charity from some of those few with resources to spare. The Privy Council was told that the fire left thirty-seven families homeless, with all their goods lost. A few days later, one of the London newspapers reported that the fire had destroyed six houses of six storeys each, displacing fifty families. The discussions of the tragedy in the burgh council were more detailed, perhaps because of the implications for local taxation. According to the burgh council's minute book, the fire struck in the 'head' of the Canongate (very near the Netherbow on the High Street, which separated Edinburgh from the Canongate), leaving a school as well as fifty houses (by this was probably meant individual tenements) 'brunt & destroyed'. The property lost was worth an annual rental of £1,600 Scots.[17] The servant Elisabeth West described the swiftness of the fire, noting that 'in a short time the whole city was all in confusion, as it was no wonder'. She piously hoped 'that the Lord would make this fire a means of conversion to some one or other, which I thought would turn our mourning into a song'. This message of corrective retribution was further stressed the following day, when West attended a sermon preached at College Kirk by John Moncrief, who used Micah 6:9, concerning the rod of the Lord, as his text:

> He told us that God's voice was crying to this city, and that he was come to the very ports, and was crying over the walls to us, that we should amend our ways, lest he should come into our city and consume us in a terrible manner.[18]

Certainly, the city offered temptations not available in the countryside. One of those, about which ministers like Moncrief were increasingly concerned, was the sort of loose philosophical talk that could lead a person into two of the gravest sins of all – blasphemy and its close relative atheism. Few offences would so certainly bring on God's wrath, and, by the time of the Canongate fire of 1696, pressure from the ministers, via parliament, had already turned the attention of the authorities towards this problem. The standard menu of sinning – fornication, adultery, sabbath-breach, drunkenness and neighbourly infighting – was certainly still much in evidence, as it had been since the earliest days of the Reformed Kirk. But it seemed to many that the extraordinary divine wrath of 1696 must have sprung from some deeper and more profound dissatisfaction with God's Most Covenanted Kingdom.

3.2 EDINBURGH'S DEISM SCARE

Despite the grave problems facing Scotland in 1696, the ongoing need to feed the Williamite war machine ensured that parliament would meet again. Its session began on 8 September and concluded on 12 October. Burnet deemed it noteworthy mainly for its sparse attendance, reporting 'a Parliament was held in Edinburgh and in a very thin house, everything that was asked was granted'. In fact, the government's agenda did not sail through quite that smoothly, but ultimately two years' additional taxation was granted, with only the second year raising any controversy. Although Johnston and Tweeddale, voices of moderation, had been driven from office the previous winter, there was no effort to modify the accommodation offered to the Episcopal clergy that they had guided through the previous year's parliament.[19] Indeed, the partisans of covenanted religion seemed to have scaled back their particular confessional expectations while at the same time focusing on a target that few would have the temerity to defend. As the General Assembly had reiterated in January, they wanted the laws against irreligion strictly enforced.

The Scottish Secretary Lord John Murray, now newly minted as Earl of Tullibardine, opened the parliamentary session by informing the estates that the king wanted them 'to pass Acts for suppressing of Profanity, and for curbing of vice, and it is expected ... that they be afterwards impartially put in Execution by those of the Government'. This was echoed by the new Chancellor, Patrick Hume of Polwarth. Both men offered these instructions after giving thanks for the king's deliverance from the assassination plot, and noting the need to vote supply for war.[20] The responsibility for the Act against 'profaneness' was delegated to the Committee for Security, as had been the case the previous year, although the records do not give the committee's membership in the 1696 session. The Act was given its first reading on 5 October, and was passed on 9 October 'after some amendments'. As passed, it was much more specific than the list of generalities offered by Tullibardine and Hume of Polwarth. The Act warned of the dangers posed by 'drunkenness, Sabbath breaking, swearing, fornication, uncleanness, *mocking and reproaching Religion and the exercises therof*' (emphasis added). All prior laws against these offences were to be revived and magistrates were to enforce them. If local magistrates did not comply, the Privy Council was to fine them and replace them with others who would. Cooperating magistrates would get to keep a share of the fines paid by offenders. Further, 'His Majesty and the said Estates of Parliament Recommend to the Lords of Privy Council to take such farder effectuall course as shall be found requisite for restraining and punishing of all sorts of profanity and wickedness ...'[21] In the past, such resolutions had amounted to no more than statements of pious intent that were soon forgotten. Not so this time. In a remarkable display of resolve, the Privy Council set out to offer an example of what parliament was urging, starting as soon as the session of parliament ended.

The day after the adjournment, a committee of the Privy Council gathered to hear accusations of allegedly blasphemous statements made by John Fraser, said to be a bookkeeper to the merchant Alexander Innes. Here it looked as though the council had a case involving exactly the sort of thing parliament had denounced and the General Assembly wanted to see punished. On 13 October the council heard testimony from witnesses in the case, including Fraser himself. Another meeting was called for two days later, and, with many who had sat in parliament still in town, the meeting of 15 October was remarkably well attended. A typical meeting of the Privy Council that year might draw between ten and fifteen councillors. But, on 15 October, twenty-one men gathered to hear the evidence in the Fraser case. This was a heavily aristocratic group, including one duke (Queensberry) as well as eight earls. Both Scottish secretaries – Tullibardine and Sir James Ogilvy – were present, so the Scottish administration in Whitehall was fully represented, and the provost of Edinburgh attended as well. Nineteen of those present had also sat in the parliament.[22] Clearly, this was intended as a display of enforcement by Scotland's most important magistrates, all gathered in one room.

Given the blasphemy statutes of 1661 and 1695, the charges against Fraser were serious. Witnesses alleged that Fraser

> did upon one or other days of July Agust or September last bypast take the boldnes in and by his discourse to deny Impugne Argue or reason against the Being of God saying that ther was no God to whom men owed that reverence worship and obedience so Much talked off. And that ther was a being who created the worlde yet that creator did not make any of his creatures to be Damned for any evill that they should doe. Lykeas the said John denyed Impugned or argued ag[ainst] the immortality of the soull affirming that the soull of man dyed as the soull of a beast and that ther was noe more account of it as lykeways that ther was no Devill. And when it was answered that it were to be wished the Devill would come and take him away that night that he might believe ther was a devill he wished the same and that he might but see him. And as to the holy Scriptures he

ridiculed them saying he believed none of them, arguing against their divyne authority. And affirmed they were only made to freighten folks and to keep them in order and when asked what religion he could be off that held such principles he answered of no religion at all but wes just ane Athiest and that was all his religion.[23]

Fraser's prosecution was led by Sir James Stewart, the king's advocate, and the devout, if politically inconsistent Stewart, known to devote his entire Sundays to church attendance and prayer, with only short breaks for meals, must have thought that there could be no more clear-cut case of blasphemy.[24] The charges against Fraser specifically mentioned the illegality of questioning 'the providence of god in the governance of the world' – wording included in the 1695 Blasphemy Act. Here was someone whose punishment could unite a fractured nation, reaffirming its allegiance to covenant principles while also placating an angry God.

Fraser appears to have sensed the danger of his position. He defended himself by claiming he had been misunderstood. His response suggests that the charges grew out of a conversation between him and the couple from whom he rented lodgings, and they – a Robert Henry and his wife – were probably the source of the accusations. His description of the conversation gives us a sense of the sort of loose philosophical talk in Edinburgh that had the authorities so concerned, the kind of heterodox literature that was being read by some, and also of the dangers of speaking too freely in front of strangers in a time of acute crisis.

According to Fraser, he, Henry and Henry's wife had been conversing one August evening at about nine when the topic turned to a sermon Fraser had heard the previous day. Fraser said he did not know the couple well, since he had only recently started lodging with them, and thus was 'not knowing the measure of his Landlord or Landlady's knowledge or understanding in matters of divinity'. This was probably a coded way of saying that he did not realise that they did not share his critical spirit, or interest in deist writings. In the course of the conversation, Fraser mentioned the arguments of Charles Blount, as set forth in his *Oracles of Reason* (1693). Fraser said he mentioned the arguments of Blount (whom he labelled 'a nottorious Blasphemer') against the divine origins of Scripture and the workings of Providence, in order to give Henry the opportunity to refute them. But Henry's wife thought (perhaps correctly?) that Fraser agreed with Blount, and stormed out of the room, followed by her husband. As a result, Fraser said 'he had not the opportunity to undeceave them as to their apprehensions of him till the next morning', when he told Henry 'that he was a fool to have mistaken what he was saying of Blunt the night before and that he ought not to have misconstructed his principles by imputing

Blunts Athiestical tenents to him'. In fact, he invoked the Dutch jurist Hugo Grotius' *Truth of the Christian Religion*, a book that he appears to have owned, as an antidote 'to defeat what any such Athiest was able to say'. But Henry's wife reported him to the authorities anyway. It is impossible to say whether she knew much of anything about Charles Blount, but she knew what she did not like, and, as it turned out, the conversation that August evening had touched upon some of the most controversial heterodoxies of late-seventeenth-century Britain.

Blount (1654–93) was the leading English deist writer of the period, and is regarded as second only to Lord Herbert of Cherbury (1583–1648) in shaping English deism, a form of religion that drew on the ancient Epicurean tradition associated with the philosopher Lucretius. But Blount went beyond Herbert in his seeming rejection of all Christian relevation, as well as his libertinism and his general incendiary tone, which has been described by one commentator as 'sustainedly destructive' of traditional doctrine. Deists were sceptical about the literal truth of Scripture, denied the authority of most revealed religion, and attacked the role of the clergy.[25] While their belief in some form of God meant they were not atheists in the modern sense of the word, Fraser's testimony reminds us of the loose application of the term 'atheist' in the early modern period.[26] Blount had published *Oracles of Reason* in 1693, the same year he committed suicide, allegedly distraught over the Anglican Church's refusal to allow him to marry his dead wife's sister due to their consanguinity. In the work, he ridiculed the Genesis accounts of creation and Adam and Eve's expulsion from the Garden of Eden:

> And really it seems a very cruel and very hard thing in this respect that God should be said to have tormented, nay, and ruined Mankind for so small a Fault, and that too committed through the Levity of a Woman's Mind. Wherefore some are of an Opinion (which I am not much averse to) that *Moses* laid so fast a Punishment on so small a Crime, only to the end he might procure the greater Deference and Authority to his own Laws, which often decree with the strictest severity things Frivolous, and in their own Nature, Indifferent.[27]

Oracles also contained 'a Summary account of the Deists Religion', which stated, among other things, that 'whatsoever is Adorable, Amiable and Imitable by Mankind, is in one Supream infinite and perfect Being: *Satis est nobis Deus unus*'. His influence on the controversial statements attributed to Fraser can be seen in his claim that people need not fear punishment after death, because God is the first and original good and therefore could not have 'malevolent intent'.[28]

Blount also seems the likely source for Fraser's statements about the soul. Using various ancient philosophical texts and some Old Testament material, Blount argued that the soul separates from the body at death and returns to the *Anima Mundi*, or common soul of the world. Thus the soul might have a sort of immortality, but not in any separate, individualised sense. His ranking of the relative authority of scripture versus ancient philosophy on this question was implied in his statement that 'for Rewards and Punishments hereafter, the Notion of them has not been universally receiv'd; for the *Heathens* disagreed in the Doctrine of the Immortality of the Soul'.[29] In addition, Blount challenged the Christian reckoning of the age of the earth, using non-scriptural sources to argue that the world had to be more than six thousand years old. He also attacked the Trinity under cover of an admiring letter to the philosopher Thomas Hobbes (dated just before Hobbes's death in 1679), suggesting that the Arian position that Jesus was merely human (denounced as a heresy in 325 by the Council of Nicea) was much more reasonable and logical than the Trinitarian stance, which had been the prevailing Christian doctrine ever since.[30]

Whether or not Fraser accepted any of these ideas, he had clearly read them and thought about them enough to present them to others. Now he needed to convince the assembled councillors that, however much he might have read and discussed blasphemous works, he was no blasphemer himself. Lest they had any doubts as to the sincerity of this Christian beliefs, Fraser assured them that

> with the deepest and most profound veneration doeth he acknouledge the BEING of God and the persons of the Blessed Trinity with the allwise and powerfull providence of the most holy God over all the creatures and their actions. And doeth own the divyne authority of the holy Scriptures as the rule by which he is directed to glorifie his God as the end of his creation.[31]

Although Fraser pled that he had been ignorant of the parliamentary statutes against blasphemy at the time of the August conversation, the specificity of this *ad hoc* confession of faith shows that he had since become familiar with the particular wording of the 1695 statute, and wanted to deny holding the beliefs it condemned. Further, he argued that, even if the councillors were to conclude that he was guilty of the heterodox statements attributed to him, his crime was, at worse, a first offence punishable only by public repentance under the statute's terms. But he opined that even public repentance was too harsh, given his youth, the fact that he was the first person charged under the statute, and that such a high-profile punishment 'would rather propogat the same [atheist views] ... and bring others to search after such blasphemous books who now knowes nothing of the same'.[32]

This sophisticated and ingenious defence suggests that Fraser was receiving legal advice. He also knew how to draw on the sympathies of his audience. He reminded the Privy Council that his father, Robert Fraser in Peterhead, had 'testified to his firmnes to the protestant religion according to the Presbyterian persuasione by the hardship he enderent and repeated fynes he payed in the late reigns as is knowen to some of their lo[rdshi]ps Number'.[33] Thus he tied his own heritage into the struggles of 1660–89, reminding the Presbyterian majority in the room that his father's cause had been their cause, and that like many of them he had suffered for it. In a society where kinship bonds still meant a great deal, and in which many leading families (that of the Chancellor Hume of Polwarth comes to mind) treasured their steadfastness to the covenants, this would have resonated powerfully, particularly since Stewart of Goodtrees, leading the prosecution, had not always been so politically faithful. The message was clear: he was from a good family, and could have been one of their own sons gone briefly astray.

While Fraser was not wealthy, he was better off than most. In 1694 he had been living in the Tron parish (where his neighbours would have included the free-thinker Archibald Pitcairne), in the household of his master Innes, then said to be a writer (that is, a solicitor). Fraser's assets were substantial enough that he paid his own poll tax assessment of six shillings that year, a reflection of his income and professional status (Innes was assessed at £6). More significantly, he had money to invest. On 28 March 1696, he had stepped forward to buy £100 worth of shares in the African Company, marking him as an early backer of what would become the Darien colony. Many of the privy councillors present at his hearing, including Queensberry, Hume of Polwarth, Cockburn of Ormiston, Sir John Lauder of Fountainhall, Sir James Murray of Philiphaugh, Sir Archibald Murray of Blackbarrony, Sir William Anstruther of Anstruther and Sir John Hamilton of Halcraig, were his fellow investors.[34]

If Stewart had been seeking the highest penalty for Fraser's offence, as the charges against him suggested, he was disappointed. This was not a defendant the assembled councillors were prepared to put on trial for his life. Nevertheless, Fraser was not let off the hook entirely. The Privy Council decreed that he be locked in the tolbooth until he satisfied the presbytery of Edinburgh through his public repentance in sackcloth. His hopes of keeping his punishment private were firmly dashed.[35] He was still in the tolbooth at the end of December, after Thomas Aikenhead had been condemned to death for his blasphemies, although he seems to have been given partial liberty at that time in response to Innes's plea to the Privy Council that his accounts were in arrears since Fraser could not attend to them, 'which occasioned considerable damadge' to his business enterprises. At that time, Fraser was allowed to leave the tolbooth during the day to hear sermons and to work on Innes's accounts. But he was not released for good until the following February, when he had performed all the required public repentance.[36] Meanwhile, the Privy Council decided to get closer to what some might have seen as the root of the problem: the spread of heterodox books.

3.3 DANGEROUS BOOKS AND THE WAR OF IDEAS

The Privy Council had occasionally taken interest in the book trade previously through the licensing of particular books, although this was usually intended to protect the intellectual property rights of authors or publishers. Occasionally, the council would condemn a work, as it did in May 1696 when it ordered the burning of an unnamed book 'Reflecting upon the government of Church & State', or in June, when it did the same to three pro-Catholic pamphlets discovered in Edinburgh. Thus censorship, when it happened, had traditionally taken place after the fact, rather than in advance of the publication and sale of a work, and authorities were usually more concerned about what they viewed as political sedition or Catholic works – which were interpreted as attacks on the principles of 1688–9 – than other forms of printed heterodoxy. Now the council vowed to prevent the sale of certain books in advance, and to take a more systematic approach. After sentencing Fraser to his public repentance, it issued an order 'to search the housses and shoppes of booksellers for erroneous and prophane books'. The council also decreed that all stationers in Edinburgh or its suburbs compile 'exact catalogues of the books to be sold by them or which are or may be in their chopes or houses or other pleces' and turn those lists in to the clerks of the Privy Council by Martinmas (11 November). Thereafter, they were to submit the titles of any new books acquired for sale before offering them to the public. Any books not so listed would be subject to confiscation. Three people were appointed to oversee this process – Gilbert Rule, the firmly Presbyterian principal of the town college, James Webster, minister of the Tolbooth and of an even more evangelical mind than Rule, and Robert Ferguson, one of the burgh's bailies. Considering this committee's composition, it seems clear that the Privy Council was determined to narrow the terms on which any debates touching on matters of religion and natural philosophy could be conducted.[37] It was this unusually thorough plan to police the marketplace of ideas that received first mention in the report on Fraser's case in London's *Protestant Mercury*: 'here [in Edinburgh] has been a great search made among our Booksellers, for some Infamous Libells, occasioned by a Merchants Apprentice of this city, owning publicly the Tenets of *Blunt*'.[38] So much for Fraser's hopes of punitive anonymity!

Another factor not specifically mentioned in the deliberations of the Privy Council, but that was probably on the minds of its better-informed members, was the fact that England's Licensing Act had been allowed to lapse in 1695, thus effectively ending censorship south of the border. The London presses were now relatively free to publish heterodoxy (like the works of Charles Blount), and Scotland's authorities might have been justified in fearing an influx of dangerous English-language publications. One of the most controversial books unleashed on English readers late in 1695 was *Christianity Not Mysterious*, which by the time Scotland's Privy Council was establishing its censorship committee had been reprinted, expanded and officially avowed by its theretofore anonymous author: the sometime student and MA recipient from Edinburgh's town college, John Toland.[39] The Irishman Toland's previous sojourn in Edinburgh (and, before that, Glasgow) might have made this, his first major work, particularly interesting to Scots readers of eclectic tastes. While Toland in his preface approvingly quoted the late Archbishop of Canterbury John Tillotson (d. 1694), and claimed that he was attacking atheists and infidels, his arguments outraged traditionalists. An investigation of the book by a Middlesex grand jury would force its author to flee back to Ireland, where his work would earn the condemnation of the Irish House of Commons in 1697. One critic claimed Toland (who had been born in 1670) had boasted that 'he would be *Head* of a Sect before he was thirty years of Age'.[40] Toland's book criticised those who spent much time arguing over distinctions within Christianity, such as transubstantiation or belief in the Trinity, as well as those who said they could believe in things that contradicted reason – that is, mysteries – because 'by opposing one light [Scripture] to another [reason]' such people 'make God the Author of all Incertitude'. Such contradictions would, according to Toland, lead people to scepticism, particularly since traditionalists mistakenly insisted on taking Scripture literally.[41] Toland wrote that 'mystery' had entered Christianity because the Jews had been reluctant to give up their rituals and even more so because the early Church had wanted to draw in pagans, so it incorporated many pagan cults. A recent study of Toland's work has commended the subtlety of his approach, noting that he 'consistently presented himself as a man of learning and theological erudition'.[42] But this did not fool his devout opponents. While on the surface his critiques of ceremonialism, aimed primarily at high-church Anglicans and Catholics in England, might seem compatible with a Presbyterian outlook,[43] this was more than overcome by his attitude towards Scripture and his rabid anticlericalism:

> So jealous were the clergy of their own Order, lest any of 'em should irreligiously unfold those sublime Mysteries to the profanely inquisitive LAITY, that they thought fit to put it as much out of the power of the Holy Tribe itself, as out of ours, to understand them; and so it continues, in a great measure, to this day.[44]

Such views, which saw little difference between 'godly' Protestant clergy and Catholic priests, would not have pleased men like Rule and Webster if they had found them represented in Edinburgh's bookshops. They would have been inclined to agree with Toland's leading Irish critic, Peter Brown, who wrote that Toland

> swells with the fancy of having run down three kingdoms only with one *cross Question*, which is the foundation of all his Book, *viz How can a Man believe what he doth not know?* ... it is such wretches as he who ... plentifully furnish the Atheistical and Prophane, with all the matter of their objections against Scripture. But I hope in time God will put it into the hearts of our Governours to remedy these disorders.[45]

This had already happened in Scotland. Unfortunately – at least from the perspective of anyone interested in studying Scottish reading habits – none of the inventory lists prepared for the censorship committee appears to have survived.

Obviously, Charles Blount's book was circulating in Edinburgh, and it certainly was the sort of work this committee wanted to confiscate and ban. It is plausible that Toland's was as well; it was purchased in London on behalf of the college library that year.[46] But it would be helpful to know what other controversial books might have been available to Edinburgh's reading public. While the paucity of sources makes it impossible to offer a detailed picture, stray pieces of evidence allow for some suggestions. For example, upon the death of the physician and botanist Sir Andrew Balfour (1630–94), the contents of his library were put up for sale, with the auction held in early February 1695. Among those planning to purchase books were Archibald Pitcairne, who hoped to find a copy of J. C. Vanini's *De Admirandis Naturae Reginae Deaeque Mortalium Arcanis* (Paris, 1616) for his London friend Robert Gray.[47] The anti-Christian nature of this work had led to its condemnation shortly after publication by French authorities, and Vanini himself was executed for his atheism in 1619. It is not clear why Pitcairne thought he would find the book at the Balfour auction, as it was not listed in the published auction catalogue. Possibly this was because it was too notorious to list, although there were other books listed for auction that day that would have troubled the Privy Council's censorship committee of 1696, and might have been of interest to someone like John Fraser if he could read Latin or French. These included several editions of Lucretius' *De Rerum Natura*, a work widely cited by deists like Blount, various works by Hobbes and Descartes, and a French edition of Richard Simon's *Critical History of the Old Testament*, as well as two responses to it by Dutch theologians.[48] Simon, a French cleric, had argued against the Mosaic authorship of the Pentateuch, suggesting that it had been produced by a series of 'public scribes' such as Ezra, a view shared by Hobbes and Baruch/Benedict Spinoza. This was an attack on one of the fundamental Christian (and Jewish) beliefs about the provenance of Scripture.[49]

But Balfour's had been a private library, and most of its volumes were not in English. Someone well connected, prosperous and comfortable in several languages like Archibald Pitcairne could have partaken of its fruits, but this was less likely for the likes of John Fraser, for whom the comparatively downmarket philosophy of Charles Blount might have been more accessible. The library of the Faculty of Advocates (the ancestor of the National Library of Scotland) was similarly exclusive, although it is conceivable that, as a sometime 'writer' (advocate), Fraser's master Innes might have had access to its volumes. In 1696 these included works by Hobbes (and his critics), Simon (and his critics), Blount's disciple Charles Gildon's *History of the Athenian Society* (1691), and several volumes in the satirical series *Letters Writ by a Turkish Spy* (1691–), which made comparisons between Islam and Christianity that portrayed the latter in an unfavourable light. Recent commentators have seen the *Turkish Spy* as largely a deist work, which was also sympathetic to pantheism or atomism.[50] The advocates also purchased Thomas Burnet's *Sacred Theory of the Earth* (1684), which had influenced Blount, arguing that the Genesis story in the Old Testament was intended as allegory and that there had been natural causes for the flood of Noah. Other purchases by the advocates included compilations (in French) on Confucian philosophy, Epicurean morality and anti-Trinitarian views.[51] Clearly, they felt their members would not be endangered by exposure to a wide spectrum of opinions, including non-Christian views and those explicitly critical of Christianity. Several of the privy councillors who created the censorship committee in October 1696 (including Stewart of Goodtrees, who as king's advocate would have presented the case against Fraser) were members of the Faculty of Advocates and thus would have had access to these books themselves.

In a similar vein, the border laird George Home, a frequent visitor to Edinburgh who was devout enough to feel that he had to justify his non-attendance at a Tuesday afternoon sermon in January 1695 (it was snowing heavily), owned a copy of Blount's *Two first books of Philostratus, concerning the life of Apollonius Tyaneus* (1680), which offered in its account of Apollonius of Tyana (*c.* AD 3–97) an alternative to Jesus as saviour, and a French edition of the Qur'ān, both of which he was happy to loan to a friend.[52] Alastair Mann has opined that after the Restoration of 1660 'a Scottish society, which before had been primarily besotted with religion, elite politics, kings and faction, was gradually being infused with a new sense of polite culturalism, and mainly because it was reading more'.[53] Given what had happened to Fraser and what would happen to Thomas Aikenhead, this may be an overly optimistic assessment. On the contrary, it appears that the Covenant would still be a very powerful force, particularly in the crisis atmosphere of 1696. But it is undeniable that the landowning and professional elites in and around Edinburgh were reading a lot and reading eclectically. The danger arose when someone not sufficiently connected to those with power and influence expressed agreement with one or more of the era's more unorthodox authors. Could the town college and its library (whose collection will be discussed later) have become a seminary of 'atheistical deism', as one pamphlet would put it?[54] Or, if reading led to discussion, to what extent might Edinburgh's taverns, coffee houses and merchants' stalls become the settings for loose philosophical talk, which might even reach the ears of non-readers?

The homegrown Scottish press was not ignoring the need to combat heterodox views. While the shelves of wealthy readers and professional or academic libraries were lined with books published in Paris, Amsterdam and London, local publishers churned out less expensive works aimed at the general reader. The major compendium of Scottish-published book titles from the period lists a total of 172 books, pamphlets and proclamations published in Scotland in 1695, dipping to 160 in 1696 and 93 in 1697 (probably the effects of the economic downturn) before recovering somewhat to 135 in 1698. While the real numbers were probably a bit higher, owing to the fact that some published items have not survived, the general picture this gives is probably accurate.[55] The vast majority of these works were published in Edinburgh, and most of them were uncontroversial, such as the almanacs that came off the presses every year offering very specific (but probably not very accurate) weather predictions, and precise dating of where matters stood with regard to biblical time – one almanac of 1696 noted, for instance, that it had been 5,645 years since the creation of the world, 3,989 since the Flood and 3,600 since the destruction of Sodom and Gomorrah.[56] Some titles were mere broadsheets, often published proclamations by authorities such as the Privy Council. Other cheap works were published as volleys in professional feuds, as when Archibald Pitcairne defended his reputation against several medical colleagues who had accused him of an over-reliance on mathematics as well as drunkenness, atheism and 'bantering the Scripture'.[57] But another of the year's early publications was the text of the sermon that David Williamson, minister of West Kirk parish, had delivered before Tweeddale and other high officials the previous June as parliament was in the midst of the session that would, among other things, pass the new blasphemy Act. Chastising sinfulness in general (a common Presbyterian refrain), Williamson's warnings about the 'fruits of Atheism' and God's consequent punishments, cited in the previous chapter, must have seemed grimly prophetic amid the crop failures, threatened invasions and near-assassination of the king in 1696.[58]

Scottish book-buyers seeking material to combat the ideas of those who, like Blount and Toland, had argued that Scripture should not be taken literally could find it in *A Vindication of Our Blessed Saviours Genealogy from the Cavils of Antiscripturalists*.[59] Its anonymous author said he wrote it to help a 'young Gentleman, who by his travelling unto several parts of Europe, had found too many occasions of conversing with bad company, and was by them tempted to an ill opinion of the Holy Scriptures'. Like John Fraser, he found a good guide in Hugo Grotius.[60] While this work, published by George Mosman, official publisher of the Reformed Kirk, was not the most highbrow pamphlet, it was sophisticated enough to impress the young schoolmaster Thomas Ruddiman, who later became a friend of Archibald Pitcairne and eventually preceded David Hume as keeper of the Advocates Library, and who included with his copy of the *Vindication* his own manuscript 'Account of the four generall Religions in the world & by what nations they are preached'.[61]

More at the tabloid end of orthodox polemics was a brief pamphlet by the minister Alexander Telfair describing the haunting of a house in his Kirkcudbrightshire parish. Mosman published this one also, and was so certain of its commercial promise that he took the trouble to get a one-year exclusive licence to sell the work from the Privy Council, commencing in January 1696. Telfair entertained his readers with accounts of the house being deluged with stones and spontaneously catching fire several times. A mysterious boy was seen at the window and eventually bones of unknown origin appeared in front of the house, along with a letter written in blood warning the people of Scotland to 'flee to god' and repent.[62] As if the moral were not clear enough, Telfair included a preface, dated December 1695, stating that he was moved to write his account because of the need for the conviction and confutation of that prevailing spirit of Atheism, and Infidelity in our time, denying both in Opinion and Practice the Existence of Spirits, either of God or Devils; and consequently a Heaven and Hell; and imputing the voices, Apparitions and Actings of Good, or Evil Spirits, to the Melancholic Disturbance or Distemper of the Brains and Fancies of those, who pretend to hear, see or feel them.[63]

Aware that such sceptics would question the veracity of his reports, Telfair took pains to list witnesses to the hauntings, giving his work the flavour of an advocate's brief. This publication apparently had commercial prospects outside Scotland as well; a London edition of the pamphlet was advertised in the *Flying Post*, which, in a news report from Edinburgh on the case, claimed that the blood letter had been 'brought to this City and laid up amongst the curiosities in the Library of the University'.[64]

Scots publishers were also happy to reprint English contributions to this war of ideas, particularly those which supported traditional Christian positions. In 1695 one of them offered *The Charge of Socinianism against Dr Tillotson Considered*, published anonymously in England the previous year by the Anglo-Irish Jacobite clergyman Charles Leslie. This primarily attacked the allegedly latitudinarian and anti-Trinitarian views of John Tillotson, late archbishop of Canterbury, and his successor Thomas Tenison, along with Gilbert Burnet, bishop of Salisbury (and James Johnston's cousin) – all of them Whigs and supporters of the Revolution settlement that Leslie opposed. John Toland, as mentioned earlier, had praised Tillotson's rationality, the same quality that spurred Leslie's condemnation. Leslie accused Tillotson of denying the need for mysteries in Christianity and of claiming that they were just 'a Gratification to the Humour of Mankind who were fond of Mysteries' and that the Incarnation of Christ 'was to comply with their notion of a sensible Deity; and his Passion with their custom of Human sacrifices [and] his Exaltation with their custom of Deifying Men'.[65] Leslie charged that Burnet's position on Christ's divinity was ambiguous and that both Tillotson and Burnet had questioned the certainty and eternity of Hell.[66]

But most significantly for our purposes, this new Scots edition of the pamphlet included an additional section that attacked the views of 'that Execrable Charles Blount, one of the Atheistical Club, and very intimate with Dr Tillotson'. Leslie charged that Blount's *Great is Diana of the Ephesians* (1680, reprinted in 1695) was a litany of 'Blasphemies and Prophaneness', whose author, under cover of offering a history of the 'Gentile sacrifices' set out 'to Blaspheme, and, like a *Mad Dog*, to curse and Reproach the whole Institution of God, as well under the *Law* as the *Gospel*' – that is, in the era of the Old Testament as well as the New.[67]

Just as Leslie freely associated Tillotson's broadly inclusive Anglicanism with Blount's philosophical scepticism, he was quick to connect both with political radicalism: 'there are none of these *Latitudinarians* that are not *Commonwealth-Men*; they are against *Monarchy* in *Heaven* or on *Earth*; and indeed against all *Government*.' He was equally certain that government needed to strike back against them, given that blasphemers 'have no fear of the law at present'.[68]

> Shall the Honour of the *King* be Guarded with *Death* and God be Blasphem'd *Impunè* [sic] in Print and in the Streets! Has not this Propagated *Atheism* to the Degree we now see it: Not only to pass unpunished; but to be thought a *Grace* in Conversation, and the mark of a Wit![69]

Leslie must have found the tolerance (not to mention the Whiggery) of England's authorities frustrating, but his Scottish audience had concluded that something needed to be done, at least as far as heterodoxy was concerned. God's anger was all too evident by late 1696.

3.4 THE ACCUSATION OF THOMAS AIKENHEAD

On 10 November 1696, on the eve of the deadline for booksellers to turn inventory lists over to the Privy Council and three days after the devastating fire in the Canongate, Thomas Aikenhead, sometime student in the town college, was brought before the council, charged with blasphemy. The council's records do not say much about the case, in marked contrast to Fraser's appearance the previous month.[70] This initial hearing was also much more sparsely attended than Fraser's, with just thirteen councillors present, only four of them aristocrats. Twelve of these men had attended Fraser's hearing as well. Fraser's hearing, which had drawn twenty-one councillors, nine of them aristocrats, had coincided with the conclusion of a parliament that had pledged to enforce the law against irreligion; now many of its members (nineteen of whom had attended Fraser's hearing) had scattered to their homes. But what the council of 10 November lacked in numbers it would make up for in determination. Hume of Polwarth was there as Chancellor, as was Stewart of Goodtrees as king's advocate, presenting the libel against Aikenhead. Stewart of Goodtrees was assisted by Sir Patrick Hume, identified as king's solicitor. They read the charge against Aikenhead, which was not copied into the council register, but which probably resembled the eventual indictment.[71] The specific charges will be discussed later, but it is clear from the indictment that Aikenhead's reputation for blasphemy, particularly among his fellow students, had been developing for several months. Appearing on his own behalf before the council, apparently without legal representation, he made some answers to the charges, but these were not recorded. The council concluded that the charges were serious and ordered that Aikenhead be tried 'for his life' before the High Court of Justiciary, instructing Stewart of Goodtrees to continue preparing the case against him. Three others present would participate directly in Aikenhead's trial – Adam Cockburn of Ormiston as Justice Clerk, and John Lauder of Fountainhall and Archibald Hope of Rankeillor as judges. Whatever answers Aikenhead gave, they must not have elicited the councillors' sympathies in the same way Fraser's had. He was sent to Edinburgh's tolbooth (where he may have already been incarcerated) to await trial.

There are several possible reasons why the accusations against Aikenhead led to a capital trial, while those against Fraser resulted in the humiliating, but ultimately just symbolic, punishments imposed by the Edinburgh Presbytery. For one, Aikenhead did not have the sort of family background likely to result in lenient treatment; unlike Fraser, he could not point to a family history of steadfastness to the covenanting cause, as will be seen later. Nor could he demonstrate any connection to Scotland's landed, merchant or professional elite; he had not invested in the Darien scheme, and had no employer who would plead for his freedom. Further, as will be seen from the analysis of his trial, the charges against him were more detailed than those against Fraser, and there were more witnesses (and more highly educated witnesses) available to testify against him. The English nonconformist clergyman William Lorimer, who had been in Edinburgh during the winter of 1696–7, later contrasted Fraser's humility before the authorities with Aikenhead's 'sullen and obstinate' attitude, which he claimed persisted for some time after his initial accusation. One contemporary London newspaper reported that Aikenhead had agreed with some of the charges against him and continued to maintain his principles before the council. A later report in the same paper referred to Aikenhead as an 'atheist' and Fraser as a 'deist', suggesting a perception of difference in degree of heterodoxy.[72] In the eyes of the authorities, Aikenhead probably appeared more dangerous, and also more expendable, than Fraser. They may also have viewed Fraser's punishment as a warning that the likes of Aikenhead had not heeded, necessitating sterner measures. The thirteen councillors present to hear Aikenhead on 10 November may have been in total a more devout group than the twenty-one who heard Fraser, and therefore more determined to see the law fully enforced. It is not necessary to prefer one of these factors over the others, as all of them may have contributed to the decision to try Aikenhead for his life.

Further, for a society that by and large accepted the idea of divine punishment for public sins, the signs suggested that God had, if anything, only got angrier since Fraser's appearance before the Privy Council. The Canongate fire of early November had been a serious blow, and on 25 November, Sir John Clerk of Penicuik, whose lands were not far from Edinburgh, was in town to hear the college principal Gilbert Rule preach on 1 Corinthians 10:22 ('Do we provoke the Lord to jealousy? Are we stronger than he?'). The examples Rule cited, according to Clerk of Penicuik's notes, were 'daring sins (such as 1 atheism or denying ye points of ye [Chris]tian religion, 2 mocking at holiness, 3 sinning ag[ain]st light & men of nimble witts inventing new distinctions to serve [their] carnall interests, 4 not hearking to ye gosple)', all of which 'were dreadfull in ye sight of G[od].'[73] Further evidence of divine anger was the fact that the nationwide food shortage was growing more acute. As the Chancellor Hume of Polwarth wrote to Sir James Ogilvy in early December:

> Not only is the bear [barley] crop so very scantie, but the oats in all the murish places so verie bad that the barlie that is will in all appearance goe more to meall than malt this year in such a case ar the mure countries that the half of the oats of Scotland ar good for litel. The agedest people doe not remember that the aged of the former generation told of their seeing so late a seison for there is much to reap still in severall places.

Plague had broken out in parts of the realm (although not the capital), and as Aikenhead sat in the tolbooth awaiting his trial the international political situation worsened. On 1 December Ogilvy wrote to the Earl of Melville from Whitehall that 'wee are nou again threatned with ane invasion on Scotland. God in his providence may prevent it houever wee ought to doe al that is in our pouer.' That same day the king ordered the Privy Council to put the kingdom in a defensive posture, and three days later councillors received a letter reminding then to prepare the militia, following a plan devised in May. This would have required immediate musters in Edinburgh, Glasgow, the three Lothian counties and Fife. These instructions had to be repeated two weeks later, a fact that may reflect an inability to comply, although Edinburgh's council did order a muster on 14 December. Clerk of Penicuik linked domestic and (possible) foreign scourges in his spiritual journal entry two days earlier: 'the corns are not yett shorn in Nicolson & O L[ord] pitie ye land & poure out a spirit of repentance & [there] is great fear of ane French invasion, ye militia being ordered to be in readiness.' Hume of Polwarth had been unsuccessful in his efforts to prevent bad news from reaching Whitehall; Scottish troops remained unpaid and at the end of November he wrote to Ogilvy lamenting the fact that the king had learned this. Neither Melville (a privy councillor) nor Ogilvy apparently thought Scotland was prepared to defend itself; it would require reinforcements of troops from England or Flanders. Elsewhere in the kingdom, several lairds and minor noblemen suspected of disloyalty were taken into custody, and soldiers were quartered on the Duke of Gordon. The Privy Council also worried about people travelling without authorisation.[74] All in all, it was a bad time to be a potential scapegoat.

NOTES

1. *Home Diary*, p. 117.
2. *Protestant Mercury*, 105 (4 November 1696), 109 (13 November 1696), 110 (18 November 1696) suggested fifty families left homeless; NAS MS PC2/26, fo. 309r, puts the figure at thirty-seven.
3. Christopher Whatley, *Scottish Society, 1707–1830: Beyond Jacobitism, towards Industrialisation* (Manchester: Manchester University Press, 2000), pp. 17–23; Ian D. Whyte, *Scotland before the Industrial Revolution: An Economic and Social History, c. 1050–c. 1750* (New York: Longman, 1995), pp. 286–9; Keith Wrightson, *Earthly Necessities: Economic Lives in Early Modern Britain* (New Haven: Yale University Press, 2000), pp. 261–4.
4. James Whitehead to Lord Yester, 27 July 1696, NLS MS 7020, fo. 85r; NAS MS PC1/51, fo. 12r; NAS MS PC4/2, fos 26r, 29r, 30r; WRH MS PC13/2, 7 August 1696. A boll was equivalent to about 140 lbs.
5. *HMC, Supplementary Report on the Manuscripts of the Duke of Hamilton* (London: HMSO, 1932), pp. 137–8.
6. e.g. James Baird to the Earl of Findlater, 24 November 1696, in James Grant (ed.), *Seafield Correspondence, 1685–1708* (Edinburgh: Scottish History Society, 1912), p. 208; W. G. Scott-Moncrieff (ed.), *Narrative of Mr James Nimmo, 1654–1709* (Edinburgh: Scottish History Society, 1889), p. 102; Burnet, *History*, ii, p. 179.
7. Murray to Tweeddale, 29 February 1696, NLS MS 7020, fo. 26r; Ogilvie to Tweeddale, 2 March 1696, ibid. fo. 36r; NAS MS SP4/18, fo. 162; WRH MS PC13/2, 29 February 1696, 6 March 1696; ECA MS SL1/1/35, fos 240v, 241v; WRH MS PC12/16, 7 April, 17 April 1696.
8. Rose, *England in the 1690s*, pp. 50–1. The would-be assassin was George Barclay, a former army officer. In the end, the unmasking of the plot led to nine executions.
9. WRH MS PC12/16, 25 February and 4 April 1696.
10. Rose, *England in the 1690s*, p. 92; Tony Claydon, *William III and the Godly Reformation* (Cambridge: Cambridge University Press, 1996), p. 178.

11. *Flying Post*, 145 (16–18 April 1696), *Post Boy*, 149 (18–21 April 1696). For doubts about Murray, see Johnston to the Earl of Annandale, 13 April 1695, HMC, *Johnstone*, p. 76; Riley, *King William and the Scottish Politicians*, pp. 108, 121.
12. Cockburn of Ormiston to Carstares, 31 March 1696, in McCormick (ed.), *State Papers and Letters*, p. 288; *Protestant Mercury*, 14 (6–8 April 1696); *Flying Post*, 141 (7–9 April 1696); NAS MS PC4/2 fo. 17r–v.
13. WRH MS PC13/2, 10 March 1696.
14. WRH MS PC13/2, 5 June, 7 August 1696; *Protestant Mercury*, 28 (8–11 May 1696).
15. NAS MS PC4/2, fo. 26r.
16. See, e.g., Todd, *Culture of Protestantism*, 179–81.
17. NAS MS PC2/26, fo. 309r; *Protestant Mercury*, 109 (13 November 1696); ECA MS SL1/1/35, fo. 297r–v; Scott-Moncrieff (ed.), *Household Book of Lady Grisell Baillie*, p. 6.
18. *Memoirs, or Spiritual Exercises of Elisabeth West* (Edinburgh: Ogle & Aikman, 1807), p. 37.
19. Burnet, *History*, ii, p. 179; Riley, *King William and the Scottish Politicians*, pp. 118–19.
20. *APS*, x, app. 2.
21. *APS*, x, pp. 14, 47, 65–6.
22. NAS MS PC1/51, fo. 12v; *APS*, x, pp. 3–5.
23. NAS MS PC1/51, fo. 13r–v; PC4/2, fo. 28v.
24. For Stewart, see Omond, *Lord Advocates*, i, pp. 243–80; Beisner, 'His Majesty's Advocate'.
25. Sullivan, *John Toland and the Deist Controversy*, pp. 219–20; Sarah Ellenzweig, 'The Faith of Unbelief: Rochester's "Satyre", Deism, and Religious Freethinking in Seventeenth-Century England', *Journal of British Studies*, 44 (2005), pp. 27–45, at p. 36.
26. Hunter, 'Problem of "Atheism"'.
27. Blount, *Miscellaneous Works*, pp. 49–50.
28. Ibid. pp. 88, 90.
29. Ibid. pp. 117–27, 201.
30. Ibid. pp. 97–105, 182–6.
31. NAS MS PC1/51, fo. 14r–v.
32. NAS MS PC1/51, fo. 15r.
33. NAS MS PC1/51, fo. 13v.
34. WRH MS E70/4/7, fos 3, 8; John Burton (ed.), *The Darien Papers* (Edinburgh: Bannatyne Club, 1849), pp. 372, 385, 391–3, 401, 408.
35. NAS MSS PC1/51, fo. 15v; PC4/2, fo. 29r.
36. NAS MSS PC2/26, fos 317v–318r; PC4/2, fos 37r, 38r.
37. NAS MSS PC1/50, fos 473v–474r; PC1/51, fo. 16r; PC4/2, fos 18r, 29r; Mann, *Scottish Book Trade*, pp. 168, 170, 175, 258. Mann interprets the formation of the committee as reflecting concern about Catholicism,

overlooking the fact that the council dealt with the Fraser case in the same meeting.
38. *Protestant Mercury*, 101 (26 October 1696).
39. John Toland, *Christianity Not Mysterious: Or, a Treatise Showing that There is Nothing in the Gospel Contrary to Reason nor Above it, and that No Christian Doctrine Can Properly be Called a Mystery* (London, 1696); Sullivan, *John Toland and the Deist Controversy*, p. 7; Justin Champion, *Republican Learning: John Toland and the Crisis of Christian Culture, 1696–1722* (Manchester: Manchester University Press, 2003), p. 70.
40. Toland, *Christianity Not Mysterious*, pp. i, vii; Sullivan, *John Toland and the Deist Controversy*, pp. 8–9; Peter Brown, *A Letter in Answer to a Book Entitled Christianity not Mysterious* (Dublin, 1697), p. 148.
41. Toland, *Christianity Not Mysterious*, pp. 26–7, 31–2, 34–5.
42. Champion, *Republican Learning*, p. 14.
43. Toland, *Christianity Not Mysterious*, pp. 151–6, 163–7.
44. Ibid. p. 169.
45. Brown, *Letter in Answer*, p. 168.
46. EUL MS Da.1.34, fo. 9r.
47. Johnston (ed.), *The Best of Our Owne*, p. 21.
48. *Bibliotheca Balfouriana, sive Catalogus Librorum, In quavis Lingua & Facultate Insignium Illustris Viri D. Andreae Balfourii M.D. & Equitis Aurati* (Edinburgh: Heirs of A. Anderson, 1695), pp. 6, 9, 23, 33, 35, 37, 93, 97.
49. Malcolm, *Aspects of Hobbes*, pp. 387–8, where it is argued that Simon produced in his 1678 work 'a much more sophisticated version of the theory' than had Hobbes in his *Leviathan* (1651) or Spinoza in his *Tractatus Theologico-Politicus* (1670).
50. Wooton, 'New Histories of Atheism', p. 41. For a modern selection from the original, see Arthur Weitzman (ed.), *Letters Writ by a Turkish Spy* (New York: Columbia University Press, 1970).
51. *Catalogus Librorum Bibliothecae Iuris Utriusque*, pp. 118, 127, 142–3, 150, 153; John M. Pinkerton (ed.), *The Minute Book of the Faculty of Advocates, 1661–1712* (Edinburgh: Stair Society, 1976), pp. 141–3. For Burnet's influence on Blount, see Sullivan, *John Toland and the Deist Controversy*, p. 175.
52. *Home Diary*, pp. 23, 27, 62.
53. Mann, *Scottish Book Trade*, p. 33.
54. Mungo Craig, *A Satyr against Atheistical Deism, with the Genuine Character of a Deist* (Edinburgh: Robert Hutchison, 1696).
55. H. G. Aldis, *A List of Books Printed in Scotland to 1700*, 2nd edn (Edinburgh: National Library of Scotland, 1970).
56. *An Almanack and New Prognistication for the Year of Our Lord, 1696*

... *Exactly Calculated for the Famous City of Edinburgh, by G.C., Mathema*[ticus] (Edinburgh: Heirs of Andrew Anderson, 1696).

57. [Pitcairne], *Modest Examination of a Late Pamphlet*, pp. 14–16.
58. Williamson, *Sermon Preached in the High Church of Edinburgh*, p. 35.
59. *A Vindication of Our Blessed Saviours Genealogy from the Cavils of Antiscripturalists and the accounts that two Evangelists give of it; set in so clear a Light, as may at once satisfy the well meaning Seeker, and Silence the Irreligious Disputant* (Edinburgh: Heirs of Andrew Anderson, 1696).
60. Ibid. pp. Az, 11, 18–9.
61. NLS MS 20492, fo. 4r. For Ruddiman, see Douglas Duncan, *Thomas Ruddiman: A Study in Scottish Scholarship of the Early Eighteenth Century* (Edinburgh: Oliver & Boyd, 1965).
62. Telfair, *True Relation of an Apparition*, pp. 2, 7–11.
63. Ibid. p. 3.
64. *Flying Post*, 109 (23–25 January 1696) and 112 (30 January–1 February 1696).
65. [Charles Leslie], *The Charge of Socinianism against Dr Tillotson Considered* (Edinburgh, 1695), preface. While the title page claims that the critique of Tillotson was published in 1694, it appears that no copy has survived to make it into the STC/Wing or *Early English Books Online*.
66. Ibid. pp. 17, 21.
67. Ibid. p. 25.
68. Ibid. p. 32.
69. Ibid. p. 31.
70. NAS MSS PC1/51, fo. 16v; PC4/2 fo. 29v.
71. The original appears to be NAS MS JC26/78/1/11, although there are various copies as well, such as British Library Harleian MS 6846, fos 396r–399r (two copies) and Bodleian Library MS Locke b.4, fos 88r–90r. A published version was included with the other trial records in *State Trials*, xiii, pp. 917–30, with the indictment at pp. 917–20.
72. Lorimer, *Two Discourses*, p. v; *Protestant Mercury*, 109 (13 November 1696), 124 (6 January 1697). While the latter report does not give the names of either, it is clear from the context which is Fraser and which is Aikenhead.
73. NAS MS GD18/2092/1, 25 November 1696.
74. Sir James Ogilvy to the Earl of Melville, 1 December and 24 December 1696, NAS MS GD26/13/99, items 3, 5; NAS MS SP4/18, fos 162, 302–3; NAS MS PC4/2, fos 31r–32v; Hume of Polwarth to Ogilvy, 26 November and 5 December 1696, NAS MS GD 158/964, fos 61, 72; NAS MS GD18/2092/1, 12 December 1696; WRH MS PC12/16, 4 December 1696, 18 December 1696; ECA MS SL1/1/35, fo. 293r; *The Post Man*, 252 (19 December 1696).

4

The Making of a Blasphemer

4.1 SPIRITUAL CRISES AND THE CALVINIST MIND

Nowadays the period of late adolescence and early adulthood is seen as one of intellectual and social experimentation, as young adults (many of them university students), following a pattern of seeking that has prototypes stretching back at least as far as St Augustine of Hippo, sort out their own beliefs and try out various modes of living. It is also a dangerous time, when signs of some of the mental illnesses, such as depression, associated with troubled adults can first appear. Calvinist writers of the early modern era, less inclined than we are to structure human experience in medical terms, but quite confident of Satan's existence and his nefarious objectives, often cast such maladies as a struggle over the individual's soul, with doubt and despair among the more alarming symptoms. As Louise Yeoman has observed, 'believers had to make a (usually traumatic) transition from a state of despair and possible damnation (the covenant of works) to the state of election (the covenant of grace)'.[1] What has been less noticed is the extent to which these spiritual crises became increasingly informed by the discourse of religious scepticism toward the end of the seventeenth century.

The case of Thomas Aikenhead resonates with those sceptical currents, but the fact that he was made an exemplar for the evils of disbelief should not obscure the fact that many of his contemporaries, even those whose spiritual quests ended in firm Presbyterian Calvinism, trod similar paths, if only for a time. Aikenhead's sometime classmate Thomas Halyburton recalled that, after he had transferred to the University of St Andrews, he was beset in that fashion: 'Satan, in Conjuction with the natural Atheism of my Heart, took Occasion to cast me into racking Disquietment about the great Truths of Religion, more especially the Being of a God.' Indeed, the study of philosophy 'fostered the natural Conceit we all have of our own Ability to know, and emboldened me to proceed further than was meet'. Halyburton even set out, in Cartesian fashion, to prove the existence of God using only reason. He failed to do so to his own satisfaction. Living in a lairdly household after he had finished his studies in 1696, he found himself frequently 'engag'd in Debates about the Truth of Religion, the Divinity of the Scriptures, and the most important Doctrines delivered in them, whereby I was drawn to read the Writings of Deists, and other Enemies to Religion'. Recalling this from the later vantage point of firm Calvinist faith, Halyburton wrote that such discussions were dangerous to him in particular because he was 'so unsettled' in his own beliefs at the time. He found that the doubts of his unnamed friends were 'infectious'. The result was a form of spiritual terror. 'Thus I found when I was alone, when I was in prayer and most serious, hellish oaths, and grievous blasphemous suggestions cast forcibly into my Mind, which made me tremble.' But Halyburton kept most of his doubts to himself, and after a dark winter of spiritual discontent in 1697–8 had an experience of a 'great light' and a sense that God could forgive him, putting him on a sanctified path that led into his career as a leading Presbyterian divine and a professor of theology at St Andrews.[2]

Behind Halyburton's structured conversion narrative is the story of an intellectual journey upon which many sensitive, inquisitive young people of the late seventeenth century embarked, albeit with certain features peculiar to the Calvinist culture in which Halyburton (and Thomas Aikenhead) grew up. In a similar vein, the Edinburgh servant Elisabeth West, another contemporary, wrote that in early 1695 she began to have serious doubts, and felt she was 'strongly assaulted' by Satan with thoughts that 'there is no God, there is no Christ, no Holy Ghost; it is but a fancy in the Bible, it is not God's word, it is but a contrivance of man; ministers are not the servants of God, but seducers of the people'.

West's belief that she was the only person experiencing such doubts only added to her agonies, as did reading a book about Francis Spira, the Italian and prototype figure for the sin of despair. Spira, a Protestant lawyer from a town near Padua, had been denounced to the Venetian Inquisition and recanted in 1548. Afterwards he allegedly developed grave doubts about his recantation and concluded that he was hopelessly damned as a result. Despite the entreaties of his learned friends, he apparently starved himself to death out of despair. His story was written and rewritten in many genres – prose, play and ballad – and became one of the standard Protestant cautionary tales for the evils of apostasy and despair. The version West read was probably Nathaniel Bacon's *A Relation of the Fearefull Estate of Francis Spira*, first published in 1638. 'O that I had never seen it!' she mourned, 'for I thought I would make the same end he made; but, which was worst to me, there were some atheists that wrote letters to him to confirm him in his atheism, which words could not get out of my mind; which made me lament that I ever read Francis Spira.' What brought her out of this despair was reading John Bunyan's *Grace Abounding among the Chief of Sinners* (Bunyan had also been troubled by his reading of Bacon's book on Spira) and the preaching of George Meldrum and James Kirkton in Edinburgh and Lasswade, respectively.[3]

Increased access to heterodox literature combined with the natural tendencies of young adults expanded the vocabulary of doubt. But Halyburton was discreet, and the conversations in which he was engaged apparently took place in the seclusion of a country house, rather than the bustling streets of Edinburgh, or in its taverns and coffee houses. Therefore, he was allowed to complete his quest uninterrupted, and for him it led to spiritual confidence and even a vocation. Elisabeth West appears to have shared her doubts only with her spiritual diary. Other quests were disturbed in various ways that may have altered their courses. We have already seen what happened when John Fraser spoke too freely of his own doubts and reading in the presence of his landlord and landlady. Thomas Aikenhead made the same mistake, but more frequently, and in front of more people. What is more, he seems to have combined his doubts with a brand of youthful intellectual bravado that, in the crisis atmosphere of 1696, proved a fatal combination. The authorities did not feel they could afford to indulge his spiritual quest in the hope it would end in faith (or at least conventional religiosity); it had to be cut short to save others from following similar paths, and to protect society at large.

With the blasphemies he was accused of uttering, Thomas Aikenhead seemed to represent all the sceptical currents of the day. According to the indictment prepared against him, he had claimed that theology 'was a rapsidie of faigned and ill-invented nonsense'. He also attacked the view that Scripture was divinely ordained, suggesting that the books of the Old Testament should be called 'Ezra's fables' (since he claimed that the scribe Ezra had made them up) and the New Testament should be titled 'the history of the Impostor Christ'. Jesus, he said, had tricked his followers with magic he learned in Egypt, where Moses had acquired similar skills. Aikenhead rejected the Trinity, denied the existence of spirits and 'maintained that God, the world, and nature are but one thing, and that the world was from eternity'. Challenging ideas of divine intervention or miracles, he said 'man's imaginatione duely exalted by airt and industry can do any thing, even in the infinite power of God'. Aikenhead was also said to have preferred Muhammad to Jesus, and predicted that Christianity would soon die out.[4]

These were very heretical claims, but we should not assume Aikenhead had necessarily avowed all of them in the manner described. An indictment is a legal document, intended to state the case against the defendant in the strongest possible terms, using a language and phraseology peculiar to the law. Witness testimony, from which an indictment is constructed, can (if truthful) take us closer to the actual words or deeds of a defendant, but even it is subject to the constraints of the courtroom or deposition and the questions asked. Even petitions filed by the defendant (and there would be some of these in Aikenhead's case) are usually structured as a response to specific charges or legal questions and can be evasive as to the defendant's actual views. As Cynthia Herrup has pointed out, 'law is a cultural dialect', and its enforcement 'a forum of cultural interaction'.[5] More than anything else, then, as now, a trial is a public performance aimed at convincing its audience of the defendant's guilt. In response, a strong defence can blunt the effectiveness of the performance and clear the defendant of the charges, if not from suspicion of guilt. A trial also requires preparation, and it appears that a lot of that went into James Stewart of Goodtrees's prosecution. What is less clear is what sort of preparations Aikenhead was able to make.

When Aikenhead appeared before the Privy Council on 10 November 1696 the council ordered that he be put on trial for his life before the High Court of Justiciary, but it did not set a date for that trial. By 27 November, a date of 14 December had apparently been chosen. Meanwhile, Stewart of Goodtrees summoned witnesses, seventeen in all, and it appears that Aikenhead was kept informed of their identities. As late as 9–12 December, when jurors were being summoned for the assize, the trial was still set for 14 December. But for reasons that cannot be determined from the surviving records, it was thereafter changed to 21 December and then to 23 December.[6]

All this time Aikenhead languished in Edinburgh's tolbooth, a building situated in the centre of the burgh, adjacent to the High Kirk of St Giles. While he would not have been isolated there, the atmosphere would have been insalubrious. As an accused felon, Aikenhead would have been held in the oldest part of the building, the eastern end, which at that point was already more than three hundred years old, although it had been extensively renovated in the early 1560s. Originally it had included merchants' stalls as well, but this was no longer the case by the 1690s, and the merchants hawked their wares in the nearby 'luckenbooths' (locking booths) running along the north side of St Giles', instead. A western wing had been added to the tolbooth in 1610 to house debtors. Overall, the building stood five storeys tall, and would stand until 1817, when it was demolished.[7] This

The Making of a Blasphemer

Figure 4.1 The tolbooth from the south.
Aikenhead would have been kept in the oldest section, to the right.
(Source: *The Book of the Old Edinburgh Club* and Ohio State
University Libraries. Used with permission.)

was not a pleasant place to be, and, as it turns out, Thomas Aikenhead was not the first member of his immediate family to face death's approach while housed there.

4.2 WHO WAS THOMAS AIKENHEAD?

Thomas Aikenhead was an intellectual iconoclast from an idiosyncratic and (by the 1690s) marginal Edinburgh family. But the Aikenheads' misfortunes were of recent vintage. His paternal grandfather was Mr Thomas Aikenhead, one of the commissaries of Edinburgh and a burgess. Young Thomas's father, the apothecary James Aikenhead, was made a burgess of Edinburgh through his father's right in April 1669. In October 1667 James had married Helen Ramsey, a clergyman's daughter.[8] Their first three children were daughters – Jonet, baptised in February 1668, Katharine, baptised in July 1669, and Margaret, baptised in February 1672.[9] Katharine was still alive in 1698, but at least one, and probably two, of these girls died young. James Aikenhead and Helen Ramsey buried a child (not named in the record) in Greyfriars Kirkyard, Edinburgh, in July 1675.[10] The brevity of the witness list for Margaret's baptism – only three witnesses as opposed to four and five for her elder sisters – and the fact that the baptism was said to have taken place three days before it was recorded in the register, implying haste, suggests that she may have died shortly after birth, which would mean that Katharine was the only living sibling remaining to greet her brother Thomas's entry into the world.

Thomas Aikenhead was baptised on 28 March 1676. The prominence of some of the nine witnesses listed is indicative both of his family's status and of the value placed on the birth of James Aikenhead and Helen Ramsey's first (and, as it would turn out, only) son.[11] This was an opportunity to demonstrate the family's connections to Edinburgh's professional and merchant elite. The first two men listed were Mr James Aikenhead, commissary of Edinburgh, and Alexander Aikenhead, a writer to the Signet. Doubtless these two were relatives, but the closeness of the relationship cannot be ascertained; they were probably uncles and/or cousins of Thomas Aikenhead's father. Next was Patrick Hepburn, laird of Blackcastle, also involved in the apothecary's trade, and with whom the family would have ongoing business ties. Hepburn of Blackcastle, who was related to the Aikenhead side of the family, had also witnessed the baptisms of the three elder daughters. Also witnessing young Thomas's baptism were Mr James Scott, sheriff-clerk of Edinburgh, the merchants Thomas Wilson, William Paterson, George Lawson and James Harvie, and finally a Thomas Aikenhead who was apparently young Thomas's uncle.[12]

Hepburn of Blackcastle, Mr James Scott, Alexander Aikenhead, Paterson and Lawson also appeared as witnesses in March 1677 when James Aikenhead and Helen Ramsey baptised another child – Thomas's younger sister Anna. They were joined then by Dr Archibald Stevenson (an Edinburgh physician who was apparently related to Helen Ramsey), the laird David Oswald of Eastbarns and the merchant James Edmonston.[13] The family connection to Stevenson was particularly interesting given Thomas Aikenhead's eventual fate, since Stevenson's daughter Elizabeth later married the free-thinking (and Jacobite) physician Dr Archibald Pitcairne, and the couple were living under the same roof as Stevenson in the Tron Parish in 1694.[14]

These witness lists indicate that Thomas Aikenhead's family was relatively prosperous at the time of his birth. It had strong roots in Edinburgh, with several male relatives in important positions. But this comfortable position would deteriorate during Thomas Aikenhead's childhood. Through bad luck or incompetence (or perhaps just a poorly timed death), his father would squander his wealth, and the scattered references to Thomas's parents that can be found in local records suggest they were an argumentative pair, likely to alienate friends and business associates. In December 1681, when young Thomas would have been five, the couple became involved in a legal dispute with Ramsey's brother Thomas, minister of Mordington. The causes and outcome of this case are unclear, but it was the first in what would become a pattern of disputes within the extended family.[15] The medicines James Aikenhead sold also caused problems. In April 1682 a complaint brought to the Privy Council by the king's advocate on behalf of a maidservant to a local advocate alleged that James Aikenhead was making and selling 'poysonous tablets … [to] work strange wantone affections and humours in the bodies of women'. Elizabeth Edmonstone, daughter of the laird of Duntreath (and the person actually being charged in the case), had sent a servant to buy the aphrodisiacs from Aikenhead and then had given them to Jonet Stewart 'as a sweetmeat tablet'. Stewart fell ill, suffered a fever for twenty days and was unlikely ever to recover fully. Apparently a Dr Irving had saved her life with another medicine, and the Privy Council referred the case to the College of Physicians. Defending their own professional territory, the physicians ruled that aphrodisiacs were not to be dispensed without their advice.[16]

Within a year, James Aikenhead was dead. He died without a will, so a 'testament dative' for him was registered on 30 March 1683. It indicated that he had died in debt to the tune of £1,131, much of that owed to Patrick Hepburn of Blackcastle, who, along with the apothecary George Borthwick, was appointed executor. Hepburn of Blackcastle had rented a shop to Aikenhead starting in 1673, and alleged that the latter had started falling behind in payments in 1677. Hepburn took legal action in November 1682, but the rent remained unpaid at the time of James Aikenhead's death.[17] Aikenhead's widow Ramsey, apparently estranged from her brother, must have found herself (and her children, including seven-year-old Thomas) in a terrible position. She sought to carry on her husband's trade in the same location, but Hepburn of Blackcastle soon turned against this arrangement, if indeed he had ever really accepted it. At 11 p.m. one evening in August 1683 he forcibly evicted her from the shop, leading her to complain to the Privy Council against Hepburn 'for wounding her and beating her' in the removal. Hepburn denied using violence 'tho shee gave [him and his servants] very opprobrious language'. Although Hepburn had a decreet of lawful removal against her, the council held him guilty of riot because of the late hour of the incident.[18]

It appears that Ramsey was able to reoccupy the shop, perhaps hoping that her son Thomas could eventually take it over. But this was not to be. On 18 March 1685 she was ordered into ward in the tolbooth for non-payment of debts owed to Hepburn. This time Hepburn complained that, although he had a legal eviction against her dating to August 1683, she had been defiantly occupying the shop since then. A merchant named Thomas Aikenhead, probably her former brother-in-law, refused to serve as her cautioner, so she spent more than a month in the debtors' wing of the tolbooth, and was freed on 29 April on condition that she stay away from Hepburn, the shop and his servants. This was a moot point, however; she was dying, and within four days she was dead, buried in Greyfriars Kirkyard.[19] Her spell in the tolbooth probably hastened her into the grave.

Young Thomas was thus orphaned at nine, with no wealth within his immediate family on which to rely. His surviving sisters Katharine and Anna would have been in similarly bad straits, although Katharine was nearly sixteen. In his later recollections of his intellectual journey, Aikenhead recalled that it was when he was about ten years old that he began 'searching [for] good and sufficient grounds whereon I might safely build my faith', a search that eventually led to the scepticism that would prove his undoing. While his parents' dealings seem to have alienated some of the extended family, Thomas received financial assistance from Sir Patrick Aikenhead, whose precise relationship to Thomas is unclear, but who was working as a factor for the Earl (later Marquis) of Tweeddale in 1685 – the same religiously moderate Tweeddale who later became Chancellor and who had (with mixed results) managed the parliament of 1695 on King William's behalf. Interestingly, Sir Patrick Aikenhead was also a grand-nephew of Hepburn, James Aikenhead's creditor and Helen Ramsey's nemesis, and served as executor of the estates of both Hepburn and his father in 1696. By the spring of 1695 Patrick Aikenhead was identified as a clerk of Edinburgh's Commissary Court, and was still in Tweeddale's employ as well.[20] In March 1692 he signed over to young Thomas Aikenhead a property in the fourth storey of a tenement house 'lately rebuilt' on the south side of the High Street near the Netherbow. The flat was said to be eighteen feet deep, and to include the garret above. This would have been one of the new stone buildings that burgh authorities were encouraging developers to put up, and it would have made Thomas a resident of the Tron parish, with neighbours including Pitcairne and John Fraser, who also was charged with blasphemy in 1696. While the document detailing the transaction stated that Thomas paid 'ane certain somme of money' for the property, he probably did not have much wealth to his name, so this was probably a case of charity within the extended family, witnessed in this instance by Alexander Aikenhead, writer to the Signet, and the same merchant Thomas Aikenhead who had refused to post caution for young Thomas's mother in 1685.[21]

4.3 EDINBURGH'S TOWN COLLEGE AND THE EDUCATION OF THOMAS AIKENHEAD

A few months after acquiring this property, the sixteen-year-old Thomas Aikenhead enrolled in Edinburgh's town college. He joined eighty-five other boys and young men under the guidance of the regent Alexander Cunningham in the 'bajan' (first-year) class, which began its studies in October 1692 and formally matriculated (with the payment of a fee to the library) on 22 February 1693. Aikenhead paid the standard fee of £1 10*d*. asked of most matriculants; wealthier students paid higher amounts. His class included several students who would later testify against him, as well as Thomas Halyburton, whose own spiritual doubts were discussed earlier.[22] Aikenhead would have been a little older than most of his peers, since students usually started at about the age of fourteen. Before becoming bajans, these students would have been required to translate a Scots work into acceptable Latin, proving they knew the language of instruction well enough. The students had to be prepared to do a lot of listening. Classes began at 7 a.m. in the winter and 6 a.m. in the rest of the year (there was a break between August and October), with regents lecturing in the morning, and asking students questions, based on the lecture, in the afternoon. At the beginning of the second year, the students would have to demonstrate competence in Greek before moving on to the intensive study of Aristotle and other philosophers (on logic, metaphysics, ethics and physics) in their third and fourth years. After completing the bachelor of arts (which most never formally attained), students could go on to postgraduate study in theology or medicine.[23]

The common practice at Edinburgh until 1708 was to have the same regent lead a class through the whole four-year arts curriculum. Cunningham was fairly young, although the fact that his appointment dated to 1689 made him a holdover from the period before the firm Presbyterian Gilbert Rule had become principal of the college in 1690. His donation to the college library at the time of his appointment of a copy of the 1684 volume *The Spirit of M. Arnaud* hints at broad philosophical interests. Antoine Arnauld was a Catholic, albeit Jansenist, philosopher and theologian whose logic was condemned by a Scottish universities commission in 1695 for using 'protestant arguments as examples of sophisms'.[24] In fact,

Cunningham almost lost his post during the post-revolution visitation of the town college in 1690, which had led to the firing of its Episcopalian principal, Alexander Monro. Visitors (including the future Chancellor Patrick Hume of Polwarth) heard several bad things about Cunningham, both in their investigations of the 'atheist' mathematics professor David Gregory (who soon after took a post at more tolerant Oxford University) and their subsequent hearings on Cunningham himself. Cunningham was allegedly regularly drunk in the company of Gregory, the regent Herbert Kennedy and Dr Archibald Pitcairne; one former student said that Cunningham and Kennedy drank so much strong ale in Gregory's room one night that they had to spend the night there, since Cunningham 'had noe foot to go home'. Someone told the visitors that Cunningham 'was taken in ane Ba[w]diehouse with any oyr mans wife', for which he was briefly imprisoned in the Canongate.[25] He had also apparently published a Latin poem critical of the penal laws against Catholics (which James VII and II had refused to enforce), although in his defence Cunningham claimed that the poem had merely suggested 'that under a government where peace, learning, piety and justice doe flourish, there will be no use for bloody lawes'. Cunningham had been observed in a Catholic chapel, and had got into a brawl in a coffee house in the Canongate because of his behaviour towards the mistress of the house. He had 'caried so lassiviouslie' with the proprietress late one evening that her husband had drawn his sword, and two other men, including Kennedy, had to intervene to persuade the man not to press charges. There were also complaints that he was rough with his students,

> boxing some in the face to the effusion of bloode and caining others to that hight that complaints wer manie times intended against him before the privie councill, and for his sake all the masters wer discharged the having of staves, though it wes the constant custome befor.

Gregory and Kennedy (probably not the most trusted of witnesses!) spoke up for Cunningham, as did a local vintner with two sons in his class, who vouched that he had entertained Cunningham in his house on several occasions, and the regent had always remained sober.

Cunningham admitted to the visitors that 'he was frequently in taverns being a young man and having no familie', but said he 'behaved as the most sober in the kingdome who were in his circumstances to resort therto for his dyet. And if he wes there at any other tyme, it was about his necessar affaires and bussines.' While the visitors may have been sceptical of his loyalties, he was allowed to keep his job.[26] Halyburton, who certainly would have had no use for Cunningham's allegedly Catholic tendencies, praised his skills in helping his pupils develop their Latin.[27] Unlike his colleague Kennedy, Cunningham does not seem to have taught the new physics of Isaac Newton, preferring instead the philosophical currents running out of France, Germany and the Low Countries (including the ideas of Descartes), although he did praise the English natural philosopher Robert Boyle, as well as King Charles II (for his patronage of the Royal Society).[28] In sum, Thomas Aikenhead's first regent appears to have been a broad-minded (but not cutting-edge) scholar, close in age to his pupils, who may have had a drinking problem, which may have contributed to a streak of violent libertinism. Such men were not rare in Restoration Britain, but the parliamentary visitors of 1690 wanted to discourage Scots universities from hiring them, particularly if (as with Cunningham), there was any whiff of Catholicism about them. New regulations promulgated in the wake of the 1690 visitation stipulated that prospective regents and masters be judged not only on their 'abilities and learning ... but also ther pietie good lyfe and conversation, ther prudence, fittnes for the place, affection for the government of church and state now established and ther other good qualifications completlie.' Edinburgh's town council protested against parliamentary interference into the governance of its college, but the regime in power wanted to make sure that institutions of higher learning would encourage the covenanted piety of Gilbert Rule rather than the Restoration eclecticism of David Gregory or Alexander Cunningham.[29]

But, as it would turn out, Cunningham would not last long enough to see Thomas Aikenhead or his fellow bajans through their whole arts curriculum. As their first year was winding down, he fell ill, and suffered the next year from what Halyburton described as 'a frenzy', forcing his retirement, and leaving the class 'quite broken up'. He died in 1696.[30] The new regent, John Row, took over the guidance of Aikenhead's class in 1695, but the disruption caused by Cunningham's breakdown and death may well have shaken some of his students.[31]

Aikenhead's formal matriculation in February 1693 would have given him access to the college library. Students were not to remove books from the library, but could read them there, under the watchful eyes of the portraits of Luther, Melanchthon, Zwingli and Calvin (joined by Descartes in 1694), not to mention George Buchanan's skull, in a building opened in 1644, which also housed the bookshop of Agnes Campbell (the widow of Andrew Anderson) on its ground floor.[32] Considering the radical philosophical positions Aikenhead was accused of espousing, it is worth investigating what sorts of books he might have been able to read in this library, particularly since Robert Henderson, college librarian since 1693, was one of the witnesses summoned to his trial.[33] This is possible owing to the existence of a couple of early library catalogues, as well as a library accessions book covering most of the 1690s, and magistrand and matriculation receipt books that list how the money collected was spent (usually on books).

Hobbes and Spinoza may have been universally attacked by college regents in their lectures, but this did not make the library shy away from purchasing works by both authors, both of whom had questioned Moses' authorship of the Pentateuch.[34] Students who wanted to read these 'atheistic' authors could, although they could also read many books critical of Hobbes in particular. Back in 1668 alone, the library had purchased *Observations, censures, and confutations of notorious errours in Mr Hobbes his Leviathan and other his bookes* by William Lucy, Bishop of St Davids, *Castigations of Mr Hobbes his last animadversions* by John Bramhall, Bishop of Derry, an anti-Hobbesian work in Latin by Seth Ward, Bishop of Salisbury, another critique of Hobbes that cannot be identified, and an attack on atheism and Socinianism (that is, the rejection of belief in the Trinity).[35] In 1672, two years after purchasing Hobbes's *Opera Omnia*, the library collected another tonic against Hobbes – the unidentifiable 'Hobs Creed examined by a student of divinity'.[36] Clearly, the 'Monster of Malmesbury' was arousing both fascination and revulsion in the college library. While until 1682 these works would be available only to students who had already completed their four-year arts degree, the opening of the library to undergraduates that year cleared the way for boys like Thomas Aikenhead to read the works their regents were supposed to be warning them against.

But Hobbes's was not the only dangerous new philosophy or alternative orthodoxy a student might encounter there. In 1669 the library acquired an English translation of the Qur'ān, which it augmented with a Latin edition, with commentaries, in 1676, although this was perhaps tempered by the purchase of Grotius' *De Veritate Religionis Christiana*, also in 1669.[37] (This last work, under its English title *Of the Truth of the Christian Religion*, was recommended by John Fraser as an antidote to the deism of Charles Blount when Fraser was hauled before the Privy Council in 1696.) In 1672 the library purchased a copy of *De Veritate* by Edward Herbert, Lord Cherbury, the founding father of English deism. This work, first published in 1633, was one of those specifically attacked by Aikenhead's sometime classmate Halyburton when he, after a youthful flirtation with deism, became a model Presbyterian academic.[38] Aikenhead and Halyburton's ill-starred regent Cunningham (along with David Gregory) signed off on the library's 1690 purchase of Richard Simon's *Critical Enquiries into the Various Editions of the Bible*, a work that, like those of Hobbes and

Spinoza, cast doubt on traditional beliefs about the authorship and compilation of scripture, although this edition did not include some of the more controversial claims in the Latin editions from which it was translated and condensed. Nevertheless, it appears that the library ultimately purchased those as well.[39] Six years later, the Presbyterian bookseller George Mosman imported from London for the library Jacques Abbadie's *Vindication of the Truth of Christian Religion* (1694), the English translation of a 1684 work that devoted sixty-five pages to a refutation of Simon.[40]

René Descartes was another potentially heterodox natural philosopher represented in the college library. While not seen as being as dangerous as Hobbes (after all, his portrait was purchased to decorate the library in 1694), the possibly atheistic implications of Cartesian mechanism did worry visiting commissioners from time to time. As noted above, Aikenhead's regent Cunningham favoured Descartes, and, as will be seen below, Aikenhead's critics would see Descartes as one of the authors who had led the young student astray. The devout Presbyterian divine James Hogg (1658–1734) had his own youthful flirtation with Cartesian ideas, and warned that those who ventured too far into that philosophy

> by their high aspirings beyond all just rates of sober and solid wisdom, did precipitate themselves into such deep pits of Scepticism and material Atheism (howsoever disguised), from whence they either never get out, or, at best, their applauded philosophy afforded them no habile means for making such a necessary escape.[41]

Nevertheless, Cartesian physics had been endorsed in regents' lectures to undergraduates starting in the 1670s, and in 1693 the library purchased *A Voyage to the World of Cartesius* (1692), which has been attributed to Daniel Defoe, among others.[42]

In the 1690s the library's acquisitions became more eclectic. In addition to purchasing Simon's works, the library acquired Thomas Burnet's *Theoria Sacra Telluris* (2 vols, 1681, 1689), as well as his *Archaeologiae Philosophicae* (1692). The Englishman Burnet had sought to reconcile biblical accounts of the Earth's origins with new scientific theories in a way that appears almost humorous today, but was regarded as anti-biblical by many contemporaries.[43] Like the library of the Society of Advocates, the college library also collected several volumes in the rather deist *Turkish Spy* series. In 1696, the year Thomas Aikenhead ran afoul of the law, the library bought alumnus John Toland's controversial *Christianity not Mysterious* (1695) and, even more shockingly, Charles Blount's edition of *The First Two Books of Philostratus, Concerning the Life of Apollonius Tyaneus* (1680).[44] It is no wonder that Mosman felt the need to counter such acquisitions that same year with Abbadie's *Vindication* as well as William Stephens's *An Account of the Growth of Deism in England* and John Edwards's *Some Thoughts Concerning the Several Causes and Occasions of Atheism, Especially in the Present Age* along with the latter's *Socinianism Unmask'd* and *The Socinian Creed*.[45] The culture wars of 1690s Britain were raging in the college library, and a curious student like Thomas Aikenhead could drink deeply at this well of critical thought.

While Aikenhead attended lectures for four years, he never completed the requirements for his degree. This was not unusual, as only a minority of those who matriculated took a degree. The bulk of those students from Aikenhead's class who graduated with their arts degrees did so in July 1696, and, based on the testimony at his trial, Aikenhead may have already become a controversial figure by then.[46] As he sat in the tolbooth awaiting his trial, it became clear that at least one of his classmates had developed a serious grudge against him.

4.4 THE ATTACK BY MUNGO CRAIG

One of the students who matriculated with Aikenhead and Halyburton in 1692–3 under Cunningham's tutelage and who was granted his arts degree in July 1696 was Mungo Craig, formally recorded in the register as 'Quintigernus' (Kentigern/Mungo) Craig. Curiously, he is not listed as having paid his library fee, but did pay the customary £4 Scots expected of graduates when he finished.[47] Like Aikenhead, Craig was a native of Edinburgh, although a bit older, and also of a more humble background; his father was a cordiner, and there were only three witnesses to his baptism on 18 December 1674 – a writer, a merchant and another cordiner.[48] Craig later implied that he enrolled in the town college in order to prepare for a career in the ministry, and, while some of his later claims may be doubted, this one rings true. But, in the course of his studies, he apparently spent a lot of time talking with Aikenhead, who was perhaps not the best social companion for an aspiring Presbyterian pastor. Craig would ultimately be the leading witness at Aikenhead's trial, but he did not wait until then to make his accusations public. Although he would later deny it, it may well have been Craig who first brought Aikenhead to the attention of the authorities.[49] In any case, while Aikenhead was in the tolbooth awaiting trial, Craig wrote some of his accusations into a pamphlet, published for his landlord, the stationer Robert Hutchison, whose property (including, apparently, a shop) was at the head of the College Wynd, between the High Street and the college buildings.

This brief work, titled *A Satyr against Atheistical Deism with the*

Genuine Character of a Deist, was a cheap quarto booklet of sixteen pages, bearing the marks of hasty production, including misnumbered pages and no running headlines on the pages. Clearly, Craig and Hutchison wanted to get this work out in a hurry, probably before Aikenhead's trial reduced its currency and therefore its marketability. While mostly appearing to describe the 'deist' as a stock, late-seventeenth-century philosophical villain, it nevertheless began with denunciations specifically related to Aikenhead, and noted that he was at the time of writing and publication imprisoned 'for the same Damnable Apostacy' – namely 'Atheistical Deism' – with this seeming oxymoron set off in black-letter type (increasingly rare in late-seventeenth-century printing) to emphasise its monstrosity.[50] While most deists would have recoiled at being labelled 'atheist', to a pious critic like Craig, the distinction was immaterial; they were '*Epicurean* Beasts', even worse than Catholics. They were

> *Witts* of the Age, who can Gigantick Feats
> Perform at Reasoning; whereas they know
> As little as an Ass, what's truely so
> Those be the course-grained *Philosophs*, who stuff
> Their Heads with Contradictions & pure Buff
> *Chimaera's* coin'd in Hell and horrid Fopp'ry
> Surpassing Transubstantiating Pop'ry[51]

In contrast, Craig credited Christians with 'Socratick Modestie' and praised Christianity as a 'Rationall and Holy Faith'.[52] But that faith was under attack:

> *O Times! O Manners!* May I justly cry
> Will *Scotland* nourish such Apostacy?
> *A Covenanted People!* and ev'n while
> Such Glorious sun-shine overspreads the Isle!

While a reader might have wondered how the crises of 1696 qualified as 'Glorious sun-shine', Craig warned that worse things might be in the offing, recalling biblical examples of punishing plagues, not to mention the destruction of Sodom and Gomorrah. Magistrates needed to take action:

> Come! Let a Rational and Holy Flame
> Of zeal to Christ and God's most glorious name
> Our Nations Honour, and our Christian Right
> Inspire God's Deputes with Coelestial Light
> Who sit at Justice: That they may attone
> with Blood, th'affronts of heav'ns offended throne;

And turn away that Deluge of God's Ire
Which threatens us worse than devouring Fire[53]

Describing 'the Genuine Character of a Deist' – with Aikenhead in mind – Craig claimed that such a person never grants that he has lost an argument, having 'a compleat Coat of Armour consisting of Loud Laughter, huffing and nauseating disdain for a sheild'. The deist scorns all churchmen, and stuffs his brain 'with all the ridiculous Fopprie, that either fell by Inadvertancy, Contention, Malice or Ignorance from the pens of Ancient and Modern Philosophers'. The examples of erring philosophers that Craig cited give us a sense of where he thought Aikenhead's ideas came from – Hobbes, Spinoza, Aristotle's theory that the world was eternal, Epicurus' denial of providence or the immortality of the soul, Descartes's view 'that matter and motion being granted, all cou'd fall out as they are, without the concurrence of an intelligent over-ruling Power', and Blount's '*Oracles of Nonsense*'.[54] These were all authors and ideas thatAikenhead could have encountered in the college's curriculum and/or its library.

Craig further ridiculed Aikenhead by offering the reader '*A Catalogue of the Works promised to the world, by* T. Aik. Gent. *the meerest* Don Quixot *in Nature, but one of the principal Patrons and Promoters of the Witty, I would have said* Witless sect'. While the list doubtless contains some exaggeration, its contents suggest that Aikenhead was something of an eclectic visionary with grandiose ideas that hovered on the frontier between natural philosophy and Renaissance magic, tipping into fevered imagination. Perhaps following in his father's pharmacological footsteps, Aikenhead allegedly told Craig that he was developing an 'Antidote against all external and internal Causes of Death' – a drug that could even raise a man from the dead '*Tho' he were speldered* [i.e. split] *like a dry Haddock*', a phrase that Craig said was Aikenhead's own. Craig jokingly referred to the concoction as '*Aurum Potabile Aikinheadaeum* i.e. *Chimaericum*'. In addition, he said Aikenhead had promised a flying machine ('*Machina Dedalaea*') 'whereby we may have easy commerce with the other *Vortices*, and especially with the *World in the Moon*'. Craig also wrote that Aikenhead claimed to be formulating a cheap way of making the philosopher's stone in four hours for four shillings, which, Craig jokingly suggested, would eliminate the need for taxation to pay for war. Surely so 'Frothy and Crackbrain'd a Fellow' could also be capable of spewing 'a compleat Aggregat of all the Blasphemies that ever were vented, maintained, or excogitated, by the Atheistical Ministers of Satan in all Ages, with an Overplus of his own Coining'.

Craig's attack certainly heightened Aikenhead's notoriety and probably brought some customers into Hutchison's shop. We must be aware of the likely exaggerations in the work, and also recognise the extent to which this pamphlet would have constructed Aikenhead's image as the antithesis of orthodoxy on the streets and in the taverns and coffee houses of Edinburgh. Indeed, the pamphlet pledged that, if anyone doubted that Aikenhead had voiced such absurdities, 'the Book-binder [Hutchison] promises, in name of the Author, to produce a considerable Number of Witnesses, who can give their Oath that they heard [Aikenhead] boast of ... ridiculous notions'.[55] Craig's pamphlet presented Aikenhead as an object of ridicule and execration, and probably would have prepared jurors and the execution audience for the dramas that followed, convicting him first in the court of public opinion. Stuck in the tolbooth, the subject of this controversy could do little about it. He was, however, receiving encouragement from outside that further exacerbated his predicament. William Lorimer, an English clergyman visiting Edinburgh that winter, and who was not entirely unsympathetic to Aikenhead, later reported that supporters would call up to his cell window at night 'to tell him he had a good Cause, and to exhort him to stand to it, and suffer for it bravely'. Such interaction between prisoners and the public outside was not unusual; in August, a 'hill preacher' named Hepburn had apparently managed to preach several sermons from the window of his cell in the tolbooth 'and by his Canting Method had got about him a great Congregation, especially of the Female Sex', spurring the authorities to order his removal to Stirling Castle. Lorimer thought the support Aikenhead received only spurred the authorities to prosecute the case more vigorously. Lorimer also visited Aikenhead before his trial, accompanied by a son of Gilbert Rule, the college principal, and claimed Aikenhead admitted 'that he had been rash and foolish, and was sorry for what he said, and desired my prayers'.[56]

Craig also apparently visited Aikenhead during this period, accompanied by Patrick Middleton, another student at the college who also ended up testifying against him. The prisoner probably did not receive these guests with open arms. Craig, later defending his own conduct in the case, wrote that, while Aikenhead had in his cell a copy of Sir Charles Wolseley's *The Reasonablenes of Scripture-Beleif* (London, 1672), he judged from the prisoner's tone while discussing this orthodox work that he was not convinced by it. Craig said he recommended that Aikenhead read Hugo Grotius' works in defence of Christianity (apparently widely regarded as an antidote to heresy – recall John Fraser's endorsement of the Dutch jurist before the Privy Council) as well as those of 'Dr More', presumably Henry More (1614–87), whose works included *An Antidote against Atheisme* (London, 1653).[57] Both Aikenhead and Craig would write about each other with mutual bitterness, and it is hard to imagine that this conversation in Aikenhead's cell could have been anything but tense. Nevertheless it is possible that this visit, as well as the visit from Lorimer and Rule, was part of an effort to get the prisoner to back away from his more controversial views, particularly those challenging the Trinity and the authority of Scripture. One can also speculate that, if this conversation had gone differently, Craig might have testified differently at Aikenhead's trial. But, given that he had already attacked him in print, Craig's accusations may have already reached the point where they could not really be withdrawn.

On another front, Aikenhead's relatives were abandoning him. At the end of October (probably aware that young Thomas was marked for prosecution), Sir Patrick Aikenhead, his former benefactor, signed a debt of £410 2s. owed to him by Thomas over to one Thomas Mercer, a writer in Edinburgh. This money was said to be owed 'for payment of board in coll[ege] buying and maiking of his cloaths and other necessary'. It suggests that Thomas had lived well if not extravagantly; his contemporary Thomas Boston paid £128 15s. 6d. for his degree at the college, including regents' fees, college dues, and room and board.[58] Before his imprisonment, Aikenhead was apparently lodging in rooms owned by George Dickson, a tailor; perhaps he had been removed from the lodgings near the Netherbow that Patrick Aikenhead had earlier sold him, or perhaps he was living in part off income from that property that Patrick Aikenhead was administering on his behalf.[59] Patrick Aikenhead may have been seeking to avoid suing his own relative for the debt, or he may simply have been trying to get something of value from Mercer in exchange for an obligation that was looking very difficult to collect on. On 7 November, Edinburgh's Commissary Court ruled that Thomas Aikenhead now owed Mercer the money.[60] Given his appearance before the Privy Council three days later, this debt was probably not Aikenhead's main concern, but it is further evidence of the depth of his predicament. A successful defence would require money and influential friends; he clearly lacked the former, and the latter were abandoning him. His own stubbornness and rash habit of speaking his mind rather too freely were not making his situation any easier, but contentiousness and debt seem to have been family tendencies. Whiling away the endless hours between visitors in the tolbooth, casting his eyes over works meant to show him the errors of his opinions, he probably spent some time recalling his mother's final days in that same establishment. But his finale would be much more public. His case was already being reported in the London media, and Scots authorities were determined that his example would be remembered.[61]

NOTES

1. Louise Yeoman, 'The Devil as Doctor: Witchcraft, Wodrow and the Wider World', *Scottish Archives*, 1 (1995), pp. 93–105, at p. 94.
2. *Memoirs of the Life of the Reverend Mr Thomas Halyburton*, pp. 41–4, 52–3, 67–71.
3. *Memoirs, or Spiritual Exercises of Elisabeth West*, pp. 19–21, 23, 28–9; for Spira and his popularity in Anglophone Protestant culture, see Michael MacDonald, '*The Fearefull Estate of Francis Spira*: Narrative, Identity and Emotion in Early Modern England', *Journal of British Studies*, 31 (1992), pp. 32–61, and M. A. Overell, 'The Exploitation of Francesco Spiera', *Sixteenth Century Journal*, 26 (1995), pp. 619–37. It is possible that the book West read was John Sault's *The Second Spira* (1693), although that work described the travails of one 'F.N.', assailed by deism, rather than those of Spira himself. I am grateful to Professor Erin Kelly for introducing me to Spira as a literary phenomenon.
4. A printed version of the indictment can be found in *State Trials*, xiii, pp. 917–20. The original manuscript appears to be NAS MS JC26/78/1/11.
5. Cynthia Herrup, *A House in Gross Disorder: Sex, Law and the 2nd Earl of Castlehaven* (Oxford: Oxford University Press, 1999), p. 6.
6. NAS MSS PC 1/51, fo. 16r; PC4/2, fo. 29v; JC 6/14, fo. 98r; JC 26/78/1/1–2, 4–8.
7. John Fairley, 'The Old Tolbooth: With Extracts from the Original Records', *Book of the Old Edinburgh Club*, 4 (1911), pp. 75–144, at pp. 78–9, 86–8; Henry Kerr, 'The Old Tolbooth of Edinburgh', *Book of the Old Edinburgh Club*, 14 (1925), pp. 7–24, at pp. 9–10, 12.
8. Charles B. Watson (ed.), *Roll of Edinburgh Burgesses and Guild Brethren, 1406–1700* (Edinburgh: Scottish Record Society, 1929), p. 23; Henry Paton (ed.), *Register of Marriages for the Parish of Edinburgh, 1595–1700* (Edinburgh: Scottish Record Society, 1905), p. 7; New Register House (hereafter NRH) MS OPR 685.1/44, fo. 155v. For Helen Ramsey's father, who died in 1650, see *Fasti*, ii, p. 48.
9. NRH MSS OPR 685.1/6, fo. 613; OPR 685.1/7, fos 22v, 129v.
10. Henry Paton (ed.), *Register of Interments in the Greyfriars Burying Ground, Edinburgh, 1658–1700* (Edinburgh: Scottish Record Society, 1902), p. 7.
11. NRH MS OPR 685.1/8, fo. 23r.
12. NRH MS OPR 685.1/7, fo. 129v, identifies him as 'brother german' to the apothecary James Aikenhead. For Hepburn's connection to the Aikenhead family, see NAS MS CC8/2/93, 5 August 1696.
13. NRH MS OPR 685.1/8, fo. 54r. For the family connection between Stevenson and Ramsey, see NAS MS CC8/2/93, 2 February 1697.
14. WRH MS E70/4/7, fo. 8.

15. David Laing (ed.), *Historical Notices of Scottish Affairs Selected from the Manuscripts of Sir John Lauder of Fountainhall*, 2 vols (Edinburgh: Bannatyne Club, 1848), i, p. 343.
16. *Register of the Privy Council of Scotland*, third series, 16 vols (Edinburgh: HM General Register House, 1908–), vii, pp. 389–90; Laing (ed.), *Historical Notices ... Lauder of Fountainhall*, i, p. 353.
17. NAS MS CC8/8/77, fos 126v–128r.
18. Laing (ed.), *Historical Notices ... Lauder of Fountainhall*, i, p. 451.
19. John A. Fairly (ed.), 'The Old Tolbooth: Extracts from the Original Records', *Book of the Old Edinburgh Club*, 11 (1922), pp. 21–73, at pp. 46, 48, 57; Paton (ed.), *Register of Interments*, p. 7.
20. Bodleian Library MS Locke b.4, fos 99r–101r, printed in *State Trials*, xiii, pp. 930–4, at p. 931; NLS MSS 14410, fos 102–3, 129, 174; 14593, *passim;* NAS MS CC8/2/93, 5 August 1696.
21. ECA Moses Bundle 93, item 3968; Pitcairne and Fraser were residents of the Tron parish in 1694. See WRH MS E70/4/7, fos 3, 8.
22. EUL MS Da.1.33, fos 119–20.
23. Shepherd, 'University Life in the Seventeenth Century', pp. 2–4; Cant, 'Origins of Enlightenment in Scotland', pp. 44–5.
24. Christine Shepherd, 'Philosophy in the Arts Curriculum of the Scottish Universities in the 17th Century' (Ph.D. thesis, University of Edinburgh, 1975), fos 74, 103–5.
25. NAS MS PA10/4, 28 August 1690; Hannay, 'Visitation of the College of Edinburgh', pp. 83–4.
26. NAS MS PA10/4, Cunningham's defence (undated, unpaginated); Hannay, 'Visitation of the College of Edinburgh', pp. 96–9.
27. *Memoirs of the Life of the Reverend Mr Thomas Halyburton*, p. 34.
28. Shepherd, 'Philosophy in the Arts Curriculum', fos 68–9, 233.
29. NAS MSS PA10/2, 27 September 1690; PA10/4, 20 August 1690.
30. *Memoirs of the Life of the Reverend Mr Thomas Halyburton*, p. 34; Hannay, 'Visitation of the College of Edinburgh', p. 99.
31. *Catalogue of the Graduates of the Faculties of Arts, Divinity, and Law, of the University of Edinburgh*, pp. 153–4.
32. Jonquil Bevan, 'Seventeenth Century Students and their Books', in Gordon Donaldson (ed.), *Four Centuries: Edinburgh University Life, 1583–1983* (Edinburgh: Edinburgh University Press, 1983), pp. 16–27, at pp. 17–18; EUL MS Da.1.34, fo. 2r.
33. NAS MS JC26/78/1/5.
34. Shepherd, 'Philosophy in the Arts Curriculum', fos 153, 161; EUL MSS Da.1.18, fo. 44; Da.1.32, fo. 75; Da.1.33, fo. 87. Hobbes's *Leviathan*, which the library owned, specifically rejected the possibility that Moses wrote the first five books of the Hebrew Scriptures.
35. EUL MS Da.1.32, fo. 68.
36. EUL MS Da.1.32, fos 75, 82.

37. EUL MS Da.1.32, fos 72, 98.
38. EUL MS Da.1.32, fo. 83; Halyburton, *Natural Religion Insufficient*, title page.
39. EUL MSS Da.1.32, fo. 130; Da.1.33, fo. 115; Richard Simon, *Critical Enquiries into the Various Editions of the Bible* (London, 1684), 'To the Reader'. For Hobbes, Spinoza and Simon and the controversy they engendered, see Malcolm, *Aspects of Hobbes*, pp. 387–92.
40. EUL MS Da.1.34, fo. 6r; Malcolm, *Aspects of Hobbes*, p. 388.
41. *Memoirs of the Public Life of Mr James Hogg*, pp. 12–13.
42. EUL MSS Da.1.33, fo. 95; Da.1.34, fo. 1r; Shepherd, 'Philosophy in the Arts Curriculum', fos ii, 61; Christine Shepherd, 'Newtonianism in Scottish Universities in the Seventeenth Century', in R. H. Campbell and Andrew S. Skinner (eds), *The Origins and Nature of the Scottish Enlightenment* (Edinburgh: John Donald, 1982), pp. 65–85, at 66–7.
43. EUL MSS Da.1.33, fo. 111; Da.1.34, fo. 1r; Hunter, 'Aikenhead the Atheist', p. 328.
44. EUL MSS Da.1.32, fo. 134; Da.1.34, fos 1r, 7r, 9r.
45. EUL MS Da.1.34, fo. 6r.
46. *Catalogue of the Graduates of the Faculties of Arts, Divinity, and Law, of the University of Edinburgh*, pp. 153–4.
47. EUL MS Da.1.33, p. 120; *Catalogue of the Graduates of the Faculties of Arts, Divinity, and Law, of the University of Edinburgh*, pp. 153–4.
48. NRH MS OPR 685.1/7, fo. 246r.
49. Craig, *A Lye Is No Scandal*, pp. 3, 10.
50. Craig, *Satyr against Atheistical Deism*, title page.
51. Ibid. pp. 5–6.
52. Ibid. pp. 7–8.
53. Ibid. p. 10.
54. Ibid. pp. 12–14.
55. Ibid. p. 3.
56. Lorimer, *Two Discourses*, pp. v–vi; for Hepburn, see *Post Boy*, 201 (18 August 1696); *Protestant Mercury*, 74 (24 August 1696).
57. Craig, *A Lye Is No Scandal*, pp. 11–12.
58. It may be worth noting that Boston reported that he ate so little he suffered fainting spells. Thomas Boston, *Memoirs of the Life, Time and Writings of the Reverend and Learned Thomas Boston* (Edinburgh: Murray & Cochrane, 1776), p. 18.
59. Dickson is identified as Aikenhead's landlord on a list of witnesses summoned to his trial. See NAS MS JC26/78/1/8.
60. NAS MS CC8/2/93, 7 November 1696.
61. *Protestant Mercury*, 109 (13 November 1696).

5

Trial and Execution

Thomas Aikenhead's trial and eventual execution would be major public events, allowing Scottish authorities the opportunity to confront the 'atheism' they feared was festering in the capital, to demonstrate their commitment to 'godliness' and to clarify the boundaries of acceptable speech and debate. For many of them, this was the time to uphold the covenants with the full force of the law, to show that the Revolution of 1637–43, reconfirmed in 1689, still defined Scotland's body politic. Aikenhead would face ridicule, execration and eventually – at least from some observers – pity. The hostile reaction he faced is indicative of the discursive monopoly enjoyed by traditional Christianity (no big surprise there) but also of the support he was receiving from some quarters, which raised the possibility of an epidemic of 'atheism' unless decisive action was taken to contain this contagion. His own response to the ordeal alternated between bravado, denial and contrition; as a legal strategy it would prove disastrous. That bravado and his public notoriety made this a battle in which the authorities felt they had to win a crushing victory, and they would bend the law in order to do so. There would be no half measures or compromises, as there had been with John Fraser, and the grim determination of those determined to see Aikenhead hang would divide the Privy Council nearly down the middle.

5.1 THE OFFICIALS AND THE PROSECUTION

The trial convened in Edinburgh's tolbooth on 23 December 1696, after several delays for reasons that are not readily apparent, but that may have involved locating the necessary witnesses, a process that occupied officials for much of the first half of December.[1] The presiding officials at the trial were the judges Colin Campbell of Aberuchil, David Hume of Crossrig, John Lauder of Fountainhall and Archibald Hope of Rankeillor, assisted by the Justice Clerk Adam Cockburn of Ormiston.[2] Campbell of

Aberuchil's mother was a daughter of Sir Patrick Hepburn of Blackcastle, meaning he was the grandson of the man to whom Thomas Aikenhead's father James had owed so much money when he died, and who had been a witness to Thomas Aikenhead's baptism. Campbell of Aberuchil was also the co-executor, along with Sir Patrick Aikenhead, of a philosophy scholarship (a 'bursary') that had been established at the town college out of a bond for £1,000, which had been granted by Hepburn of Blackcastle. Given the connections of family and debt, it seems very plausible that Thomas Aikenhead may have been a beneficiary of the bursary. In any case, Campbell of Aberuchil knew him and his family well, and would serve as a legal guardian (again, along with Sir Patrick Aikenhead) for Thomas Aikenhead's sister Anna.[3] Hume of Crossrig had studied law in the Netherlands, and was one of the first justice lords appointed by William after he took the Scottish throne. Lauder of Fountainhall was an eminent jurist and collector of historical materials and one of the leading members of the city's Tolbooth parish, holding a prime pew in the north-west quarter of St Giles'. He and Hope of Rankeillor had attended the Privy Council on 10 November, so they had seen Aikenhead that day and had participated in the vote to put him on trial for his life, as had Cockburn of Ormiston. The last of these three had a particularly strong reputation for Presbyterian orthodoxy and distrust of those with any connections to the pre-1690 regime. One contemporary (John Macky) described him as 'a bigot to a fault, and hardly in common charity with any man out of the verge of Presbytery, but otherwise a very fine gentleman in his person and manners'. As Justice Clerk, he would have had the responsibility of copying the testimony of witnesses into the court record. It seems almost certain that he favoured Aikenhead's trial and execution, while Lauder of Fountainhall was more inclined toward mercy, as we will see.[4]

It appears that James Stewart of Goodtrees, the lord advocate, was also determined to pursue the case as aggressively as possible. He had a reputation for great legal acuity, adroit political manœuvring, and firm Presbyterianism. He was known to devote his Sundays fully to church attendance and prayer, with short breaks for meals. While such piety was not rare in seventeenth-century Scotland, it would not have engendered much sympathy for the likes of Thomas Aikenhead, and, given the penchant for trimming that 'Wily Jamie' had displayed in the past, it is safe to say that he also saw political advantages in the prosecution of the case.[5] He had turned on his patron, the Scottish Secretary James Johnston, at the end of 1695, and would not do anything to endanger his place high in the Scots administration. Stewart of Goodtrees was assisted in the prosecution by Sir Patrick Hume, king's solicitor, and a kinsman of the Chancellor Sir Patrick Hume of Polwarth.[6]

Thus the prosecution was in able and experienced hands. It does not appear that the same was true of the defence. In fact, nowhere in any of the official documents from the case is it explicitly noted that Aikenhead even had legal representation. This is highly unusual for a Justiciary Court trial in this period. In almost all other cases, even those with relatively poor defendants, one or more advocates for the 'pannel' would appear on his or her behalf. Interestingly, and perhaps not coincidentally, two men convicted of robbery two days before Aikenhead's trial and before the same set of judges also had no counsel listed.[7] The only hint that Aikenhead might have had an advocate came from one London newspaper, which referred to 'his Council' in a report on the case.[8] All that can be said for certain is that, if he had a lawyer, the man in question was ineffective and remains anonymous as far as the historical record is concerned.

The indictment listed the charges against Aikenhead as described in the previous chapter, holding that 'by the lawes of this and all other well-governed Christian realms, the cryme of blasphemy against God, or any of the persons [sic] of the blessed Trinity, or against the holy Scriptures, or our holy religione, is a cryme of the highest nature, and ought to be severely punished'. It then went on (ominously, for Aikenhead's case) first to cite the 1661 statute against blasphemy, particularly where it mandated death for any person 'not being distracted in his witts [who] shall raill upon or curse God, or any of the persons of the blessed Trinity'. Only after that did it invoke the 1695 statute, with its milder scale of punishments but detailed enumeration of possible blasphemies: 'whosoever shall in their wryteing or discourse denye, impugne or quarrell, or argue, or reason against the being of God, or any of the persons of the blessed Trinity, or the authority of the holy Scriptures, of the Old and New Testaments, or the providence of God in the government of the world.' This suggests that Stewart of Goodtrees and Hume were hanging the bulk of their prosecution on the earlier, more draconian law. Since the later statute made no specific mention of 'railling' against or 'cursing' God or any aspect of the Trinity (those who voted for it in parliament could have been forgiven for assuming that 'railling' would be covered under 'denye, impugne or quarrell, or argue, or reason against'), they must have made the interpretation that the 1695 statute did not supersede the 1661 law as far as 'railling' and 'cursing' were concerned. They were determined to see the prisoner hang. Stewart of Goodtrees was certainly not ignorant of the details of the 1695 statute, since, as lord advocate, he would have played a role in its drafting.

The indictment went on to claim that Aikenhead had vented 'wicked blasphemies against God and our Saviour Jesus Christ, and against the holy Scriptures and all revealed religione' several times over the course of the previous year and more ('for more than a twelvemoneth by past'). These had included the claim 'that divinity or the doctrine of theologie was a rapsidie of faigned and ill-invented nonsense, patched up partly of the morall doctrine of philosophers, and pairtly of poeticall fictions and extravagant chimeras'. He also allegedly

> scoffed at, and endeavoured to ridicule the holy scriptures, calling the Old Testament Ezra's fables, by a profane allusione to Esop's fables, and saying that Ezra was the inventer thereof, and that being a cunning man he drew a number of Babylonian slaves to follow him, for whom he made up a feigned genealogie as if they had been descended of kings and princes in the land of Canaan.

In addition, he had called the New Testament 'the History of the Impostor Christ ... affirming him to have learned magick in Egypt, and that coming from Egypt into Judea, he picked up a few ignorant blockish fisher fellows who he knew ... had strong imaginations and that by the help of exalted imaginatione he play'd his pranks' (as Aikenhead allegedly reckoned the miracles attributed to Christ in the Gospels). He lodged similar charges against Moses, according to the indictment, claiming: 'Moses, if ever ... ther was such a man ... also learned magick in Egypt, but that he was a better politician than Jesus.' Further, Aikenhead rejected the concept of the Trinity 'and [said] it is not worth any man's refutation, and also ... scoffe[d] at the mistery of the incarnation of Jesus Christ, affirming blashphemously [sic] that Theantropos is as great a contradictione as Hircus Cervus'.

On a more philosophical level, the indictment alleged that Aikenhead had argued against the likelihood of eternal reward or punishment or the existence of spirits, had claimed 'that God, the world, and nature, are but one thing and that the world was from eternity; and ... that man's imaginatione duely exalted by airt and industry can do any thing, even in the infinite power of God'. Here we see both deism (in a pantheistic form) and an early example of the faith in progress that would become characteristic of the Enlightenment. The prosecution also accused him of having said that he preferred Muhammad to Jesus, that he 'hoped to see Christianity greatly weakened' and had confidently averred that 'in a short tyme it will be utterly extirpat'. The indictment was clear in its assertion that Aikenhead had made these various statements without the least provocation; he had not been lured into making them, but had 'meerly

[been] prompted by [his] irreligious and devilish malice against God and our blessed Saviour and the most concerted truths of the holy Christian religion'. This indictment pulled no punches.

5.2 THE DEFENCE

The bulk of Aikenhead's defence is contained in two undated petitions, both of them submitted before the trial and both seeking to have the indictment against him dropped. The copies of these in the process papers of the High Court of Justiciary are both in an idiosyncratic, left-leaning handwriting (except for the signatures on both and a separate two-line plea at the end of the first), and may be the originals. The fact that Mungo Craig's name is filled in a blank space, and in a different hand, in the first of them suggests that Aikenhead was getting some help in preparing these petitions at least, since he would presumably have known Craig's name already, and if he drew up the document himself he would presumably have written it in with the rest.[9] It would be interesting to know whether either or both of these petitions was drawn up after (or perhaps even during?) his visit from William Lorimer and Gilbert Rule's son, but Lorimer, while at least showing retrospective sympathy for Aikenhead, made no mention of offering him any legal advice, and at any rate as an Englishman would have been ill-prepared to write a Scots legal petition.

The first of the two petitions was more aggressive, mixing avowals of innocence with counter-accusations. In it Aikenhead protested that he could not even list the charges against him, because 'I ... from my very heart abhorre and detest them, but [also] I do tremble and abhorre either to repeat the samen myself, or to hear the samen repeated and objected against any person born of Christian parents'. Then, switching to the third person to refer to himself, in four numbered points, he affirmed (1) his 'greatest happyness that he was born and educat in a place where the gospell was professed and so powerfully and plentifully preached, upon a true impressment of which benefite he doth truely believe the salvation of his immortall soul doth intirely depend'; (2) his belief in the immortality of the soul and the resurrection of the body and its reunion with the soul on the Day of Judgement; (3) his belief in the Trinity and his certainty that such belief was necessary for salvation; (4) his belief that the Scriptures of the Old and New Testaments were 'cannonical and written and dictated by holy men inspired by the Holy Ghost, and to be of divine authority and set down as a rule for our obedience and faith, and by believing whereof a happy immortality may be obtained, and no otherways' and therefore mandated the necessity of the sacraments of baptism and communion 'and that the said sacraments are to this moment celebrated with the greatest purity in our reformed Protestant churches in Britain and Ireland'.

From these general protestations of Protestant orthodoxy, Aikenhead's petition moved on to address the particular circumstances of the accusations against him. He implied that the heterodox statements he was accused of making may indeed have come out of his mouth, but they were 'uttered or expressed by me not as my own privat sentiments and opinions, but were repeated by me as sentiments and opinions of some atheisticall writers whose names I can particularly condescend upon'. This was rather similar to John Fraser's claim before the Privy Council. But then, in the most dramatic aspect of his defence, Aikenhead fingered Mungo Craig as the person who had given him books by those writers. He accused Craig of framing him, saying that Craig 'was the chief and principall instrument who constantly made it his work to interrogat me anent my reading of the said atheisticall principles and arguments therin contained, and of which I am now very sensible and heartily sory for'. Indeed, he opined that such 'atheisticall' books as Craig showed him 'ought neither to be printed nor exposed to public view'.'A later *apologia* penned by Craig implied that Aikenhead told the court that Craig himself was only a recent convert from religious scepticism, although this claim was not made in the petition.[10] Elsewhere in the petition, Aikenhead wrote that he had been 'exceedingly imposed upon to give an account of the abominable and atheistical principles' in the books. Then, curiously, he further excused his actions on the grounds that at the time of his accusation he had been a minor 'and as yet am so and under age'. Perhaps this was a sign of desperation in his defence; in any case it was demonstrably untrue, unless one were to take twenty-one as the age of majority (which was occasionally done in cases of legal guardianship). His baptism in March 1676 would have made him at least twenty when he was formally accused, and possibly nineteen when he started publicly uttering blasphemies, if indeed the claim in the indictment that he had been blaspheming for more than a year was correct. It is possible that he did not know his own age, given the fact that both his parents were dead and that the bureaucracies of early modern societies did not require birth dates as an identification tool in the myriad ways their modern successors have. At any rate, his claim to be a minor probably confused the correspondents of two of the London papers, each of which then identified him as eighteen at the time of his execution.[11] At least one privy councillor was also mistaken about his age, as we shall see.

In addition to the claim that he had been entrapped and was not yet legally an adult, Aikenhead assured the judges that he was

> content to testify my sorrow and remorse to the world for my former escap[ade]s as to any thing contained in the indictment, hoping by the blessing and assistance of our blessed Saviour, not only to be delivered from all such snares and temptations in time coming, but likewise to lead a life suteable to the gospell and the expectation of eternal life through the blood and merits of our dear and only Saviour.

Here was a (perhaps forced) end to his journey through spiritual doubt and into (half-hearted) sanctification – a procrustean Calvinist conversion narrative, with Mungo Craig standing in for the Devil. More likely, he was hoping to offer the prospect of public confession and recantation to save himself and comfort the authorities that they had done their duty to defend the honour of God, protecting His Most Covenanted Kingdom from further smitings. The problem was that John Fraser had already done that, and the problem had not gone away.

The second pre-trial petition is shorter, but shows evidence that whoever prepared it (it is in the same hand as the first) had, since the first petition, developed a more focused strategy, perhaps in light of Stewart of Goodtrees's and Hume's argument that the 1661 statute (and thus capital punishment) should apply. First, it referred to the statements of belief contained in the earlier petition and averred that, if Aikenhead had uttered any blasphemies, it had been with 'great reluctancy' and only because others had hounded him as to the contents of what he had been reading, and that he was steadfast in his views of the 'villainy and wickednes' of these blasphemies. More significantly, it brought up again the issue of his age, claiming he 'is as yet Minor and that minority in matters of judgement & opinion or words & expressions by which no prejudice ever has or can redound to any person' (*sic*). Further, and most importantly, the petition argued that the 1661 blasphemy law had been superseded by the 1695 law, and that, under the terms of the latter, blasphemy could be treated as a capital crime only if the accused had already been twice convicted for it, and was thus 'obstinat & obdurate'. It concluded with the plea

> Yet in place of all the forsaid defences & many others competent to me ag[ains]t the Indytment I do again humbly throw my self at yo[u]r L[ordship]s feet humbly craving pardon for whatever might have escaped me as to anything contained in my Indytment in respect of my minority & want of discretione for the tyme, & for which escapes [*sic*] I am now most heartily sorry.

Perhaps a plea for mercy was his best defence, given his actual age and the fact that Stewart of Goodtrees, probably the sharpest lawyer in the room, was determined to bring about the capital punishment envisaged by the 1661 law.

5.3 THE WITNESSES

Stewart of Goodtrees compiled a list of seventeen witnesses to offer evidence against Aikenhead, although only fifteen of them were present at the trial and only five actually testified.[12] A close look at the witness lists can tell us something about the strategy the prosecution had in mind, and the circle of people who might have been familiar with Aikenhead and therefore had some knowledge of his alleged beliefs. As had been the case with Fraser, Stewart of Goodtrees and Hume must have thought the offender's landlord and landlady could offer evidence. Thus the tailor George Dickson and his wife Jonet Elder were summoned, although the lack of testimony from either suggests that Aikenhead had been discreet within their earshot, or at least that they could not recall anything specific enough to be construed as blasphemy under the relevant statutes. Another witness who appeared was Robert Henderson, keeper of the college library. He could probably have testified as to Aikenhead's reading tastes, and perhaps also to statements Aikenhead might have made about some of his more heterodox reading choices. In any case, he was not called upon to testify. Among the other witnesses who did not testify was William Eckford, a town officer in Edinburgh, who was summoned along with his wife Alison Oswald, suggesting that his knowledge of Aikenhead may have come from some social context outside his official duties. Also summoned were an officer to the signet, a smith (who was also a burgess of Edinburgh), and several writers and students. In a few cases, the dwelling places of witnesses were given: the schoolmaster Hugh Crawford (recently a student) and Mungo Craig lived with Hutchison the stationer in College Wynd, and the student John Potter lived with a Captain Woods at the Cowgate port, which was nearby. Another student, Adam Mitchell, had been a resident of the Tolbooth parish in 1694, although it is not clear where he was living in 1696.[13] It appears that Aikenhead's statements were most likely to have been made and heard in the south-eastern quadrant of the old town, where the college was located and in which many of its students lodged. Crawford and Craig also would have been acquainted with Aikenhead for several years (despite statements Craig made later); the three of them matriculated together, in the bajan under the tutelage of Alexander Cunningham, in February 1693.[14] Potter was an Edinburgh native, and a recipient of a bursary from the burgh council to further his studies, owing in part to his father having died in the upheavals of 1688–90.[15]

The five witnesses who ended up testifying against Aikenhead were Mitchell, John Neilson, Patrick Middleton, Potter and Craig. Neilson was identified as a 'writer' – probably a clerk in one of Edinburgh's courts – and all the others as students. Given his reported age ('near to twenty years'), Neilson had probably recently been a student as well. Potter was said to be eighteen, Mitchell and Middleton twenty, and Craig twenty-one. These were all Aikenhead's contemporaries, and it seems likely that they were among his social companions. Middleton and Craig had even visited Aikenhead in the tolbooth while he was awaiting trial. As will be evident from their testimony, these five provided the information on which the indictment was based.

In the court record, Mitchell's testimony was given first, and he assured the court that he had been 'several tymes in company' with Aikenhead during the previous year. On those occasions, he said, he had heard Aikenhead claim that 'divinity or the doctrine of theology was ane rapsodie of feigned and ill invented nonsense'. Additionally, Aikenhead had questioned the veracity of the Hebrew Scriptures, 'calling them Ezra's Romances', and had claimed that Jesus 'wrought no miracles but what any other man might have wrought by ane exalted fancie'. Mitchell said Aikenhead had explicitly denied the divinity of Christ, rejecting the whole idea of 'Theantropos or God-man as a contradiction, and that it was as absurd as Hircus Servus, that is a goat and ane hart in one animall'. He insisted that Aikenhead had claimed 'the Apostles were a company of silly witless fisher-men and ... he wondered the world was so long deluded with their contradictions and nonsense'. Jesus and Moses were both magicians, Aikenhead allegedly said, but Moses was 'the better artist and politian of the two'. Mitchell added that Aikenhead had also attacked the notion of the Trinity 'and that oftner than any other thing', suggesting that to Mitchell he seemed a Socinian before he seemed to be anything else. Mitchell's testimony also contained the claim that Aikenhead had argued 'that man's imaginatione, raised by art and industry to a high pitch, could doe as much as our blessed Saviour did'.

Neilson's testimony appears next in the record, and offers more detail, while also repeating several of the claims in Mitchell's evidence. For example, Neilson expanded upon what Aikenhead had allegedly said concerning Ezra, charging that he had attributed the entire authorship of the Old Testament to the scribe, and that Neilson had

> several times heard [Aikenhead] say that Ezra being a cunning man, he drew a number of Babylonian slaves to follow him, for whom he made up

a feigned genealogie, as if they had bein descendit of kings and princes in the land of Canaan, and imposed upon Cyrus who was a Persian and stranger, persuadeing him by the pretendit devyce of a prophecie concerning himself, and gott a great quantity of gold from Cyrus, and gold vessels that was never in the temple, upon pretense that they had bein taken out of the temple of Jerusalem.

In fact, Neilson said he had heard Aikenhead argue 'that if ther was any punishment after this life, surely Ezra and his followers, whom he called Ezraits, were damned'. It appears that Aikenhead, perhaps influenced by Hobbes or Spinoza, had something of an obsession with Ezra and his putative forgeries; Neilson offered the colourful anecdote of Aikenhead, one chilly night the previous August, strolling down the High Street and wishing aloud 'to be besyde the place Ezra called hell to warme himself there' – perhaps as much a testimony to Edinburgh's late summer weather as to Aikenhead's blasphemous manner of speaking. Middleton, who was also apparently present on the occasion, located that particular declaration in front of the Tron Kirk on the High Street – Aikenhead's parish kirk. Neilson also alleged that Aikenhead had cursed Ezra 'and all the inventors of the Scriptures' (*sic*), partly because of the fact that 'the Scriptures were full of contradictions'.

According to Neilson, Aikenhead claimed Jesus had chosen his twelve disciples for their gullible natures, knowing 'by his skill in phisognomy' that there are 'none having stronger imaginations than ignorant people'. Neilson followed Mitchell in saying that Aikenhead had denied the divinity of Jesus (Neilson said he had heard this 'several tymes' from Aikenhead) but added the detail that Aikenhead had likened the idea of the Trinity to a square triangle. Further, he 'heard [Aikenhead] say that within some hundreds of years the whole world would be converted to his opinion, and the Christian religion would be wholly ruined'.

Middleton's testimony followed, and offered a slightly different version of Aikenhead's denunciations of Ezra. Rather than being Babylonian slaves. Ezra and his followers were Jews, but 'vagabounds, such as Egyptians [which in early modern Scotland generally meant gypsies], Goths or Vandals' who deceived Cyrus, the Persian king, into giving them gold and sending them back to Jerusalem. Other aspects of Middleton's testimony repeated what the first two witnesses had testified, but added further detail, or in some cases additional allegations, such as the avowal that Aikenhead had suggested that Muhammad (rather than Moses) 'was both the better airtist and polititian than Jesus'. Whereas the first two witnesses had detailed Aikenhead's attacks on the veracity of the Hebrew Scriptures, Middleton added that he had heard Aikenhead 'scoff at the Scriptures of the New Testament, and say the history of them was a fable, and the [book of] Revelatione was ane alchimy book for finding out the philosophers stone'. This was not the only eclectic interpretation Middleton attributed to Aikenhead; he said the prisoner also averred 'he could make himself immortall, and that the ascention of our Saviour was but a progresse to the world in moon'. It was also in Middleton's testimony that those attending the trial would have first heard of Aikenhead's apparent pantheism, in his claim that 'God, the world, and nature are but one thing, and that the world was from eternity', and thus not created as described in the Genesis account. Additionally, Middleton offered a more detailed account of Aikenhead's attacks on Christian theology, saying he claimed 'the authors and propagators of the doctrine of Redemptione by Jesus was the damnedst crew in the world, and that they would have the most perplexed thoughts of any for ever'. Aikenhead said 'he hoped to see Christianity greatly weakened', according to Middleton, and 'he was confident that in the year 1800 it would be utterly extirpat'.

It appears that Middleton was followed in the witness box by Potter, but the latter must not have said anything that had not already been lodged against the defendant; the trial record simply records his appearance and his being sworn in and notes that he said 'knew nothing' ('nihil novit'), presumably meaning nothing that could add to the case. Perhaps he was reluctant to testify against someone whom he may have regarded as a friend, or perhaps he simply repeated evidence that had already been offered. What is certainly true is that this apparent reticence was not shared by the final witness whose testimony is recorded: Mungo Craig.

As noted earlier, Craig had already testified against Aikenhead in the court of public opinion, with his pamphlet published while the latter was awaiting trial. He was also unequivocal in his official testimony, which takes up more space in the record than that of any of the other witnesses except Neilson, whose testimony was only slightly longer. While, from a theological perspective, Craig did not really attribute any heterodox notions to Aikenhead that the other witnesses had not already mentioned, his testimony was very specific about the tone of Aikenhead's claims, and what the prisoner might go on to do if he were not convicted and executed. In following a legal strategy of trying to convince the judges and assize jury that the 1661 statute ought to be applied rather than the more lenient 1695 law, Stewart of Goodtrees and Hume had saved their most damning witness for last. Earlier testimony had already described Aikenhead's attacks on the veracity of the Scriptures, but Craig specified that he had heard Aikenhead 'revile the books of the New Testament, and call them the books of the imposter Jesus Christ; and ... he expressed it in a scorning and jeiring manner'. With this assertion of 'scorning and jeiring', the prosecution was presenting evidence to suggest Aikenhead was guilty of 'railling' against one facet of the Trinity – namely, Christ – and thus had committed an offence for which the 1695 statute did not lessen the capital punishment envisioned by the 1661 law. In a similar vein, Craig alleged 'he had heard [Aikenhead] curse Moses, Ezra, and particularly our Saviour Jesus, and if ther was any punishment after this life the[y] deserved the worst, and all the inventors of the doctrine of redemption'.

Here were blasphemies that cursed God himself, but also ridiculed those who sincerely believed the tenets of Christianity. The room was full of such believers, and they were charged with assessing Aikenhead's guilt. Craig presented Aikenhead as one who had no respect for them, who 'made it his frequent discourse that the holy Scriptures were stuffed with such contradictions that the stupidity of the world was admirable in having believed them so long'. He went so far as to 'curse those that baptised him and say that baptisme was a magicall ceremony that tyed children's imagination to that religion wherto they were baptised'. As presented by Craig, Aikenhead was a defendant with whom the audience present could not have felt any sympathy; it would have felt insulted. If the assize jurors still had any doubt about their responsibility, Craig assured them that not only had Aikenhead said he hoped 'to see Christianity greatly weakened, and shortly to be extirpated', but also pledged that 'if he were banished, he would make all Christianitie tremble, and would wryte against Christianity …' The clear implication was that this outcome could be prevented only by the hangman's noose.

5.4 THE JURY AND THE VERDICT

Who were the assize jurors who now held Aikenhead's life in their hands? A total of forty-five men had been summoned for service on the jury, although six of them did not appear on 23 December for the trial; five of those were fined for their absence and the other (John Pringle, late deacon convener of Edinburgh's crafts) was excused because of illness. One of those fined, William Menzies, a merchant and former baillie, appealed his fine on the grounds that he had appeared as summoned, but had been called out of court because he had to attend to business in the Dean of Guild Court, and then could not get in the outer door when he returned to Aikenhead's trial, suggesting that the room was packed. Another absentee was the merchant and former baillie James Graham, who was wealthy enough to be assessed in the highest level of wealth in the 1694 poll tax, but was one of Aikenhead's neighbours in the Tron parish. It is worth noting, given the role that books and reading played in the Aikenhead case, that three of the forty-five men summoned were involved in the book trade – the bookseller James Wardlaw and the stationers John Grierson and George Mosman – and all three appeared for the trial.[16]

Of the thirty-nine assizers present on the day of the trial, fifteen were then chosen for the jury itself. The final fifteen chosen seem representative of the original forty-five in terms of status and occupation, and this is reflected in the fact that only one of the three from the book trade – Mosman – was on the final list of fifteen. But, unfortunately for Aikenhead, Mosman was a leading publisher of Presbyterian works, the official printer for the Reformed Kirk of Scotland, and a kirk session elder in the rather evangelical Tolbooth parish, and was thus unlikely to feel much sympathy for an allegedly heterodox blasphemer.[17] Joining Mosman on the final fifteen were several men who had been legal officers of the burgh – five former baillies, two former deans of the craft guilds, one former convener of the craft guilds and one former treasurer. Partial poll tax returns from 1694 (covering only two of the burgh's parishes) indicate that four of those former officers were wealthy merchants (said to be worth more than 10,000 merks) from the Tolbooth parish, and it seems likely that most of the others were similarly well off. Two other jurors were from the Tolbooth parish – Mosman and the wright Patrick Thomson, who had been burgh treasurer – but those two were assessed in the next tier of wealth, between 5,000 and 10,000 merks.[18] The final jury also included a former kirk treasurer, a wigmaker, two lairds and one man simply identified as a merchant. On the whole, it was a prosperous and prominent group. As its chancellor, or head, the assize chose the merchant and former bailie (and future Tolbooth elder) George Clerk, and the former bailie Adam Brown served as its clerk.

The jury would have listened to the indictment, the testimony of the five witnesses and anything Aikenhead might have said in his defence. Nothing of the last is recorded in the trial record, but one London newspaper reported that he attacked the witnesses for being 'Socinians' and as guilty as he was, 'which did not avail'. Then the assize was 'inclosed' – sent off to deliberate, and told by the judges to return with a verdict by noon the next day.[19] Aikenhead was taken back to his cell in the tolbooth. We cannot know how long the assize deliberated over the prisoner's fate, but the fact that its unanimous verdict was dated on 23 December suggests that the jurymen did not stay up too late worrying about the decision. The next day at noon Clerk and Brown appeared before the judges with the verdict. They and their colleagues felt it was

> proven that the pannall, Thomas Aikenhead has railled against the first persone, and also cursed and railled our blessed Lord the second persone of

the holy Trinity, and farder finds the other crymes lybelled proven, viz. The denying of the incarnatione of our Saviour, the holy Trinity, and scoffing at the holy Scriptures.

Thus Aikenhead was found guilty of the most serious charges in the indictment, based primarily on the testimony of Mungo Craig. Officially, the punishment would now be determined by the judges, with the assistance of the justice clerk, based on the applicable statutes. But the specific finding in the verdict, that he had 'cursed and railled' against Jesus, meant that Stewart of Goodtrees had won a complete victory in this case, even if the evidence for this 'cursing and railling' was only in the testimony of a single witness. As a group, the judges did not take long to make up their minds. After reading the verdict, they announced that they

> decerne and adjudge the said Thomas Aikenhead, to be taken to the Galowlee betwixt Leith and Edinburgh, upon Friday the eight[h] day of January next to come, betwixt two and four a clock in the afternoon, and there to be hanged on a gibbet till dead, and his body to be interred at the foot of the said gallows, and ordaines all his moveable goods and gear to be escheat and inbrought to his majesty's use.

According to one report, Aikenhead immediately asked for 'a longer Respite, which occasioned the Court to ask, whether it was in hopes to save his life, or the better to prepare himself for Death? He answered for the latter; but it was refused him.'[20]

The celebration of Christmas, or Yule, was discouraged in Presbyterian-dominated Scotland anyway, and the poor harvest, coupled with invasion fears, intensified the gloom that seemed to overhang the kingdom as 1696 drew to a close. But it is hard to imagine a bleaker holiday season than the one that lay before Thomas Aikenhead as he was led back to the tolbooth on the afternoon of that 24 December.

5.5 SEEKING MERCY

Aikenhead was not yet resigned to this fate, and it appears that at least one of the judges was wavering as well. Aikenhead petitioned the Privy Council twice after his conviction, first on 31 December and then again on 7 January, the eve of his execution. Interestingly, the council rejected petitions from John Fraser, seeking relaxation of his confinement, at each of those meetings as well. The Privy Council's minute book laconically reports that Aikenhead was 'craveing a repryve' in each instance, and that both of his petitions were rejected, but the (undated) text of only one has survived. The two meetings were well attended, with eighteen and nineteen councillors, respectively, compared to the thirteen present in November when the council ordered his trial. While the lord advocate and the justice clerk (both of whom would have opposed any mercy) attended both meetings, the only one of the four justice lords from the trial who attended either was Hope of Rankeillor, and he was present only on 31 December.[21] But Lauder of Fountainhall, also one of the four justice lords, visited the prisoner in the tolbooth during this period, along with Sir William Anstruther, another privy councillor. Anstruther was present all three times the council considered Aikenhead's fate, and his reaction to the young blasphemer – whom he believed to be only eighteen – is revealing. Although Anstruther described Aikenhead as 'an anomaly, and monster of nature' because of his crimes, he also found him 'not vicious, and extreamly studious'. He reported that when he and Lauder of Fountainhall had visited Aikenhead, they 'found a work on his spirit, and [he] wept that ever he should [have] maintained such tenets, and desired a short repriev, for his eternall state depended upon it'.[22]

Anstruther did not precisely date this visit to Aikenhead, but it may be connected to the prisoner's attendance in the Tolbooth Kirk (the part of St Giles' set aside for the Tolbooth Parish) on Sunday, 3 January. Lauder of Fountainhall attended that parish, and Aikenhead would have heard the fiery evangelical James Webster preach there. The correspondent for London's *Protestant Mercury* confidently asserted that at this service Aikenhead 'seem'd to be convinced of his fatal Error, and 'tis believed, he will accordingly be respited for some longer time'.[23] The tone of this report, compared with the text of the one post-trial petition from Aikenhead that has survived, suggests that the surviving petition is the later one – that of 7 January. In that petition, Aikenhead said he accepted the justice of the sentence against him, but he again claimed to be a minor, and again argued that others had led him astray. It was his 'misfortune to have got some atheistical books belonging to others in his custody, the reading whereof did prompt him to these extravagances for which he is now most justly sentenced'. But,

> se[e]ing it hath pleased Almighty God, to begin so far in his mercy, to work upon your petitioner's obdured heart, as to give him some sense and conviction of his former wicked errours, and that he doth expect through the mercys of our blessed Saviour's death and merits for the salvation of his immortal soul, and that if time were allowed, he doth expect through the merits of Jesus, by a true remorse and repentance, to be yet reconciled to his offended God and Saviour.

He asked the council to delay his execution so 'that I may have the opportunity of conversing with godly ministers in this place, and by their assistance be more prepared for an eternal rest'.[24] It was conventional for the condemned to acknowledge the justice of the sentence against them, but it is possible that the preaching and counsel of clergy like Webster (and before him, Lorimer or George Meldrum) were bringing about a change of heart. On a more practical level, he may have hoped that a delay in the sentence would eventually bring about a change of heart on the part of the authorities, allowing him to make public repentance for his heterodoxies and live, as Fraser was doing. It was not unusual for the Privy Council to change sentences; indeed on 5 January it changed the death sentence the High Court of Justiciary had imposed on Thomas Weir for robbery and breaking of sheaves to banishment, on the grounds that Weir had been 'led asyde by Ill company'.[25]

Anstruther said he argued on Aikenhead's behalf before the council, and the matter came down to the tie-breaking vote of Hume of Polwarth as Chancellor on the eve of Aikenhead's execution, meaning that nine of the councillors present on 7 January must have favoured granting the petition. A newspaper account confirmed that Aikenhead lost this bid for mercy by one vote, 'and thereupon he was ordered to prepare for Death'. One wonders what the outcome would have been if Lauder of Fountainhall had attended. Anstruther wrote that Polwarth was unwilling to support any reprieve 'unless the ministers would interced[e]'. A General Assembly of the Kirk had convened on 2 January, and conducted business on the morning of 7 January, although there is no specific mention of Aikenhead in its records.[26] Recalling this later, Anstruther opined

> I am not for consulting the church in state affairs [and] I doe think he would have proven and eminent christian had he lived, but the ministers out of a pious tho I think ignorant zeal spok and preached for cutting him off. I find capital punishments inflicted most against crimes that disturb the society and government, and not against the heinusness of the sin against God.[27]

This was another way in which the Aikenhead case would prove exceptional.

As Chancellor, Hume of Polwarth was certainly in a delicate position. He did not yet have an aristocratic title (this would come in late April when he was made Earl of Marchmont). His job was to hold together a government that included several men whose social standing was higher than his. He had seen, a year earlier, how Stewart of Goodtrees and (in Whitehall) William Carstares had turned on his former patron James Johnston, and therefore would have been wary of giving either of them any cause to criticise his own actions. His relations with Cockburn of Ormiston also appear to have been frosty. Nearly two weeks after the final decision on Aikenhead's appeal, Polwarth assured his ally the Earl of Tullibardine, then resident in Whitehall, that, when Tullibardine received a full account of the matter, he would 'see that it was not onlie most just but also most necessary in our circumstances', suggesting political expediency as well as righteousness.[28]

The attitude of the General Assembly is revealed in a petition it submitted to the Privy Council in early December, seeking the declaration of a national day of fasting and humiliation for 21 January. The eventual proclamation issued by the Privy Council mentioned the visible wrath of God in the outbreak of plague, the famine and the danger of a French invasion, suggesting that these were 'all the just deservings and effects of our continewing and abounding sins'. But the original petition from the ministers, given in by George Meldrum and William Crichton (the latter of whom would be moderator of the assembly which met in early January), was accompanied by a letter that was much more specific about the sins in question. They were:

> Atheism [in bold ink] and Blasphemy, the commission of many abominations without shame or blushing, to wit abominable uncleanness, drunkenness, swearing, lying and blood toutching blood by frequent murders, our apostacy [in bold ink] and defection from the Lord.

Three days after Aikenhead's execution, the General Assembly would follow up on these sentiments with another 'Act against Profaneness', which added deism to the usual catalogue of sins needing attention, along with blasphemy and the others.[29]

As one committed to the heritage of the covenants himself, Polwarth would have wanted to maintain the support of the Presbyterian clergy, and also would have been personally offended at what Aikenhead represented. He frequently copied down his own spiritual meditations as well as those of others, and had hidden himself in the family vault under Polwarth Kirk for a month before fleeing into exile after the discovery of the Rye House Plot in 1684, reportedly comforting himself by reciting psalms. One observer described him as 'zealous for the Presbyterian Government in the church and its *Divine Right*, which was the great Motive that encouraged him against the crown' in the 1680s.[30] He was politically insecure and religiously assured – not the sort of magistrate who was likely to favour an appeal from Thomas Aikenhead. As he summed up his reasoning in a letter to both Tullibardine and Sir James Ogilvy, the other Scottish secretary, near the end of January:

The young man had passed his course at the Colledge and was twenty years of age. His crime was capitale by our law and I thinke there is non[e] of our communion who have a due regaird to these articles of our faith which relate to our Lord Jesus Chryst and our redemption who will thinke the procedur too severe against Akinhead especially at this time when we understand blasphemous notions and opinions ar vented such as were never heard of here for ought we know since Cristianity was professed in this nation. If in any case the rule principiis obsta is to be regarded it was in this.[31]

Clearly, Polwarth did not believe Aikenhead was as young as he claimed to be, nor did he view his ostensible conversion as genuine. Like Stewart of Goodtrees, Cockburn of Ormiston and seven other privy councillors, he was determined to see the sentence carried out.

5.6 LAST WORDS

Aikenhead's procession to the scaffold has already been described in this book's introduction. But now, having examined what we know of his background and the nature (and contemporary meaning) of the blasphemies for which he was convicted, we should look closely at two statements he presented to onlookers – and apparently read aloud, at least in part – on the last day of his life. The first was a lengthy and somewhat rambling intellectual biography, and the second a more conventional statement of contrition.[32] The discordance between these two could not have offered much help to those in the audience (or since) looking for signs of either true remorse or bold intellectual defiance. In fact, it only added to the debate over his execution. One eyewitness alluded to his 'great disorder (as is said) of speech', opining that this 'gave but little evidence of his sincere repentance'.[33] In this respect Aikenhead remained an enigma to the end, although the inconsistencies that created this enigma may have been more the result of terror than duplicity.

Aikenhead's intellectual autobiography is the closest we can come to an unmediated statement of what he really believed. His prior petitions were intended either as defences against specific charges or else (in the case of the two made after his conviction) pleas for mercy, with their contents thus structured in response to particular circumstances. But in this long statement offered on the last day of his life he could write his mind more freely, having little to lose. The statement was not published, but circulated widely enough in manuscript that both John Locke and Thomas Halyburton (Aikenhead's former classmate) acquired copies.[34] Early in it, Aikenhead proclaimed the need for free enquiry in the style of a Galileo or many of the *philosophes* who people the intellectual histories of the Enlightenment:

> Verity or truth, generally in all things is a quality most appetable, but especially in matters of great consequence, where fancy cannot have place … Hence it is a principle innate and co-natural to every man to have an insatiable inclination to truth, and to seek for it as for hid treasure, which indeed had its effect upon me, and my reason therin so mastered me, that I was forced of necessity to reject the authoritys and testimonys, both of my parents and others.

This fealty to 'reason' crippled his subsequent efforts to 'build my faith upon uncontrovertable grounds' because 'the more I thought theron, the further I was from finding the verity I desired; so that after much ponderings I found my education altogether wrong'.

Aikenhead reckoned that his quest began when he was only ten years old, which would have been shortly after his mother's death left him an impoverished orphan. He said he found it 'impossible for me or any that I conversed with, to produce any grounds really sufficient to confirm' the teachings of Christianity, 'but with the greatest facility sufficient ground could be produced for the contrair'. This is what led him to make the statements for which he was convicted. He granted that many sceptics used their suspension of belief as an excuse for libertinism – for 'numerous villanys and immoralitys' – but in his case he was motivated only by 'a pure love to truth [*sic*], and my own happiness'. He was particularly interested in the roots of morality. He claimed that moral concepts or laws were developed by humans 'as that [*sic*] of kingdoms, commonwealths, or what the most part of men think convenient for such and such ends and purposes'. And yet, he said, through a process of circular reasoning, people then attributed all the qualities that they saw as 'good' to God (thus both creating and reinforcing their conception of God), and all that was evil or imperfect to something else.

Following along the lines of Charles Blount and (closer to home) John Fraser, this led him to question the nature and necessity of divine punishment:

> If God did not pardon men's sins, ther would be no use of his mercies, and certainly if God have mercy (as undoubtedly he has) and if it be infinite, he it [*sic*] must of necessity pardon (as the least of its operations) the greatest sins that the highest dependent being can be capable of. And it must not be said, that this overthrows justice, for that is most false, seing that mercy presupposes justice, and the sentence to be given, and then it steps in and satisfies justice.

The God that Aikenhead was describing was a deistic God, entirely bound by logic, and only minimally related to the God of the Christian and Hebrew scriptures.

> We can say that God will not destroy and damn one, that from his heart loves him, prayeth to him, and praiseth him, and doth other acts of natural religion; for thus [i.e. otherwise] it would follow that in hell, ther were prayers, praises and the love of God, and such like, yea and that the creature had more love to the creator, than the creator hath to the creature. All of which are most absurd. And it is impossible for any intelligent being not to love God, seing that he is with his most appetable attributes, 'ipsissimum bonum'. So then it would follow that men could be saved and enjoy God by the natural law ... And that ther were no need of revelation, or of any other way of salvation, espeichially such a way as christianism.

Aikenhead thus adopted a deism founded on natural law. Blount (who was indeed a probable source for some of these ideas) would have agreed. John Toland would have shared Aikenhead's suspicion of the 'mysteries' of Christianity, but would not have gone as far in his embrace of 'natural religion.'

Aikenhead also freely professed his inability to accept the Christian idea of the Trinity. In this, he 'thought that the common distinction of a seeming contradiction could not have place'. The concepts of Father, Son and Holy Spirit tended to 'overthrow the simplicity of the same [God] if they be distinct among themselvs ... and so the Trinity should differ nothing from the politheism of the Gentiles, by making three distinct infinits'. He averred that he had sincerely tried to accept traditional Christian teachings on this point, 'but I found always that the more I thought, the further I was from it'.

Following this explanation of his philosophical scepticism, Aikenhead offered a warning:

> Now these things I have puzled and vexed myself in, and all that I could learn therfrom, is, that I cannot have such certainty, either in natural or supernatural things as I would have. And so I desire all men, espeichially ingenious young men, to beware and take notice of these things upon which I have splitt. I declare my abhorrence and detest of any of my failings or offences concerning the forsaids, and its my earnest and only desire and prayer to God for his mercies sake in the name of Jesus Christ, (by which way I only expect pardon of my sins, and reconciliation with God) to forgive me my offences and trespasses.

He recognised that others might doubt the sincerity of his remorse, noting that 'tho' it do not appear much by outward signes and tokens, yet I cannot express how much I detest, abhor and am troubled' at the heterodox beliefs for which he had been condemned. He assured listeners and readers that 'I die in the full perswasion of the true Christian Protestant Apostolick faith, according to the tenor of my petitions given into the lords of justiciary and councill'.

But, while acknowledging that he was guilty of the charges against him, he insisted that he was innocent of the 'abominable aspersions' made against him in Mungo Craig's pamphlet. He again charged that Craig was 'as deeply concerned in those hellish notions (for which I am sentenced) as ever I was'. Then he seemed to offer himself up like a sacrificial lamb:

> as the Lord in his providence hath been pleased in this exemplary manner to punish my great sins, so it is my earnest desire to him, that my blood may give a stop to that rageing spirit of atheism which hath taken such footing in Britain, both in practice and profession. And of his infinite mercy recover those who are deluded with these pernicious principles. And for that end that his everlasting gospell may flourish in these lands, while sun and moon endureth.

This spirit of contrition was continued in the brief letter to his 'freinds (whom I from good ground may term parents)' – in early modern usage this usually meant relatives – which he also offered that day. In this, he insisted he had only been seeking a reprieve in order to prepare himself better for death. He acknowledged his 'great sins, which I hope shall be all forgiven by the mercy of God, through the merits of my Redeemer Jesus Christ, tho alace my time hath been short since my sentence, so I have trifled away and misspent too much thereof', suggesting that any conversion to traditional Christianity had come rather late. He expressed the hope that his intellectual autobiography 'will give satisfaction to you in particular, and to the world in generall, and after I am gone produce more charity than hath been my fortune to be trysted hitherto with, and remove the apprehensions, which I hear are various with many about my case'.

In closing, he defended his reputation on one other point, not mentioned in any of the other sources. He said: 'I am suspected to have practised magick and conversed with devils, which I here declare ... to be altogether false and without any solid ground.' In any case, it seems unlikely, given his apparent deism and insistence on the test of reason, that such a charge could have had much basis. Perhaps this was a reference to the claims in Craig's *Satyr* that he had promised to develop antidotes against death and an inexpensive version of the philosopher's stone. Aikenhead was willing to grant his past scepticism, but would insist that his beliefs were built on a rational foundation.

5.7 DEATH AND REMORSE

Aikenhead then prayed with the ministers Webster and George Meldrum. Webster's fiery style and uncompromising high Presbyterian stance might not have been particularly comforting. A few years later he would hound an eleven-year-old girl to whom he was ministering on her deathbed over whether she had ever played on the Sabbath. Meldrum, on the other hand, might have offered some solace. The diarist Elisabeth West, a contemporary of Aikenhead, credited Meldrum's 'meek and comfortable' style of spiritual counsel and preaching with helping her overcome the spiritual doubts that had troubled her in the mid-1690s. One later account even suggested that Meldrum had sought a pardon for Aikenhead or, failing that, at least a reprieve. The minister and antiquarian Robert Wodrow opined that Meldrum's 'charity was knoun throu all the Kingdom'.[35] Perhaps one of the two ministers handed Aikenhead the Bible that he then carried with him as he walked to the Gallowlee, accompanied by the clergy and surrounded by 'a strong Guard of Fuzileers, drawn up in two lines'. Once the procession reached the Gallowlee, a journey that would have taken the better part of an hour, it stopped so that Aikenhead could sing the Fifty-First Psalm, and he again affirmed that he now accepted all traditional Christian beliefs, including the Trinity and, appearing 'surprised & terefied for death', asked onlookers to pray for him. Then he was hanged, twisting in the January breeze as a short Edinburgh afternoon descended into twilight. His body was buried at the foot of the gallows.[36]

How did the onlookers react to this spectacle? It was a full display of the powers of the covenanted (at least in the minds of some of its leaders) Presbyterian state, protecting itself from both internal disunity and the smitings of an obviously angry God. The hanging of a scapegoat like Aikenhead might paper over many of the cracks that had emerged in the public religiosity of post-revolutionary Scotland. In such a drama, all were expected to play certain roles, none more critical than that of the condemned man himself. Because the extent of his remorse would be debated in the aftermath of the hanging, it is worth comparing the perceptions of eyewitnesses as to how well Aikenhead played his part. Sir John Clerk of Penicuik's description, cited earlier for its reaction to Aikenhead's intellectual autobiography, is the most sceptical of all the surviving accounts with regard to Aikenhead's true repentance. Clerk of Penicuik, an extremely devout Presbyterian himself who regularly took notes on sermons and recorded his dreams about scriptural passages, would have been difficult to convince. He described Aikenhead as a 'wretched creature', and hoped that the experience of watching the hanging would help him root 'atheism & unbeliefe' out of his own heart.[37] But others, including some Presbyterian clergy, were more inclined to accept the sincerity of Aikenhead's last words. George Turnbull, minister at Alloa, was in Edinburgh for the General Assembly. Coming from a covenanting family and having shared his father's exile in the Netherlands, Turnbull was not likely to show much sympathy for a heterodox blasphemer. But even he granted that Aikenhead 'recanted his errors, and seemed to dye penitent'. A similar assessment was offered by Alexander Findlater, minister at Hamilton, to his co-minister Robert Wylie in a letter written in the late afternoon or evening of the day Aikenhead died. Findlater reported that 'I did see Aikinhead this day execute for his cursing railling against our saviour calling him a magician & that he hade learnd it in Agypt but he abjured all his former error and dyed penitantly'. This did not mean that Findlater opposed the sentence. Indeed, he noted, 'I think G[od] was glorified by such ane awful & exemplary punish[men]t'.[38] It is possible that ministers like Turnbull and Findlater, who believed in the didactic powers of public execution, and thought this one was entirely justified, were looking for (and perhaps exaggerating) signs of repentance that they desperately wanted to see. But several laymen, less religiously sensitive than Clerk of Penicuik, also saw remorse from the condemned man.

The next day David Crawford wrote to the Earl of Arran, reporting on Aikenhead's execution as the only news he had that was 'worth yor Lo[rdship]s trouble'. Less specific than Findlater about the charges, he said Aikenhead was 'hanged for Atheism [but] at his death he confessed his being deluded and hoped to be saved by the mercies and mediation of J. Christ'. The correspondent for London's *Post Man* averred that Aikenhead 'according to all humane appearance, dyed with all the Marks of a true Penitent'. Other eyewitnesses assured William Lorimer (who apparently did not attend the execution) that Aikenhead 'died very penitent, pouring out his soul with great Brokenness of Heart in prayer to God in Christ'. The architect Robert Mylne wrote in his copy of Mungo Craig's *Satyr* that at his execution Aikenhead 'acknowledged God, father son and Holy Ghost and sang a psalm. But some Presbyterian ministers followed him to death.'[39] Based on this small sample, it appears that the condemned man generally fulfilled the role expected of him. But that version of events would be challenged, as we will see.

One stipulation of the sentence against him was that all Aikenhead's movable goods would be escheated to the Crown. These probably did not amount to much, but there is evidence that his relatives were at least able to hang on to the real estate that was once his. In November 1698 Thomas

Aikenhead's sisters Katharine and Anna signed over to Patrick Aikenhead their ownership of the fourth-storey lodging near the Netherbow, which Patrick Aikenhead had signed over to Thomas in 1692. The disposition referred to Katharine and Anna as Thomas's heirs, with no mention of the nature of his demise, and stipulated that they were giving the property to Sir Patrick Aikenhead in exchange for an unstated sum of money. Thus, despite his legal condemnation, Aikenhead's sisters were able to inherit this property from him. The fact that Anna was being legally represented early in 1697 by Sir Colin Campbell of Aberuchil, one of the four justice lords who had presided at her brother's trial, may have helped ensure this bit of judicial mercy. Possibly the sisters also inherited Thomas's debts to Sir Patrick Aikenhead (another of Anna's legal representatives), and this property transaction was intended to pay them off. Both sisters signed their names quite clearly, suggesting that Thomas was not the only literate child of James Aikenhead and Helen Ramsey.[40]

As the debate over his execution developed, Aikenhead's remains lay interred at the Gallowlee, along with those of others executed there. But they did not stay there for ever. The hill on which the Gallowlee stood was made of sand, and a century or so after Aikenhead met his end there, the sand was taken away to be used as an ingredient in the mortar needed in the construction of Edinburgh's New Town.[41] Perhaps it is appropriate that Aikenhead's bones helped to bind together the stones in that architectural embodiment of Enlightenment reason and order. He would have been more popular there.

NOTES

1. NAS MSS JC26/78/1/2–8.
2. Except where indicated, all trial details come from *State Trials*, xiii, pp. 917–38, which appears to be based on Bodleian MS Locke b.4, fos 86r–108v, a set of documents collected on the Aikenhead case by John Locke.
3. George Brunton and David Haig, *The Senators of the College of Justice* (Edinburgh: Clark, 1832), pp. 433–4; Andrew Dalzel, *History of the University of Edinburgh from its Foundation*, 2 vols (Edinburgh: Edmonston & Douglas, 1862), ii, pp. 316–17); NAS MS CC8/2/93, 2 February 1697.
4. Brunton and Haig, *Senators of the College of Justice*, pp. 438–40, 442–5, 478–80; *Memoirs of the Secret Services of John Macky, esq.* (London, 1733), p. 225.
5. Omond, *Lord Advocates*, i, pp. 243–80; *Memoirs of the Secret Services of John Macky*, p. 208. For a more sympathetic portrait of Goodtrees,

which also details his work as a political theorist, see Beisner, 'His Majesty's Advocate'.
6. NAS MS JC26/78/1/1.
7. NAS MS JC6/14, fos 98v–99r, 103v.
8. *Protestant Mercury*, 122 (30 December 1696–1 January 1697).
9. The two petitions are NAS MSS JC26/78/1/12–13. Only the first of them is included in *State Trials*, and it can be found at xiii, pp. 921–3. I base the claim that these petitions are pre-trial on their contents.
10. Craig, *A Lye Is No Scandal*, pp. 11–12.
11. NRH MS OPR 685.1/8, fo. 23r; *Post Man*, 265 (16 January 1697); *Post Boy*, 266 (16 January 1697).
12. The lists are NAS MSS JC26/78/1/5, 7–8.
13. Marguerite Wood (ed.), *Edinburgh Poll Tax Returns for 1694* (Edinburgh: Scottish Record Society, 1951), p. 12.
14. EUL MSS 'Matriculation Roll Transcripts: Arts, Law, Divinity, 1623–1751', fos 228–32; Da.1.33, fos 119–20.
15. ECA MS SL1/1/34, fo. 39r.
16. NAS MSS JC26/78/1/8–10; for Graham's wealth and residence, see WRH MS E70/4/7, fo. 4.
17. Mosman was an elder in Tolbooth Parish in 1693–7. See NAS MS CH2/140/2, fo. 3.
18. Wood (ed.), *Edinburgh Poll Tax Returns*, pp. 5, 9, 10, 22, 24, 31.
19. *Protestant Mercury*, 122 (30 December 1696).
20. Ibid. 122 (30 December 1696).
21. NAS MSS PC1/51, fos 42v, 44v; PC4/2, fos 34r–v; *Post Boy*, 262 (7 January 1697); *Protestant Mercury*, 124 (6 January 1697).
22. Anstruther to Robert Cunningham, 26 January 1697, Bodleian MS Locke b.4, fo. 98r–v, printed in *State Trials*, xiii, pp. 929–30.
23. *Protestant Mercury*, 125 (8 January 1697).
24. Bodleian MS Locke b.4, fo. 97r, printed in *State Trials*, xiii, p. 928.
25. NAS MS PC 1/51, fo. 44r.
26. *Post Man*, 265 (16 January 1697); Pitcairn (ed.), *Acts of the General Assembly*, pp. 258–61.
27. Anstruther to Robert Cunningham, 26 January 1697, Bodleian MS Locke b.4, fo. 98r–v, printed in *State Trials*, xiii, pp. 929–30.
28. Polwarth to Tullibardine, 14 December 1696, NAS MS GD158/964, fo. 80; Tullibardine to Polwarth, 23 December 1696, NAS MS GD158/1103/2; Polwarth to Tullibardine, 19 January 1697, NAS MS GD158/964, fo. 113.
29. NAS MSS PC1/51, fos 31v–32r, 34r–v; PC13/2, 12 December 1696; Pitcairn (ed.), *Acts of the General Assembly*, pp. 241, 253, 262. The 1694 Act against Profaneness had mentioned blasphemy but not deism, although the latter had been covered by a separate Act early in 1696.
30. NAS MSS GD158/560, GD158/1570; Scott-Moncrieff (ed.), *Household*

Book of Lady Grisell Baillie, pp. xv–xvii; *Memoirs of the Secret Services of John Macky*, pp. 216–17.

31. Polwarth to Tullibardine and Ogilvy, 26 January 1697, NAS MS GD158/964, fo. 122.
32. Neither is part of the Justiciary Court record, but John Locke collected a copy of each, and those copies were published in *State Trials*, xiii, pp. 930–4.
33. NAS MS GD18/2092/1, 8 January 1697.
34. Locke's copy is Bodleian MS Locke b.4, fos 99r–101r, and Halyburton commented extensively upon it in his *Natural Religion Insufficient*, especially at pp. 119–23.
35. *An Account of the Last Words of Christian Kerr* (Edinburgh, 1702), p. 15; *Memoirs, or Spiritual Exercises of Elisabeth West*, pp. 8, 23; Lorimer, *Two Discourses*, pp. v–vi; Wodrow, *Analecta*, i, pp. 175–7.
36. NAS MS GD18/2092/1, 7 January 1697; *Post Man*, 265 (16 January 1697).
37. NAS MS GD18/2092/1, 8 January 1697. For other evidence of Clerk of Penicuik's religiosity, see ibid., 11 October, 25, 26 and 29 November, 18 December 1696, 4 March 1697; NAS MS GD18/2090, 26 June 1692.
38. Paul (ed.), 'Diary of George Turnbull', p. 370; Findlater to Wylie, 8 January 1697, NLS MS Wodrow Quarto XXX, fo. 245r.
39. David Crawford to the Earl of Arran, 9 January 1697, NAS MS GD406/1/4204; *Post Man*, 265 (16 January 1697); Lorimer, *Two Discourses*, p. vi; Notes in NLS and British Library copies of Craig, *Satyr against Atheistical Deism*.
40. ECA MS Moses Bundle 108, item 4498; NAS MS CC8/2/93, 2 February 1697.
41. James Grant, *Old and New Edinburgh*, 3 vols (London: Cassell's, 1883), iii, pp. 154–5.

6

The Aftermath:
Public Opinion in Scotland and England

In the short run, the hanging of Thomas Aikenhead may have had the desired effect on would-be blasphemers in Edinburgh, driving underground any discussion of philosophical alternatives to traditional Christianity for a while. There was no comparable case in its aftermath. In fact, Aikenhead would be the last person executed for blasphemy in Scotland or England. But the case generated controversy in both kingdoms. In Scotland, it became connected with other contemporary efforts to punish the putative enemies of God, and to convince sceptics of the reality of supernatural evil. In England, it became something of an embarrassment for Scottish officials and highlighted what to some English critics seemed the intellectual backwardness of Scottish society. But others in England praised the actions of the Scots authorities, and hoped the magistrates of England would take a similarly firm stand against heterodox viewpoints. It would cast a long shadow over the Scottish Enlightenment, particularly for those who came to see it as a last gasp of clerical domination in the city that would be the centre of that movement. More immediately, it seems to have fatally wounded Mungo Craig's career.

6.1 THE DEFENCE OF MUNGO CRAIG

As we have seen, nobody did more than fellow student Mungo Craig to blacken Thomas Aikenhead's reputation and to supply the evidence that sent him to the gallows. But it appears that this smear campaign also sullied the reputation of its primary author to the extent that he had to defend himself in print. This he did with *A Lye Is No Scandal*, another cheap octavo pamphlet, which advertised itself as having been written on 15 January 1697 – one week after Aikenhead's execution.[1] Like Craig's earlier *Satyr against Atheistical Deism*, it bears the marks of a hurried production (including misnumbered pages); it was probably prepared to capitalise on interest in the Aikenhead case as well as to vindicate its author. While the style and typography are similar to those of the *Satyr*, suggesting that this was another offering from Craig's landlord, the stationer Robert Hutchison, for sale in his shop in the College Wynd, it gives no indication of who published or sold it, or even if it issued from an Edinburgh press.

Based on the protests Craig offered in this pamphlet, it looks as though some of Aikenhead's countercharges against him had hit their mark. 'Some say that I was the first who instill'd these [heterodox] principles in him', he wrote. 'Others assert that I lent him Athiesticall Books' – both indications that Aikenhead's claims were being repeated around Edinburgh. In response, Craig argued that in his dying speech Aikenhead had averred that he had adopted his blasphemous views when he was ten or eleven, well before he met Craig. But this was a misrepresentation of what Aikenhead had actually said. In fact, Aikenhead had recalled that since he was ten he had 'been ever, according to my capacity, searching good and sufficient grounds whereon I might safely build my faith'. At any rate, it seems unlikely that a ten- or eleven-year-old boy would have developed the elaborate series of unorthodox views for which Aikenhead was convicted.[2]

Craig's twisting of the words of Aikenhead's last speech suggests a desperate need to clear himself lest he be charged with a similar crime. He dissociated himself from Aikenhead's social circle, claiming he had kept company with the dead man only between February and April 1696, and after that had seen him only two or three times, seeming to overlook the fact that they had matriculated together in the same bajan at Edinburgh's town college in 1693. He was also careful to avow religious orthodoxy, asserting that 'ever since I could make any considerable use of Reflexion and Memory, I have observed the Finger of God in every step of my life', and characterising Aikenhead's accusations against him as a 'humbling dispensation wherewith the Lord has been pleased to try me, for ends best known to his Holy Majesty'. Craig even implied that he was studying in order to enter the ministry. He took pains to dispute statements Aikenhead had made in court that suggested that Craig had only recently, under the influence of the writings of Sir Charles Wolsley, Henry More and Hugo Grotius, overcome his own religious scepticism.[3]

While labelling Aikenhead 'that poor creature lately Executed for *Apostacy*', Craig nevertheless cast doubt on the sincerity of his repentance. He wrote that he was surprised by Aikenhead's charges against him 'because [they] came from one who was to die, and pretended to reced from his former Principles', ignoring the fact that Aikenhead had first made the claims in pre-trial petitions. He said Aikenhead had given little satisfaction to the ministers who had visited him in the tolbooth, and that his intellectual autobiography was 'very unbecoming a dying man in his circumstances, being so far stuff'd with the Affectation of a Bumbast and Airy Stile'. In any case, Craig noted with a rather confident circular argument, Aikenhead was a convicted blasphemer, 'and the spirit of God makes us Infallibly certain that such should be false accusers'.[4]

Craig assured doubters that Aikenhead was guilty of the blasphemies for which he was convicted, and that witnesses 'heard them in different places, and at several occasions, uttered by him, in the spirit of Malice and Bitterness, with frequent Repetitions, without any Provocation, yea, contrary to the sound Admonitions of those, who, with abhorence, were his Auditors'. Craig seemed indignant that anyone might question his conduct in the affair:

> Ah Christians! Who gives Ear to this groundless Calumny, what for a Monster conceive ye me to be, were I guilty of any such thing. In pointing out that Sin in such black and dismal colours, as I did in that Satyr, in denouncing so many Wo's [sic] against the guilty, and in Attributing to them such Hellish properties. Can it enter into your minds that a man cou'd ever screw up his Soul to such a hight of Hypocrisie, and shake from him so far the aw and dread of a Supream being?[5]

Apparently, it could. A resolution passed in the Kirk's General Assembly, meeting at the time of Aikenhead's execution, suggests a fear that authorities needed to keep better track of students like Mungo Craig and his friends. It stipulated that, owing to 'several weighty causes', a central register should be kept of all divinity students, whether or not they had passed their trials (demonstrations of the ability to preach properly on assigned scriptural texts), and even of students merely attending lectures given by divinity professors. Edinburgh's burgh council had acted on a similar concern the previous September, when it mandated that in the future all students who attended the college on bursaries (scholarships) from the burgh would have 'to signe the Confession of Faith ratified in this current parliam[en]t as ane specimen of their principles'. The notoriety Craig gained from the Aikenhead case may well have forced him to change his career plans; there is no record of him ever having served as a minister in the Church of Scotland, and *A Lye Is No Scandal* marks his final appearance in the historical record.[6]

6.2 MORE BLASPHEMY AND THE REVIVAL OF THE WITCH-HUNT

While Aikenhead would be the last person in Scotland (or Britain) executed for blasphemy, he was not the last person officially charged with the crime.

Over the course of 1696, the Privy Council became involved in disputes involving the Fife laird Patrick Kinninmont of that Ilk, and several others, particularly his wife. Kinninmont appears to have been prone to violent behaviour, and had allegedly become involved in an adulterous relationship with a female servant in his household. Efforts to apprehend him and bring him to justice dated back to May 1696 at least, and Kinninmont's wife managed to get a hearing before the council that July. He did not appear before the council until late January 1697, and he was then locked in Edinburgh's tolbooth.[7] But the Lord Advocate Stewart of Goodtrees had difficulties finding witnesses willing to appear and testify against him, because so many of them were 'under Kinninmonts influence'. Witness intimidation may have been the real issue here; people probably feared testifying against a man allegedly capable of 'shotting James Bardget with a pistoll betwixt the legs & in the throat', and breaking into one James Robertson's house, wounding Robertson and his wife and daughter.[8] Without witnesses, it would be impossible to convict him of such assaults. So Stewart of Goodtrees changed tactics, and focused his legal strategy against Kinninmont on charges of adultery and blasphemy, both of which were, in certain circumstances, capital crimes. A 1563 Act of Parliament, rarely invoked, had made 'notoure' (well-known) adultery punishable with death.[9]

The indictment against Kinninmont, dated 22 November 1697, charged that, in addition to openly 'keeping company and bed' with his servant for several months, he had blasphemed 'by calling a man bougar of God, and scume of Christ', and called Jesus a bastard. On one occasion, it claimed, he had told one James Dewar he would cut off his ears 'unless he would deny Christ his Saviour'. Kinninmont had also 'wickedly said ... if any man had God on the one hand and Christ on the other, [he] could stow the luggs [ears] out of his head, and ... would see who woud say it was ill done'. While such statements certainly offended Christian religious sensibilities, they did not have the philosophical underpinnings of Aikenhead's blasphemies. Five justice lords presided at Kinninmont's trial, including all four who had directed Aikenhead's. But Kinninmont had two attorneys defending him, and it showed in his defence. They attacked the indictment for not specifying the place or time the alleged blasphemies were uttered, and noted that, without witnesses attesting to actual copulation between Kinninmont and his servant, the charge of adultery could not be proven. Most significantly, with regard to the alleged blasphemies, they argued that

> in caise that ever any of the expressiones lybelled did escape the pannall (which he absolutely denyes and abhorres) the same hes certainly bein when

the pannall hes bein excessibely drunk; and it is weell knowen that men in drunk and after cups are mad and furious ...

Noting that the 1661 blasphemy statute held that blasphemy could be a capital crime only if the person blaspheming was 'not distracted in their witts', Kinninmont's attorneys argued that drunkenness caused such distraction. While the judges expressed doubt as to the legitimacy of this defence, on 13 December Stewart of Goodtrees dropped the remaining charges. Kinninmont, a drunken, violent laird who could afford good legal representation, would not go the way of Aikenhead.[10]

But there were other enemies of Christianity to be pursued. Thomas Aikenhead's scepticism represented a relatively new challenge to Scots Christianity, but Scots authorities had been enthusiastic, if not quite obsessive, participants in the general European witch-hunt of the sixteenth and seventeenth centuries. While the scale of witch-hunting in Scotland did not approach that of parts of France or the southern Holy Roman Empire, the widespread use of torture in Scottish witchcraft investigations, along with the cooperation and encouragement of many Presbyterian clergy, combined to create a Scottish hunt that was far more intensive than that of England. And, while the last execution for witchcraft in England took place in 1685, the re-establishment of official Presbyterianism in Scotland in 1690 brought witch-hunting back on the agenda. Both Ian Bostridge and Michael Wasser have recently pointed out that the aftermath of the Aikenhead case saw one of Scotland's last witch-hunts, a juxtaposition noted more than 150 years ago by the historian Thomas Babington Macaulay. Wasser has characterised both as instances of 'moral cleansing' in a period of 'moral panic, economic crisis and political instability'.[11]

Scattered reports of witchcraft allegations were brought to the attention of the Privy Council as early as July 1696, but they became thick and heavy starting in early December, as Aikenhead was awaiting trial. On the very day that the council refused Aikenhead's final appeal with Hume of Polwarth's tie-breaking vote it recommended that the Lord Advocate prepare a commission to try witches at Paisley.[12] This hunt centred on the apparent bewitchment of Kristen Shaw, the eleven-year-old daughter of a laird from Renfrewshire, just south-west of Glasgow. After medical treatment failed to solve her alleged symptoms, which included the vomiting of pins and hot coals, her family and the local minister turned to witchcraft as the likely explanation, leading to accusations against about thirty-five individuals, and the eventual trial and execution of four women and three men in the spring of 1697.[13]

Contemporaries were quick to draw a connection between the diabolical attacks on Kristen Shaw and the dangers of deism and religious scepticism. Supporters of this witch-hunt painted doubters with the same brush used against the likes of Thomas Aikenhead. Sir Francis Grant, who was the prosecutor in the case against the seven witches, published a tract defending traditional witchcraft theories and the prosecution of Shaw's alleged tormenters against the doubts of modern-day 'sadducees' in 1698.[14] In his preface, Grant (who was also the nephew of the minister George Meldrum, who attended Aikenhead on the scaffold) argued that just because judges and juries had erred in the past and wrongly convicted witches did not mean that witchcraft did not exist, any more than the mistaken conviction of criminal suspects meant that crime did not exist. He mentioned 'Mr Aikenhead' as one who had denied that 'there are spirits and a Devil to Torment Sinners', but claimed 'he died in full conviction of it'. In fact, Grant took Aikenhead's apparent change of heart in his final days as 'visible Testimony super added to the greater Gospel-proofs' in these matters.[15]

Infusing his account with a touch of apocalyptic rhetoric, Grant wrote that

> These things we doubt not will meet with a very different Reception, especially in this unhappy Age and place of the world, where *Britain* may be termed the Unfortunate Island; *Africk* never having been more fertile in the production of *Monsters*, since its observ'd that through all the Successions of Men, there was never before any Society, or Collective body of *Atheists* till these dreggs of time; though there might have been here and there some mishapen Births.

Like the Privy Council as it considered the cases of John Fraser and Aikenhead, Grant saw the circulation of certain types of books as a major problem:

> Seeing Devils take so much pains to contract for the souls of Witches; the Saducee's [*sic*] tho judicially blinded in their Reason, are hereby rendred inexcusable by very sense; ill Books, which corrupt and ensnare curious Fancies, who are seldom endow'd with accurate Judgments, ought to be restrain'd.[16]

After his narrative of the case, Grant appended documents such as statements made by advocates at the trial and attestations from a doctor and an apothecary who examined Shaw. In his conclusion, he addressed readers with the argument that reason was on his side, rather than that of the sceptics:

> Thus I have given you hints that your own Reason (which I know to be refin'd) may improve and apply, so as to dissolve the quibles which the

petty witts, who have not soul enough of themselves to penetrate into the depth of that which is abstruse may raise against it: It being their common Talent either to skipp over things superficially, or else to Attaque some of the slightest outworks, and then to Triumph as if they had obtain'd the Victory.[17]

Grant saw this case in the context of a general cultural conflict between faith and doubt, with the former reflecting a deeper understanding, and the latter championed by Satan. The Glasgow Synod, proclaiming a fast in April 1697, primarily because of the apparent re-emergence of witchcraft, saw things in similar terms. It lamented that

> our holy lord hes been highly provoken ... to loose Satan's chaine so farr as to permit him to manifest and exercise a visible rage and malice against some par[ticu]lar persons and families in this corner of the Kingdom, as is evident in the troubill & disturbance that hes bein given to that gentlemans daughter.

This was due to many sins, which the synod listed. Interestingly, they did not include fornication, adultery or drunkenness, which were so often named in such proclamations, but they did include 'horrad atheisticall principles & practices'.[18] It would be some time before Scots authorities abandoned belief in the reality of witchcraft; as late as 1730 William Forbes, writing in his *Institutes of the Laws of Scotland*, would accept the idea that a witch could conjure a storm, or kill a child by laying a hand on its nurse's breast.[19]

The revival of the witch-hunt and the Aikenhead case would be linked in the broader British debate over judicial interventions in such matters; indeed, Grant's account of Kristen Shaw's bewitchment was published in London as well as Edinburgh, and his characterisation of Britain as the 'unfortunate island' highlights that larger context. He, like the ministers Webster and Meldrum, would also become involved in the 'Reformation of Manners' campaign, which would draw adherents throughout Britain.[20] In the meantime, some of those involved in the Aikenhead case would continue to weigh in on issues related to scepticism and toleration in Scotland. Sir William Anstruther, the privy councillor who visited Aikenhead in the tolbooth, took up his pen (with the support of the Presbyterian publisher and Aikenhead juror George Mosman) in 1701 because he felt he had to inveigh 'against the *spreading contagion* of *Atheism*, which threatens the Ruine of our *Excellent* and *Holy Religion*'. He lamented that people are quick to defend their liberties and property, but 'stand *tamely by*' when God is insulted and 'our Religion *overturned*'. Perhaps recalling Aikenhead's account of his own intellectual journey, Anstruther opined that 'what by *degrees* and *Insensibly leads* severals [sic] to *Atheism* is *Scepticism*, which as one terms it is the *lethargy of the understanding*, which *benums* and chills our *intellectual faculties* with a *cold despair* of ever attaining to any certain verity ...'[21]

In tones reminiscent of Grant's critique of scepticism, and even Craig's *Satyr*, Anstruther attacked Christianity's critics as shallow, charging that '*Atheists* affect to be called *Witts*, but possess not so much of it, as to discover they are only termed so by *Ironie*, being *the most foolish*, and *most Unreasonable Companie of Man-kind*'. Like Craig, he identified the idea of the eternity of the world as one of their cardinal principles, and associated his targets with Epicureanism.[22] But he thought the problem was most common among younger men:

> I have observed that sometimes a petulancy of wit, a wantonness of Spirit and Humor of Raillery upon sacred things, hath insensibly seduced men into *Atheism*, and laughed themselves out of all Principles ... indeed this often proceeds from young men of proud and haughty Dispositions, who being conscious to themselves of their own Ignorance, and sense to entertain conversation upon Subjects that are serious or solid; do cover themselves under this stratagem, that with an Impetuous Ludibrious Raillery, they endeavour to run down all that is Serious, Moral or Divine.

Although he never mentioned Aikenhead by name, terms such as 'raillery' certainly suggest he was on his mind. Having described Aikenhead as 'an anomaly, and monster of nature' in 1697, he now wrote that, given man's natural inclination to believe in God, those who do not share this belief 'are to be looked upon as Monsters, and Anomalies of Nature'.[23] It appears that the four years since Aikenhead's execution had hardened Anstruther's views on philosophical scepticism. On the other hand, his *Essays* were so poorly received that after his death in 1711 his son allegedly tried to buy up all available copies of the work and have them destroyed.[24]

James Webster, the minister of the Tolbooth Kirk in Edinburgh, who preached to Aikenhead on his final Sunday and accompanied him to the scaffold, had never displayed any sympathy for heterodox viewpoints, and his views remained consistent in his 1703 *Essay upon Toleration*. In this, he wrote that, while people should not be compelled to embrace Christianity, 'the *Sword* should be drawn, to restrain Men from Saying, or Doing any thing to the hurt and prejudice of the Souls of others'. Webster argued that the distinction between religious truth and error 'cannot be denied, without confounding the Nature of Things and Establishing of Atheism in the World'. People who do not accept this, 'introduce Universal Scepticism, or Blasphemously Assert, that God could not, or would not,

Reveal Himself Intelligibly to us ...'[25] He could not have avoided thinking of the Aikenhead case when he asserted:

> It is a Criminal Partiality, to punish the cursing of an *Earthly Father*, yet to suffer the Reproaching of a Trinity; To Cutt off a Man for a Treasonable word, yet to let go Unpunished the Blaspheming of Christ; to Hang a Man for *Forging another Persons Hand*, yet not to chastise a *false Prophet*, who uttereth gross and Damnable Lies, in the name of the Lord; To punish a *Petty Theft* and not a Man that endeavours to *Robb the Great* GOD, of a *Son*; and His *Son* of His *God Head*.[26]

For Webster, these heterodoxies were not victimless crimes, and the general tenor of his pamphlet was to suggest that even the toleration of Episcopalians would lead down a slippery slope to the toleration of anti-Trinitarianism and atheism. While no new case analogous to Aikenhead's had emerged, Webster and some of the others involved in the case do not seem to have changed their minds in the few years after 1697. Current and former Scots officials resident at court in Whitehall had more mixed feelings, however.

6.3 'A NOISE' IN ENGLAND

Only eleven days after Aikenhead had worn the hempen necktie, the Earl of Tullibardine, one of the Scottish secretaries resident in Whitehall, wrote to the Scottish Chancellor Hume of Polwarth, scolding him and his administration over their handling of the case, and lamenting the way the English news media were portraying it:

> they still make a noise here [in London] about Aikenhead, but it is either those that have little of religion themselves, or would fain have something to find fault with in our actings, because they cannot find anything material; but, as I wrote, it has been ane ommission that I was not acquainted with the particulars of his tryall and other circumstances of it, which the sollicitor ought to have given me. I would be satisfied to know what age he was of. Your lordship will see in the prints (particularly in the 'Postboy' and 'Postman') that they would aggravate the business. I cannot yet make them give account of their correspondents in Scotland, but it seems they are none of our friends.[27]

This was not entirely news to Hume of Polwarth; he had already heard something similar from the other secretary, Sir James Ogilvy. He immediately wrote back to Tullibardine that Ogilvy had told him the Aikenhead case 'is talked of by some there'. But he assured Tullibardine that when he sent him 'a full account of that matter ... you will see that it was not onlie most just but also most necessary in our circumstances'. Later that same day, he sent a similar message to Ogilvy.[28]

This exchange highlights the speed with which an event such as Aikenhead's trial and hanging could become grist for discussion in the increasingly linked media world of the two British kingdoms. The lapsing of the English Licensing Act in 1695 had spurred an explosion of 'news', with six new London papers appearing on the scene within a month to compete with the government-sponsored *London Gazette*.[29] Several of these were still publishing early in 1697, and reported on the Aikenhead case. The availability of these papers in coffee houses (whose proprietors kept them around as a lure for customers) as well as booksellers' shops ensured that their contents would be widely discussed by the denizens of London's public sphere, who now had the means to form opinions on the case as quickly as the Scottish secretaries could. At least one of these papers, the *Flying Post*, was also distributed in Edinburgh, which had its own, smaller group of coffee houses, but no local paper until the launch of the *Edinburgh Gazette* in 1699. The linked world of the coffee house and periodical press had been developing since the mid-seventeenth century (Britain's first coffee house opened its doors – in Oxford – in 1650), but had reached a kind of maturity after the Revolution of 1688–9.[30]

By the time Ogilvy and Tullibardine were writing to Hume of Polwarth, reports on the Aikenhead case had appeared in the *Post Man*, the *Post Boy*, and the *Protestant Mercury*. These were all single broadsheets, printed on the front and back. The last of these three had offered the most detailed coverage, going as far back as mid-November, when it had reported on Aikenhead's first appearance before the Privy Council. Indeed, the *Protestant Mercury* had earlier described the John Fraser case and the council's order to search the shops of Edinburgh's booksellers in the hunt for heterodox books as well. It appears to have been the only newspaper that reported on Aikenhead's trial itself; none of the others even mentioned Aikenhead until he was appealing his sentence. But, interestingly, the *Protestant Mercury* stopped reporting on Aikenhead after detailing his appearance in the Tolbooth Kirk on the Sunday before his execution. Any reader dependent exclusively on it for news would have been left with the impression that he 'seem'd to be convinced of his fatal Error, and 'tis believed, he will accordingly be respited for some longer time'.[31] Of course this did not happen, and Tullibardine's ire at the other two papers was probably due to the fact that they mentioned the rejection of his appeals and the execution itself. The account of the execution in the *Post Man* was particularly detailed, noting the need for troops to escort Aikenhead to the scaffold, his invocation of the Trinity and the fact that he died clutching a Bible, and claiming that he 'dyed with all the Marks of a true Penitent'. The *Post Man* also reported that the vote in the Privy Council on Aikenhead's final appeal went against him by only one voice.[32] It exposed the Scots authorities as divided, fearful of public disturbance and cruel.

Regular readers of the *Post Man* might not have been surprised that it was critical of the Scots authorities in the Aikenhead case. Its inclusion of an advertisement by a bookseller offering the second, enlarged edition of John Toland's controversial *Christianity Not Mysterious* that same January suggests that it was aimed at a broadminded readership – the sorts of people that Sir Francis Grant would have labelled 'sadduccees'. Toland himself had used the *Post Man* the previous summer as a forum to reveal that he was the author of that controversial work, which had been published anonymously at first.[33] The *Post Man*'s owner was Richard Baldwin, a major publisher of books on current affairs and a man of Whig sympathies. Its newswriter was J. de Fonvive, who eventually bought the paper after Baldwin's death in 1698. De Fonvive was praised by the nonconformist publisher John Dunton as the 'glory and mirror' of the London newswriters during the period. The *Post Boy*, on the other hand, was published by Abel Roper, whose publishing enterprise was much smaller than Baldwin's, and after 1702 it would become the leading tory paper in London. Its newswriter was the otherwise unknown E. Thomas.[34] Baldwin's eclecticism and Roper's tory views would have made each man, for differing reasons, unsympathetic to the Edinburgh regime headed by Hume of Polwarth.

On 26 January, Hume of Polwarth sent Tullibardine and Ogilvy a fuller statement of his views on the Aikenhead case; apparently the solicitor Sir Patrick Hume, who had assisted Stewart in the prosecution, had already forwarded copies of the trial records. This letter, already highlighted in the previous chapter, argued that Aikenhead had been twenty years old – old enough to know better – and that nobody 'of our communion who have a due regaird to these articles of our faith which related to our lord Jesus Chryst and our redenption ... will thinke the procedur too severe', particularly given how widespread 'blasphemous notions and opinions' had become.[35]

Meanwhile, Tullibardine found a sympathetic press outlet: the *Flying Post*, which had not yet reported on the case. George Ridpath, a thoroughly Presbyterian Scot (he had helped burn the pope in effigy while a student in Edinburgh in 1681), who had financial dealings with Polwarth's family, had been the paper's main writer, and early in 1697 he took over its management. Dunton described Ridpath as 'a pious and devout observer of all the ordinances of God'.[36] In late January the *Flying Post* ran an unsigned letter from Edinburgh whose author said he was trying to correct 'false representations' made about the Aikenhead case. He claimed the Privy Council had been ready to grant Aikenhead a reprieve 'if he would make an acknowledgement of his Errors, or repent of his Blasphemous and Wicket Tenets, which he refused to do', even on the day before the execution.[37] Whether or not this was true, it made the Scots authorities appear less bloodthirsty. But it also prolonged the media life of the Aikenhead case, and, in Ogilvy's words, the letter was 'used almost by all of both sides'.[38]

Clearly, Tullibardine (and Ogilvy) wanted the Scots in London to show a united front, as did Polwarth, from the distance of Edinburgh. But the former secretary of state James Johnston, a Scot in London, wrote to his friend John Locke on 27 February explicitly to take issue with the *Flying Post* letter. Locke, who was collecting materials on the Aikenhead case, had apparently read the *Flying Post*, and Johnston insisted that Aikenhead had confessed his errors. Johnston also offered Locke a brief synopsis of the two relevant blasphemy laws, those of 1661 and 1695. It was in this letter that Johnston claimed the 1695 blasphemy statute 'was obtained by trick and surprise'. Referring to Aikenhead's intellectual autobiography, Johnston noted that Aikenhead admitted scepticism, but had explicitly rejected the charges of Mungo Craig, which convinced Johnston that the latter had been false. Regarding Craig, Johnston wrote 'no doubt he is the decoy who gave him the books and made him speak as he did'. Johnston opined that Aikenhead had made no effort to 'seduce any man' over to his views, and argued that 'laws long in dessuetude should be gently put in execution'. In his view, the Scots authorities should have shown mercy.[39] Polwarth may have got wind of this deviation from the company line. At any rate, he thought Johnston was trying to embarrass the Scots administration. In mid-March Polwarth wrote an aggrieved letter to the former secretary saying 'it is talked of you that you say ther is no credit in the present constitution in Scotland & that you are not so much my friend as I think, if it be so, tell me, for I will believ it from no other hand'.[40] Johnston (not too truthfully) pled innocence in reply:

> My conversation is among the English, where I doe you what service I can when there is occasion for it, as there was lately about the business of Aikenhead, which I coloured to the English as much as I could, tho I own to our Scotch I frankly disapproved of it.[41]

This attempt to appease Polwarth must not have been entirely successful, because on 1 April Johnston wrote to him again, protesting his loyalty and vowing his intention to stay out of politics:

> The occasion of what is said is my speech to your friends against the business of Aikenhead, and your share in it, but it was to your friends, and Scotch ones. To the English ones I made the best defence I could. In short, that man's life might be taken by all laws, both of God and man; but every thing that is lawfull is not expedient, and as the presbiterians are stated here [London] they could not have given themselves a greater blow. I say not in the opinion of libertins but of the body of this nation ... They are accused by their enemies of a bitter persecuting spirit and suspected by their friends of it.

In Johnston's view, the Scots were losing the war of public opinion in London. In the same letter, he lamented the renewed persecution of witches in Scotland, noting that French courts, once well known for witch trials, 'never try them now because of the experience they have had that it is impossible to distinguish possession from nature in disorder, and they chuse rather to let the guilty escape than to punish the innocent'.[42] Eleven days earlier, he had promised Locke a copy of 'that tryall' as soon as he got one himself – probably referring to an account of either the Aikenhead trial or the Paisley witch trial.[43]

Some of this criticism of the Scots authorities may have been the result of bitterness; Johnston had lost his position as Scottish secretary just over a year before, and may have been happy to use the Aikenhead case and the revived witch-hunt to attack those now in office (the pension of £4,000 sterling he received at the end of March was probably intended in part to quell his criticisms).[44] One contemporary reported that his ouster from office 'soured him so, as never to be reconciled all the King's reign [i.e. until 1702], tho' much esteemed'.[45] But it also appears that he was becoming anglicised, and in the process, moving far away from his roots in covenanted Presbyterianism. As the son of the arch-covenanter Archibald Johnston of Wariston, Johnston had spent his early years in what Louise Yeoman has described as 'arguably the most godly family in Edinburgh, if not Scotland'. James Johnston's older brother Archibald apparently cracked under this 'strict godly regime' and descended into insanity in the late 1650s.[46] Now James, with his political career on hold for the moment, was finding refuge in voluntary exile and semi-retirement. His social circle included critical philosophers such as Locke (who published a series of three essays on religious toleration in the early 1690s, but, unfortunately, does not appear to have recorded his thoughts on the Aikenhead case), and in 1696 Johnston had married into the English aristocracy.[47] Reflecting on the Scots authorities' treatment of Aikenhead would have highlighted for him the ways in which his thinking, and to some extent his social identity, had changed. Alexander Monro, an Episcopal clergyman whose papers Johnston had once ordered confiscated because of Monro's alleged Jacobitism, reported to a friend in May 1697 that he had run into Johnston at a London party, and 'I believe he repents what is past ... nor is he now such a friend to Presbytery as he seemed to be'. Indeed, it seemed to Monro that Johnston had headed far in the other direction: 'I think him [now to be] of a more fashionable Religion, than to give himself any trouble about the New or Old Testament.'[48]

'Fashionable religion', which held Scotland to be superstitious and backwards, found a ready audience among London newspaper readers, and the Aikenhead execution seemed to support the view. In response, Scots commentators felt the need to defend their Kirk and government. When the minister Robert Wylie wrote to the Laird of Wischaw in June 1697, he could just as easily have been responding to Johnston; he defended both the Aikenhead execution and the revived witch-hunt. Wylie had 'heard much of the censures past upon the government here [in Scotland] by some pious and charitable wits at London & elswhere upon occasion of the sentence given against Aikenhead the Atheist'. But, he argued, they had misrepresented the case. Aikenhead had not been convicted for 'a retracted erour of ... judgement', he claimed, 'but a perverse malicious railing against the adorable object of christian worship'. And Wylie was adamant that Aikenhead had refused to retract his heterodox views, at least until after his conviction. What is more, he argued that the issue was not so much the truth of Christian orthodoxy as it was acceptable public behaviour:

> When these witty criticks consider that Reason, commonsense & good manners (their own Trinity) do require that no man should in the face of a people spitefully revile & insult the object of their adoration, and that a christian could not be innocent who should rail at or curse Mahomet at Constantinople [they should see] that their pleadings against Aikenheads condemnation were most unjust & founded upon mistakes of the case and matter of fact. One wold think that after all this they should be more sparing & cautious ... in passing their little rash judgements upon the late proceedings of this government with reference to the witches in Renfrew.

Wylie said the evidence in the witchcraft cases was clear 'in spite of all the Atheism & Sadducism in the world', and he could not see how the Scots government could be questioned 'unles a man hath so far renounced humanity as well as Religion as to deny invisible spirits, and the being of witches'.[49] But the problem for the Scots authorities was that this was exactly what many people in the English reading public had started to do. And the fact that this debate was being carried on in Edinburgh, London and points in between shows the extent to which Britain was becoming a media community, if not yet a United Kingdom.

It is important to note that the Aikenhead case, while drawing attention in England (copies of the trial documents were also collected by the politician Sir Robert Harley, later Earl of Oxford), was only one facet of a larger debate being carried on in print over the linked issues of toleration, deism, Socinianism (anti-Trinitarianism) and what opponents called 'atheism'.[50] Indeed, the last term was a red flag for almost everyone, even those who favoured a degree of toleration. Matthew Tindal, a former Catholic who had turned into something of a freethinker in religion, professed great admiration for Locke's letters on toleration, and held that magistrates should not compel people to avow particular beliefs within the general spectrum of Christianity. But he insisted that authorities were

> obliged to punish those who deny the Existence of a God, or that he concerns himself with Humane Affairs; it being the belief of these things that preserveth [people] in Peace and Quiet, and more effectively obliges them to be true to their Promises and Oaths, and to perform all their Covenants and Contracts.

Nevertheless, he stopped short of calling for the execution of nonbelievers, urging that any 'Atheist' be 'disarmed, and bound to his good behaviour'. He did not mention Aikenhead by name but, since he was writing in 1697, may well have had him in mind.[51]

Others were less sanguine than Tindal about where limited toleration might lead. The Anglican clergyman and sometime Cambridge academic John Edwards attacked Locke, particularly his *Reasonableness of Christianity* (1695), and claimed that 'the great indifferency and Scepticism which reign among us have open'd a door to *Socinianism*, which is a sure Project for *Deism*, and this for *Atheism*'.[52] For a critic like Edwards, the notion that Christianity could be reduced to a simple belief (Locke suggested that all that was really needed was a recognition that Jesus was the messiah) or made 'reasonable' was very dangerous. Toland's *Christianity not Mysterious* had stoked this debate as well, and indeed its scepticism about all 'mysteries' of faith was troubling even to Locke, who turned against Toland in 1697.[53] At the same time, Peter Brown, a fellow of Trinity College, Dublin, took up his pen against Toland, using the conceit of a letter to a friend who had loaned him Toland's book:

> you tell me the Book hath made some noise; and that the Author is countenanc'd, and encourag'd by some Men of sence [Locke?]. I don't much wonder at it; for every Man of sence is not a Man of true Religion …[54]

These 'men of sence' were akin to Wylie's 'witty criticks'. For Brown, the danger was the wide circulation of Toland's book, and the reinforcement it could offer to those already inclined to scepticism:

> it is such Wretches as [Toland] who ... plentifully furnish the Atheistical and Prophane, with all the matter of their objections against Scripture. But I hope in time God will put it into the hearts of our Governours to remedy these disorders.[55]

Irish authorities responded by ordering that Toland's book be burnt by the public hangman, but Brown probably also had English 'Governours' in mind.

While Toland, in arguments similar to those of Aikenhead, had criticised the idea that God would require belief in things which are logically incomprehensible, Brown labelled this view as blasphemous, insisting that God requires belief in Christ's eternal nature and divinity, the Trinity, and the physical resurrection of the body. Toland

> pleads a *Toleration*, but for what? I hope there is no Toleration for Blasphemy and Prophaneness; and tho men are allow'd to believe what they please themselves, yet sure they may be restrain'd from industriiously spreading such Impious Notions as are destructive of all *Religion* and from poenly reviling the Christian Faith as *Imposture* and *Implicit blind Credulity*.[56]

It is not clear that Brown, in Ireland, would have been aware of the Aikenhead case, but his English readers, if they read the newspapers, knew about it, and could have seen it as a prime example of the dangers he was describing. It certainly did not end with Toland; Brown thought the wandering Irishman (and, it will be remembered, Edinburgh graduate) was part of a larger conspiracy. He saw Toland's book as 'the *joint Endeavours* of a secret Club, who set themselves with a great deal of Industry to destroy all *Reveal'd Religion*. And ... they have made use of this *Man* as a *Tool* only.' He warned that their numbers were growing, that they had sent 'Emissaries into all parts', and ultimately aimed to undermine political as well as spiritual authority.[57] Other authors would try to turn readers against Toland by associating his views with those of Aikenhead, as did an anonymous critic of Toland's biography of John Milton, who charged that Toland 'seems to Ballance mightily towards *Aikenhead's* Opinion, that the *New Testament* is a Forgery'. The same writer suggested that Toland's criticisms of Presbyterians in that work stemmed from the fact that

> his passion was in a ferment upon the Remembrance that *Aikenhead*, one

of his Brethren in Blasphemy, was hang'd by the *Presbyterians* in *Scotland* some time ago, and therefore he vows Revenge upon the whole *Bulk of those* of that Name in both Nations [Scotland and England].

The author also went out of his way to argue for the justice in Aikenhead's execution, quoting from the indictment.[58]

But Toland was not the only sceptical author earning condemnation just after Aikenhead's death. Another possible source for Aikenhead's critical ideas regarding Scripture was Spinoza's *Tractatus Theologico-Politicus* (1670). This work, which along with Hobbes's *Leviathan* and various studies of Scripture by Richard Simon, had challenged Mosaic authorship of the Pentateuch, received a fresh denunciation from Matthias Earbery, an English schoolmaster. For Earbery, Hobbes was bad enough, but Spinoza 'begins at the very Root and Foundation, by taking away all Divine Authority, from Prophecy, Miracles, or Inspiration, and making all the sacred Pen-men, to be no other than either Mad-men or Imposters'.[59] Earbery's critique of Spinoza took the form of a dialogue between a young gentleman called Scepticus and his companion Logicus, 'an old Grave Divine'. Scepticus, 'of a fiery Genius, always eager after new things', had begun his study with classical authors. Finding their ideas 'too obvious and common', he then embraced the Atomism of Descartes and Pierre Gassendus (the latter had also earned obloquy from Mungo Craig). 'But coming abroad into the World and finding that Religion was the grand Theme of all Men's Discourse', Scepticus decided to explore it, particularly by reading Socinian authors. He liked them because 'they seemed to Interpret Scripture with an ayre and freedom which he of all things most affected, and extoll'd Human Reason to such a height, as was most agreeable to the Towring thoughts of his own Ambition'. But since the Socinians seemed able to make Scripture say whatever thay wanted, he developed a contempt for Scripture. Then, 'it was his misfortune … to light upon the *Tractatus Theologico Politicus* of *Spinosa*. This turn'd him a perfect Deist, he threw away his Bible and set up this Book in the room of it.'[60] This was a tale that would have sounded familiar to those who had followed Aikenhead's story, and it echoed Edwards's warning of the slippery slope from anti-Trinitarianism to deism, and possibly even worse. Not surprisingly, Anglophone readers were also being treated to a new wave of works invoking the sad fate of Francis Spira, whose apostasy was now given a deist veneer.[61]

6.4 THE ENGLISH BLASPHEMY ACT

While the Aikenhead execution had certainly been criticised in England, the verdict of public opinion was far from unanimous, and some were suggesting that the Scottish example might be worthy of imitation. Jean Gailhard, an exiled French Calvinist resident in England, explicitly commended the Scottish parliament of 1695 for its reaffirmation and extension of the 1661 blasphemy statute, quoting from the law itself.[62] Readily equating anti-Trinitarianism with blasphemy, he called on the English parliament to take a similarly firm stand in defence of correct doctrine:

> The Enemy is not only at the Gates, but in the very body of the place, and in the Bowels of the Church, and to speak in Moses's [note the attribution] words, There is wrath gone out from the Lord, the plague is begun (Num. 16:46); for blasphemous Socinianism attended by Atheism, Deism, Prophaneness, Immorality, yea, and Idolatry, etc., doth bare and brazen-faced walk in our streets ... to what purpose is Popery or Idolatry expelled, if Socinianism or Blasphemy be let in?

Gailhard reminded readers that Israel, Judah and other ancient kingdoms were destroyed by God because they tolerated idolatry and blasphemy. But, because of modern technology, England faced assaults unheard of in biblical times, in the form of the printed word:

> Some ... have been perverted by the Conversation and Books of such Seducers, wherein that Poyson [blasphemy] ... is through Sophistry spread in a specious shape and plausible manner, and to suffer such Books stuffed with Blasphemies to be imported and here printed and sold publickly, is dangerous and against [biblical] Law.

Gailhard opined that 'there is no greater sin than Blasphemy, wherefore it deserves the heaviest Punishment to make the Pain hold in proportion with the offence'. He noted that Leviticus mandated death by stoning for blasphemers, and that English authorities had not been shy to employ capital punishment against blasphemers in the past, citing the 1611 executions of two antitrinitarians (one of whom was actually killed in 1612, in what has been reckoned the last English execution of a person for their religious beliefs).[63] He then went on, in the body of his book, to denounce Toland's work, although he never named its author.

English officials were not deaf to such pleas. Many influential gentlemen there were (like Sir Francis Grant in Scotland) becoming involved in societies for the 'reformation of manners' – a movement aimed primarily against everyday vices like drunkenness and fornication but whose adherents were also concerned about the growing scourge of religious scepticism. This campaign was particularly active in London in the 1690s, and had adherents in the English parliament as well. It first took off early in the decade, but one historian of English politics has discerned 'a second and more powerful wave of enthusiasm [which] began to roll in *c*.1697, probably originating in orthodox Anglican and Presbyterian shock at the eruption of sceptical and heretical writings that followed the expiry of the Licensing act'.[64] King William signalled his support in February 1698 by issuing 'a proclamation for preventing and punishing immorality and profaneness'. This specifically mentioned blasphemy, but the placement of that particular ill between 'excessive drinking' and 'profane swearing and cursing' in the list of sins being warned against suggests the older meaning of blasphemy. Nevertheless, the newer dangers represented by philosophical scepticism were highlighted later in the proclamation, where it was noted that

> whereas several wicked and profane persons have presumed to print and publish several pernicious books and pamphlets, which contain impious doctrines against the Holy Trinity and other fundamental articles of our faith, tending to the subversion of the Christian religion

such publications were henceforth forbidden 'under the pain of our high displeasure and of being punished according to the utmost severity of the law'.[65]

This earned the King fulsome praise from Charles Lidgould, an Anglican rector in Lincolnshire, who called the monarch 'a Moses to stand in the Gap, a prince whose endeavour to put a stop to this torrent of wickedness ... will, we hope meet with its desir'd success'.[66] In an argument with which James Webster would certainly have agreed, Ligould characterised the issue as one of 'Public safety', given the likelihood of divine vengeance if authorities did not do something to silence

> those, *who sit in the Seat of the Scornful*, and call all Religion only Priest-craft, a Trade whereby *we* get our living: That regard the Holy Scriptures but as a well-laid Romance, and the great Articles of Christianity as nothing else but so many Fables: That look upon *our* Preaching to be mere Cant, our Doctrine of Heaven and Hell, of a Resurrection and a Judgment to come only a Trick to debar them the pleasure of Indulging their natural Appetites.[67]

He could easily have been thinking of someone like Aikenhead when he denounced those 'to whom all the Sacred Mysteries of Religion, as Reveal'd in Scripture, are mere Nonsense, and the Doctrine of *three Persons and one God*, a subject fit only for Mirth and Ridicule'. Even worse were others 'that believe in *no God at all*, that will own no such thing as an *Immaterial Being*, that deny therefore that there is anything within us of a different Nature from this *Corporeal Fabrick*'.[68]

The king may have received high marks from the likes of Lidgould for his proclamation, but, without a specific law on the books, there was little that authorities could do to the critics of conventional Christianity. Facing the 'high displeasure' of a post-1689 English monarch was an empty threat in the absence of specified legal sanctions. These would be developed in parliament in the month after the king's proclamation, and encompassed in the English Blasphemy Act of 1698. Its primary sponsor was Sir John Philipps, a Member of Parliament representing the Pembroke Boroughs, who belonged to one of the many societies for the reformation of manners. Shortly thereafter, Philipps would become a founding subscriber of the Society for Promoting Christian Knowledge, one of the leading Anglican missionary societies.[69] Philipps introduced the bill on 7 March 1698, and its second reading was twice delayed in the following days, before its referral to a committee of the whole on 12 March, by a narrow vote of 98–84.

The bill as proposed by Philipps held that

> Whereas many persons have of late years openly avowed and published many blasphemous and impious opinions, contrary to the doctrines and principles of the Christian religion, greatly tending to the dishonour of Almighty God, and may prove destructive to the peace and welfare of this kingdom ... if any person or persons, having been educated in, or at any time made profession of the Christian religion within this realm, shall by writing, printing, teaching, or advised speaking, deny anyone of the persons in the Holy Trinity to be God, or shall deny the Christian religion to be true, or the holy scriptures of the old and new testament to be of divine authority

they would face penalties of being debarred or relieved from public office for the first fault, and for a repeat offence would be stripped of certain legal rights and imprisoned for three years. But witnesses would have to attest to the alleged blasphemy in front of a justice of the peace within four days of the statement in question, and the case would have to be prosecuted within three months. What is more, if a person charged for the first time retracted the blasphemous statements, all penalties would be dropped.

The bill was subject to a great deal of discussion on the floor of the House of Commons, coming before the Commons as a committee of the whole on 15, 21, 24 and 30 March. At least two amendments were made before it finally passed on 30 March. First, a clause that would have required that the Act be read aloud in churches was removed, and another clause was added, adding the assertion of the existence of 'more gods than one' to the possible blasphemies warned against. In its final form, the bill passed by the relatively wide margin of 133–58. A similar bill had already passed in the House of Lords with the strong support of Henry Compton,

Bishop of London.[70] In this way, the modern forms of blasphemy that so troubled the defenders of traditional Christianity were explicitly outlawed in England, as had already happened in Scotland. Toland was allegedly 'enraged'.[71] But anyone who had taken note of the Aikenhead case would have seen that the penalties for the crime under English law were far milder than those mandated in Scotland. England would remain a well of dangerous heterodoxies.

Partisans of the harsher Scottish approach kept this in mind in the years that followed. The two kingdoms and their parliaments were formally united in 1707. Five years later, when the British parliament was considering legislation that would have formally tolerated episcopalian preaching in Scotland, King William's old Scottish chaplain, William Carstares, who had succeeded Gilbert Rule as principal of Edinburgh University, protested that this toleration was 'inconsistent with the Union', which had promised that the religious settlement in Scotland would not be altered. To him, opening the door to episcopalianism carried the threat of far worse things:

> The Toleration Scheme propos'd seems to be very defective in providing against Immoralitys and Blasphemy; for by exempting those of the Episcopal Communion from the Censures of our Church … those People will be under no Church Government, and so become Freebooters both in Religion and Morals, as 'tis known too many of 'em are already, so that all our present Acts against Profaneness, which are very good, may be eluded by those who think fit to decline the establish'd Communion.

Ignoring the fact that the Scots blasphemy statutes of 1661 and 1695 were enforceable by secular magistrates and thus were theoretically unaffected (in fact they would remain technically valid until the early nineteenth century), Carstares warned that

> as to Blasphemy, the Toleration Scheme comes infinitely short of our Laws establish'd for that end; for that takes notice of nothing but preaching and writing against the Trinity, whereas our Laws punish those who rail upon or curse God, or any of the Persons of the Trinity, by Death, except they be distracted; and the like those who obstinately deny God or any of the Three Persons, who deny the Authority of the Holy Scriptures, or the Providence of God in governing the World.[72]

Carstares knew the language of the Scottish laws well. For him, reared in the legacy of the seventeenth-century covenants, the identity of Scotland as a Presbyterian nation was linked to its right to put someone like Thomas Aikenhead to death. But the ideal of Scottish religious uniformity was now too obviously at variance with the facts, and the Toleration Act of 1712 passed the British parliament and was ratified by Queen Anne.

6.5 AIKENHEAD REMEMBERED

The case of Thomas Aikenhead would cast a long shadow over the eighteenth century, particularly as Edinburgh, where the drama played out, became one of the centres of the European Enlightenment. Early in the century, some of those involved, however peripherally, would continue to discuss the case or Aikenhead's ideas in print, but by mid-century the fate of the unfortunate student would become an object of historical curiosity or revulsion, indicating the extent to which the intellectual culture of both Edinburgh and Britain had changed.

The same year that brought (in the Toleration Act) the legal death of Scottish religious uniformity also brought the physical death of one of the leading young lights of Presbyterian divinity – Aikenhead's old classmate Thomas Halyburton, preacher and professor of divinity at St Andrews. Two years later the Edinburgh publisher Agnes Campbell (widow of Andrew Anderson) offered to the public Halyburton's contribution to the fight against heterodoxy.[73] Halyburton, whose own youthful flirtation with deism was described earlier (in Chapter 4), offered the reader a long list of works that he would discuss (and in many cases attack) in his 'rational enquiry into the Principles of the modern *Deists*', including Blount's *Oracles of Reason*, Aristotle's *Ethics*, Spinoza's *Ethics*, Hobbes's *Leviathan*, Seneca's *de Providentia* and two of Locke's essays. Included in this august canon of broadmindedness was 'Aikenhead's Speech' – the intellectual autobiography he offered on the day of his execution – which, although it was unpublished, had apparently acquired enough influence and notoriety to be worth refuting.[74]

Calling deism '*modern Paganism*' and asserting that 'an *Atheist* is a Monster in Nature', Halyburton complained that in England and Scotland after the restoration of the monarchy in 1660

> the Philosophical Writings of Mr *Hobbs*, *Spinora* [sic], and some others of the same kidney, got, one way or other, a great Vogue amongst our *young Gentry* and *students*, whereby many were poison'd with principles destructive of all *true Religion* and *Morality*.[75]

Discussing deists who argued that there are no divinely ordained standards of good and evil, Halyburton cited Aikenhead's questioning of whether humanity is capable of offending God, and noted the resemblance to claims made by Hobbes:

> The fam'd Mr *Hobbs* was not of a very different Mind, for he plainly asserts that there is nothing *Good* or *Evil in its self*, nor any Common Laws constituting what is naturally just and unjust: But all Things are

to be measured by what every man judgeth fit, where there is no Civil Government; and by the laws of Society, where there is one.

Halyburton also referred to similar reasoning by Spinoza. He then went on to quote Aikenhead's musings on the human (rather than divine) origins of moral values, and opined:

> The sum of this confus'd Discourse, which probably he learn'd from *Hobbs*, amounts to this: God has fix'd no Law to our moral Actions, by which they are to be regulate[d]. These, which are call'd *moral laws*, are only the Determinations of Governments, or the concurring Judgment of Men, concerning what they think meet to be done for their own Ends.

To this, Halyburton answered that the Law of Nature was the same as the Law of God, and accused Aikenhead of 'thin Sophistry'.[76] Not only did he challenge the originality of Aikenhead's ideas, but also his sense of timing in offering them to the world, protesting that he did not want to 'insist any further on this inconsiderable Trifler [to whom he had already devoted more than four pages of discussion!] whose undigested notions scarce deserve the consideration we have given them; and much less did they become the awful Gravity of the Place where they were delivered' – presumably because they were not in keeping with the state-sponsored rite of penance and retribution represented by a public execution. As for Aikenhead's claims that an infinitely merciful God would 'pardon the greatest of Sins' as the 'least of its [*sic*] operations', Halyburton said this was 'plainly deny'd' – presumably by Scripture.[77]

Of course, Halyburton was speaking from the grave. His admirers would even treat his death as a powerful witnessing to covenanted Presbyterianism. Campbell published two editions of his memoirs by 1715, with a preface observing that

> there is so evident, and universal a Decay in the Life and Power of Religion with the truly Godly ... when not a few, expecially of our Youth, and that not of the meanest Quality, are poisoned, I fear beyond the Power of Antidote, with profane Romances, stage-plays, and Histories of the filty and impure Amours of the vilest Rakes, and most profligate Debauchees, and with Atheistical and blasphemous Books against all Religion.[78]

Halyburton's outward peace at death was taken as proof that his faith would be rewarded. Thus at least two of Alexander Cunningham's old pupils would die exemplary deaths in the service of belief.

In 1713 the by-then elderly English clergyman William Lorimer, 'shortly to put off this my Earthly Tabernacle', felt the time had come to publish his own account of the Aikenhead affair, partly to set the record straight concerning his own role in it.[79] Lorimer, it will be recalled, spent the winter of 1696–7 in Edinburgh, on his way to take up an academic post at St Andrews. While in Edinburgh, he visited Aikenhead in the tolbooth, offering him spiritual counsel and (as he insisted in 1713) seeking, with the minister Robert Meldrum, to obtain mercy, or at least a stay of execution, for him. He had also preached a sermon before Hume of Polwarth and other magistrates on Matthew 21:37 ('But last of all He sent unto them His son, saying, they will reverence my son'). From the tone of Lorimer's account (included in a preface to two sermons, one of which was the sermon in question), it appears that this led some to charge him with having encouraged the magistrates to prosecute Aikenhead, as one who did not accept the divinity of Jesus. But he insisted that this was not the case, protesting that he did not 'desire that severity should be us'd towards any that are fallen into any dangerous Error; for I know that our most holy, meek, and gentle Saviour came not to destroy Mens Lives but to save them'. He also opined that Aikenhead had been a deist, not a Socinian. While it is conceivable that he might have edited the sermon's text for publication, nowhere in the published version did he advocate any punishment for a person who questioned Christian doctrine, arguing that, as for Jesus, 'the more Infidels dishonour him by speaking Evil of him, the more we should honour and magnify him'.[80] According to Lorimer, heterodoxy was to be battled with preaching and debate, not punitive sanctions. Even if he was whitewashing his own role, the publication of a work like this by a minister suggests that the ground of debate was shifting.

Later generations would take different lessons from Aikenhead's travails. Another child of Edinburgh, Alexander Hamilton, was born in 1712, son of a principal of Edinburgh University. After obtaining a medical degree at the university, he emigrated to Maryland and began a medical practice in Annapolis. In 1745, seeking to break the ennui of colonial boredom, he founded the 'Tuesday Club', a group of merchants, ministers, professionals and colonial officials dedicated to fellowship and mutual entertainment. When he died in 1756 he left behind a manuscript, 'History of the Ancient and Honorable Tuesday Club', a satirical work described by its modern editor as 'a splendid gauge of eighteenth-century wit, loaded with pseudo-learned essays and digressions, surprising metaphors and allusions … doggerel verses and mock trials' and a healthy dose of nonsense. Early in this 'history' he gave the club an impressive roster of officers, reaching back to its mythical foundation in 1440. Some of them are recognisable as historical figures, but with names or other details changed. One such is the purported club secretary 'Joseph Aikenhead', appointed in 1621, but 'hang'd for atheism' in 1640.[81] Surely Hamilton would have heard of the

Aikenhead case during his Edinburgh upbringing, steeped in the life of the university. Here, he gave the once-reviled 'atheist' mock-heroic status, and placed him in a much more distant past.

When the jurist David Hume, nephew of the philosopher, took up the subject of blasphemy in his 1797 *Commentaries on the Law of Scotland*, he identified it as a crime that strikes 'at the very roots of Christianity' or even 'still deeper, to the denial of those great and original truths, which are the sources of all religion'. Nevertheless, he condemned the Aikenhead verdict as a miscarriage of justice. For this, he did not blame the law or the judges in the case, but rather the assize jury, since its members found Aikenhead guilty of 'railing and cursing' against Jesus without direct proof that he had done so. No one should be 'condemned upon arguments and consequences deduced from his discourse', Hume wrote, implying that the blasphemy might have to appear in print, rather than merely be attested to by witnesses (and, in the case of Aikenhead's most serious blasphemy, only one witness).[82]

In contrast to Hume's measured criticism, the Edinburgh advocate Hugo Arnot was unequivocal in his view of the case, which he included in his 1785 collection of 'celebrated' Scottish trials. Reflecting a confidence in progress typical of the Enlightenment, Arnot introduced the collection by asserting that 'the Criminal Records of a Country are an historical monument of the ideas of a people, of their manners and jurisprudence; and in the days of ignorance and barbarism, they exhibit a striking but hideous picture of human nature'. Scotland's legal records, he argued

> show what bitter fruits are produced under the gloomy climate of a tyrannical Government, and a superstitious priesthood; and they afford us ample ground of consolation, when we compare those bitter fruits with the blessings which we enjoy under a free government, and in an enlightened age.

Writing specifically of the Aikenhead case, Arnot proclaimed that 'mercy was asleep, as well as Justice and science, so the dreadful sentence was executed'.[83] James Johnston might have nodded his head in agreement. From the perspective of the Enlightenment, the fate of the unfortunate student seemed a solemn reminder of a very different age.

NOTES

1. Craig, *A Lye Is No Scandal*.
2. Ibid. p. 15; *State Trials*, xiii, p. 931.
3. Craig, *A Lye Is No Scandal*, pp. 2–3, 8–9, 11–12.
4. Ibid. pp. 2, 9.

5. Ibid. pp. 5, 8.
6. Pitcairn (ed.), *Acts of the General Assembly*, p. 257; ECA MS SL1/1/35, fo. 286r. There is no mention of Craig in *Fasti*.
7. NAS MS PC4/2, fos 17r, 22r, 25r–v, 33v, 35v.
8. NAS MS JC6/14, fos 131r–140r.
9. *APS*, ii, p. 539. For the non-enforcement of this law, see Graham, 'Civil Sword and the Scottish Kirk, 1560–1600'.
10. *State Trials*, xiii, pp. 1273–6.
11. Bostridge, *Witchcraft and its Transformations*, pp. 3, 23–6; Wasser, 'Western Witch-Hunt of 1697–1700', pp. 146, 151. For comparisons between the Scottish witch-hunt and its English and continental counterparts, see Brian Levack, *The Witch-Hunt in Early Modern Europe*, 2nd edn (London: Longman, 1995), pp. 21–3, 95–7.
12. NAS MS PC4/2, fos 25v, 30v–31r, 34v–35r.
13. Wasser, 'Western Witch-Hunt of 1697–1700', pp. 148–9.
14. [Sir Francis Grant], *Sadducismus Debellatus, or, A True Narrative of the Sorceries and Witchcrafts Exercis'd by the Devil and his Instruments upon Mrs Christian Shaw* (London, 1698). A cheaper version, with smaller type and pages and some small textual differences, was published in Edinburgh as *A True Narrative of the Sufferings and Relief of a Young Girle Strangely Molested, by Evil Spirits and their Intsruments [sic] in the West* (Edinburgh, 1698).
15. [Grant], *Sadducismus Debellatus*, pp. i, iv.
16. Ibid. pp. v–vi.
17. Ibid. pp. 59–60.
18. NLS MS Wodrow Folio XXXIX, fo. 34r.
19. William Forbes, *The Institutes of the Laws of Scotland*, 2 vols (Edinburgh, 1722–30), ii, pp. 37, 40.
20. [Sir Francis Grant], *A Letter from a Magistrate in the Countrey to his Friend* (Edinburgh, 1701).
21. Sir William Anstruther, *Essays Moral and Divine* (Edinburgh, 1701), preface, unpaginated.
22. Ibid. pp. 2, 6–7, 14.
23. Ibid. pp. 13, 26–7; *State Trials*, xiii, p. 930.
24. Brunton and Haig, *Senators of the College of Justice*, pp. 443–4.
25. James Webster, *An Essay upon Toleration* (Edinburgh, 1703), pp. 6–7.
26. Ibid. p. 9.
27. Tullibardine to Polwarth, 19 January 1697, *HMC, Fourteenth Report, Appendix, Part III, Manuscripts of the Duke of Roxburghe* (London: HMSO, 1894), p. 130.
28. Polwarth to Tullibardine, 19 January 1697, NAS MS GD158/964, fo. 113; Polwarth to Ogilvy, 19 January 1697, ibid.
29. Michael Treadwell, 'The Stationers and the Printing Acts at the End of the Seventeenth Century', in John Barnard and D. F. McKenzie (eds),

The Cambridge History of the Book in Britain, vol. 4 (Cambridge: Cambridge University Press, 2002), pp. 755–76, at p. 772.
30. *Home Diary*, p. 113; 'Public sphere' here is meant in the sense that it is used in Jürgen Habermas, *The Structural Transformation of the Public Sphere* (Cambridge, MA: MIT Press, 1989), an English translation of his 1962 *Strukturwandel der Öffentlichkeit*. See also Bowie, *Scottish Public Opinion and the Anglo-Scottish Union*, pp. 19–25; Helen Berry, *Gender, Society and Print Culture in Late-Stuart England: The Cultural World of the Athenian Mercury* (Aldershot: Ashgate, 2003), pp. 13–18; Brian Cowan, *The Social Life of Coffee: The Emergence of the British Coffeehouse* (New Haven: Yale University Press, 2005), pp. 25, 172–3.
31. *Protestant Mercury*, 101 (26 October 1696), 109 (13 November 1696), 122 (30 December 1696), 124 (6 January 1697), 125 (8 January 1697).
32. *Post Man*, 265 (16 January 1697).
33. *Post Man*, 261 (7 January 1697); Champion, *Republican Learning*, p. 70.
34. John Dunton, *The Life and Errors of John Dunton, Citizen of London*, 2 vols (London: J. Nichols, 1818), ii, pp. 428–9; De Beer, 'English Newspapers from 1695 to 1702', pp. 122–3.
35. Polwarth to Tullibardine and Ogilvy, 26 January 1697, NAS MS GD158/964, fo. 122.
36. Dunton, *Life and Errors*, ii, p. 430; De Beer, 'English Newspapers from 1695 to 1702', pp. 122–3; Scott-Moncrieff (ed.), *Household Book of Lady Grisell Baillie*, p. 5.
37. *Flying Post*, 26 January 1697.
38. Ogilvy to Carstares, 18 June 1697, in McCormick (ed.), *State Papers and Letters*, p. 310.
39. Johnston to Locke, 27 February 1697, in De Beer (ed.), *Correspondence of John Locke*, vi, pp. 17–19. The letter is also in *State Trials*, where Howell gives the author as Locke, but De Beer demonstrates the likelihood that it is Johnston writing to Locke rather than the other way round. The materials on Aikenhead that Locke collected are Bodleian MS Locke b.4 fos. 86r–108v.
40. Polwarth to Johnston, 15 March 1697, NAS MS GD158/964, fos 171–2.
41. Johnston to Polwarth, 17 March 1697, HMC, *Roxburghe*, p. 131.
42. Johnston to Polwarth, 1 April 1697, HMC, *Roxburghe*, p. 132.
43. Johnston to Locke, 20 March 1697, in De Beer (ed.), *Correspondence of John Locke*, vi, pp. 56–7.
44. NAS MS SP4/18, fos 361–2.
45. *Memoirs of the Secret Services of John Macky*, p. 206. While Macky obviously respected Johnston, and praised his honesty, marginal notes attributed to Jonathan Swift in the BL copy of Macky's *Memoirs*

describe Johnston as 'a treacherous knave' and 'one of the greatest knaves even in Scotland'.
46. Yeoman, 'The Devil as Doctor: Witchcraft, Wodrow and the Wider World', p. 100; Louise Yeoman, 'Archie's Invisible Worlds Discovered: Spirituality, Madness and Johnston of Wariston's Family', *Records of the Scottish Church History Society*, 27 (1997), pp. 156–86, at pp. 169, 181.
47. Polwarth to Ogilvy, 18 June 1696, NAS MS GD158/964, fo. 27.
48. William K. Dickson (ed.), 'Letters to John MacKenzie of Delvine from the Rev. Alexander Monro, 1690–1698', *Scottish History Society Miscellany V* (Edinburgh: Scottish History Society, 1933), pp. 193–290, at p. 203.
49. NAS MS GD103/2/3/17/1. John Locke also acquired a copy of this letter – it is Bodleian MS Locke b.4, fos 107r–108v.
50. For a very thorough analysis of this debate, including its connections to Dutch thought, see John Marshall, *John Locke, Toleration and Early Enlightenment Culture* (Cambridge: Cambridge University Press, 2006), esp. part 3. Harley's papers contain two copies of Aikenhead's indictment, and single copies of his intellectual autobiography and the letter to his friends. All of these materials are said to be 'from James' – possibly Johnston. See BL Harleian MS 6846, fos 396r–401v.
51. [Matthew Tindal], *An Essay Concerning the Power of the Magistrate, and the Rights of Mankind, in Matters of Religion* (London, 1697), pp. 5–6.
52. John Edwards, *The Socinian Creed: Or, a Brief Account of the Professed Tenets and Doctrines of the Foreign and English Socinians ...* (London, 1697), preface.
53. Champion, *Republican Learning*, pp. 74–5.
54. Brown, *Letter in Answer*, p. 2.
55. Ibid. p. 168.
56. Ibid. pp. 170, 175.
57. Ibid. pp. 176, 209.
58. *Remarks on the Life of Mr Milton*, pp. 16–18.
59. Matthias Earbery, *Deism Examined and Confuted, In an Answer to a Book intitled Tractatus Theologico Politicus* (London, 1697), 'to the reader'.
60. Ibid. pp. 1–3.
61. MacDonald, '*Fearefull Estate of Francis Spira*', pp. 43–4.
62. Jean Gailhard, *The Blasphemous Socinian Heresie Disproved and Confuted* (London, 1697), unpaginated preface.
63. Ibid., unpaginated 'Epistle Dedicatory'. The two executed were Bartholomew Legate and Edward Wightman, burned at Smithfield (London) and Lichfield, respectively. See Levy, *Blasphemy*, pp. 96–9.
64. Berry, *Gender, Society and Print Culture*, pp. 30–4; David Hayton,

'Moral Reform and Country Politics in the Late Seventeenth-Century House of Commons', *Past and Present*, 128 (August 1990), pp. 48–91, at pp. 53–4.
65. *Calendar of State Papers Domestic Series, of the Reign of William and Mary*, 11 vols (London: HMSO, 1895–1937), ix, p. 107.
66. Charles Lidgould, *A Sermon Preach'd in the Cathedral-church at Ely … on occasion of His Majesty's Proclamation against Atheism, and Profaneness, etc.* (London, 1699), p. 18.
67. Ibid. pp. 3–4.
68. Ibid. pp. 11, 14.
69. Hayton, 'Moral Reform and Country Politics', p. 55.
70. Danby Pickering (ed.), *The Statutes at Large, From Magna Charta to 1761*, 24 vols (London, 1762–9), x, pp. 177–8; *Votes of the House of Commons*, 80 (15 March 1698), 88 (24 March 1698), 93 (30 March 1698); *Journals of the House of Commons* (London, 1803), xii, pp. 147, 154–5, 160, 168–9, 177, 183; *Journals of the House of Lords* (London, 1774), xvi, pp. 217–18, 220.
71. *Remarks on the Life of Dr Milton*, p. 50.
72. [William Carstares], *The Scottish Toleration Argued* (London, 1712), pp. 3, 22. For the ultimate repeal of the blasphemy statutes, see Henry L. Brown, 'The Old Scots Law of Blasphemy', *Juridical Review*, 30 (1918), pp. 56–68, at p. 68.
73. Halyburton, *Natural Religion Insufficient*.
74. Ibid., title page and 'Index of Authors and Books quoted'.
75. Ibid., introduction, p. 25, main text, pp. 6, 31.
76. Ibid. pp. 119–121.
77. Ibid. pp. 123, 131.
78. *Memoirs of the Life of the Reverend Mr Thomas Halyburton*, unpaginated preface.
79. Lorimer, *Two Discourses*, p. iii.
80. Ibid. pp. iii, vii, 77–8.
81. Alexander Hamilton, *The History of the Ancient and Honorable Tuesday Club*, ed. Robert Micklus, 3 vols (Chapel Hill: University of North Carolina Press, 1990), i, pp. xxvi, 65.
82. David Hume, *Commentaries on the Law of Scotland Respecting the Description and Punishment of Crimes*, 2 vols (Edinburgh, 1797), ii, pp. 513–18.
83. Arnot, *Collection and Abridgement of Celebrated Criminal Trials in Scotland*, iii, p. 368. The first edition of this collection was published in 1785.

Conclusion

He was a young man, not far past twenty years old, living in the seventeenth century, a time when confessional orthodoxy was jealously guarded on that splintered sectarian landscape comprising western religion. Naturally curious and sceptical of received wisdom, he developed views that called into question the sacred truths held by his community, a community accustomed to defining itself in terms of its special relationship with God. This God was, among other things, the God of Moses, but he questioned whether Moses had really done the things attributed to him. He denied the existence of spirits. Other young men professing to be his closest friends pressed him to tell them his real views concerning Moses, Scripture and the Law. They told him he need not worry about what he said to them; they were grappling with their own doubts about these beliefs and traditions, and the discussion would help to enlighten them. They certainly would not report what he had said to others. They asked him to tell them what he thought about the traditional belief that the soul is immortal, and about the relationship between God and nature. He told them what he thought about these things, and they denounced him to the authorities. He was cast out, in a procedure that invoked the harshest judgment ever pronounced on a member of his community.

But that was not the story of Thomas Aikenhead, even though it sounds like it. Rather, it was the story of Baruch (or Benedict) Spinoza, excommunicated from the Portugese Jewish Community of Amsterdam in 1656 with 'the harshest writ of *cherem*' every employed there. The writ referred to his 'evil opinions and acts', and his 'abominable heresies', as well as his 'monstrous deeds', but was vague about what all these were.[1] Since his community did not control the legal system, the worst punishment it could impose was the *cherem* – a form of excommunication – which would have led to him being shunned by his coreligionists, or at least those who respected the ban. So he lived on to become one of the century's leading philosophers, writing works that rejected belief in the anthropomorphic Judaeo-Christian God in favour of a God 'identical with the active, generative aspects of nature'. This would not be a God who punishes or rewards, or who could be moved by prayer.[2] His writings also argued that

Moses, one of the most authoritative figures in the tradition into which he was born, could not have written the parts of the Hebrew Scriptures attributed to him. Both of these theories would appear in the statements attributed to Thomas Aikenhead.

It would be rash to argue that, had Aikenhead lived, he would have become a philosopher on a par with Spinoza; indeed, it is probably much more likely that he would have disappeared into obscurity and conventional Calvinism, perhaps later writing a spiritual autobiography in which he recalled (and lamented) his youthful flirtation with deism. Or, like his neighbour and kinsman-by-marriage Archibald Pitcairne, he might have remained suspicious of conventional belief, periodically tweaking the noses of Edinburgh's clergy with his irreverence.[3] But this was not to be; the timing of his brush with fame, in the crisis atmosphere of 1696, his lack of influential friends and the determination of authorities to demonstrate their own orthodoxy combined to usher him to the gallows. Mungo Craig warned that Aikenhead had vowed to write books against Christianity; James Stewart of Goodtrees and Patrick Hume of Polwarth wanted to make sure he did not get the chance. By doing this they could demonstrate the continued 'godliness' of their unstable coalition, and paint as an enemy of God anyone with the temerity to question their actions.

The determination of Scotland's rulers and ministers to see Aikenhead hang can be contrasted with the way the Spanish Inquisition – an institution notorious for its repressiveness and zealous protection of orthodoxy – handled the difficult case of Bartolomé Sánchez, a woolcarder from Cardenete, in the mountains of eastern Castile, who in the early 1550s started questioning the Trinity, suggesting that the Virgin Mary was herself divine, attacking the clergy and the Church, and eventually claiming that he himself was the 'Elijah-Messiah', sent by God because Jesus had failed. These were blasphemies on a par with those of Aikenhead, although they did not reject the conventional view of God as active in the world. While the Inquisition came close to having Sánchez burned alive, in the end it did not do so. Instead, its officials went to great lengths to demonstrate that the wool-carder was insane, in the face of his protests (and those of numerous witnesses) that he was not, and despite his repeated offences. Granted, it seemed unlikely that Sánchez would ever be able to increase his audience through the medium of print, but in his case and several similar instances, the Inquisition opted for leniency, choosing to err on the side of caution.[4] In contrast, there is no evidence that anyone involved in the Aikenhead case questioned his sanity, either as a way of explaining his statements, or as a way of mitigating his punishment. The regime that ruled Scotland in the 1690s was far too insecure for that. Unlike the authorities of sixteenth-century Spain, it knew that its hold on power and religious authority was tenuous, and chose to demonstrate both its power and its religious authority by hanging a scapegoat that nobody would be bold enough to defend. Even the argumentative Friulian miller and heresiarch Domenico Scandella, known as Menocchio, who developed an alternative cosmology and allegedly proclaimed that his calling was to blaspheme, was given two chances by the Inquisition before he was burned at the stake as a relapsed heretic in 1599.[5] The Roman and Spanish religious authorities could afford patience; they did not need to prove their legitimacy.

Interest in the Aikenhead case revived in the 1850s, when Thomas Babington Macaulay devoted several pages to it in his multi-volume *History of England*. With his classic Victorian belief in history as progress, Macaulay denounced Edinburgh's ministers as Aikenhead's 'murderers', and presented the hanging (and the simultaneous revival of the witch-hunt) as the last gasps of a kind of superstition that had chained the Scottish intellect through much of the early modern period. He saw a spark of something new in the vote by the Scots parliament in 1696 to establish a school in each parish, confidently asserting that 'before one generation had passed away, it began to be evident that the common people of Scotland were superior in intelligence to the common people of any other country in Europe'.[6] This led to an extensive debate in several periodicals, although the issue at hand was not the educational attainments of the Scots population. The Revd Thomas McCrie, a professor in the Presbyterian College in London (and son of the Edinburgh minister who had written biographies of John Knox and Andrew Melville), wrote an article in Edinburgh's *The Witness* that accused Macaulay of hating Scotland, despite his family roots in the Grampian region (and, it might be added, his trumpeting of the Scots educational system), and of unfairly presenting the Presbyterians who took the reins of Scottish government in 1689–90 as extremists. McCrie noted that the 1661 statute under which Aikenhead was executed was 'passed in the reign of the immaculate Charles II' (technically true, although it was merely a restatement of an Act passed by the Covenanter Parliament in 1649), and claimed that Scottish Catholic and Episcopalian regimes had been more repressive (debatable in that many of the religious dissidents prosecuted by those regimes had taken up arms against the state). The article was quickly republished as a pamphlet, reflecting the renewed public interest in the Aikenhead debate.[7]

McCrie's attack on Macaulay and defence of the Aikenhead prosecution drew a spirited response in a pamphlet by John Gordon, a Unitarian minister in Edinburgh. He protested that he would not even bring up the issue if not for 'the manner in which Mr Macaulay's narrative has been treated by an influential organ [i.e. *The Witness*] in the city where I reside'.[8] But he felt it was necessary because 'the interests of religious liberty are involved in the correction of that wrong'. His pamphlet had to be published in London, he said, because no Edinburgh publisher would take it on, claiming 'the prosecuting spirit which of old hung blasphemers, now displays itself in the more innocent form of terrifying booksellers'. For Gordon, like Macaulay, it was the ministers involved in the case (including Lorimer) who were most responsible for Aikenhead's death. Gordon was sceptical of Lorimer's claims that he and George Meldrum had sought clemency on Aikenhead's behalf, citing the published version of the sermon Lorimer gave in Edinburgh late in 1696, in which he warned that there were 'mouths open against Christ to dishonour him', including those who said that he was merely a man, or even 'a great imposter'. Lorimer had preached that this was blasphemy, and, in the latter case, blasphemy committed 'very spitefully and maliciously'. Gordon charged that this sermon contributed to the outcry against Aikenhead, and particularly to the capital charge that he had 'railed' against one of the persons of the Trinity.[9]

Just as Gordon found English publishers more open to his views than Scottish ones, he claimed (as did Macaulay) that English authorities would not have treated Aikenhead so harshly. He credited Aikenhead with 'considerable metaphysical talent', and confidently asserted (without any real evidence) that Locke would have interceded with William III to halt the execution had he known of it in time. 'The light [of toleration] which had pierced to the villages and hamlets of [England] had not touched either the heads or the hearts of the Christian teachers in this metropolis of Calvinistic Presbyterianism,' he argued, adding that even Oliver Cromwell had in 1655 prevented the execution of the socinian John Biddle for blasphemy.[10] He might have added to this Cromwell's intervention on behalf of the Quaker James Naylor, who had scandalised puritans in the English parliament in 1656 by re-enacting Christ's entry into Jerusalem, with female followers strewing palm fronds before him, and the English port of Bristol standing in for the Hebrew capital; thanks to Cromwell he was merely flogged and branded rather than executed.[11] The comparisons Gordon did make between Scots repression and English toleration earned him criticism in a later issue of *The Witness* for representing 'the anti-Evangelical, pro-Popery portion of the press'. That same (anonymous) writer blasted Hugo Arnot, who in 1785 had included, and lamented, the Aikenhead case in his collection of Scottish criminal trials, as 'that prince of infidel scoffers'.[12] The traditions of covenanted Presbyterianism still had great influence in many sectors of Scottish public opinion.

This debate quickly spilled into Edinburgh's newspapers. The *Scotsman* published a review of Gordon's book, lamenting

> at this day in Scotland, it is with shame and confusion of face that it must be owned that there are Presbyterians false enough to the name of Protestant … who hold that the murder of Thomas Aikenhead by the Edinburgh Clergy for religious error is a thing not to be rashly or severely condemned.

The anonymous reviewer praised Gordon, writing that he

> acts as a calm judge between Macaulay and the writer in *The Witness*, and finds the former convicted of having discharged the duty of an honest historian, and the latter guilty of stuffing history with falsehood in order to help the cause of priestcraft against religious liberty.[13]

A reader calling himself 'Ignotus' published a letter in the *Scotsman* on 5 April 1856, attacking *The Witness* as a publication that 'systematically befouls all those who argue for the truth of this matter – accusing them at one time of being infidels, at another of being Catholics. Those who read the *Scotsman* will not be misled by this atrocious one-sidedness'.[14] Gordon himself published a letter four days later that included material from a letter that someone calling himself 'A Presbyterian, But No Bigot' had written to him after seeing him lecture on the Aikenhead case. This correspondent had suggested that the Lord Advocate Stewart of Goodtrees was the real villain in the drama, while 'the clergy, at the very worst, were but the unconscious actors in the Lord Advocate's abominable tragedy'. He also pointed to the English witch-hunt to suggest that Gordon might have overestimated the tolerance of the southern kingdom. In response, Gordon opined that, while it was impossible to tell if the ministers of Edinburgh had been those who first demanded Aikenhead's execution, at a minimum it was clear that they did little, if anything, to prevent it.[15] At about the same time, a writer in London's *Saturday Review* blasted McCrie's pamphlet, wondering 'what human being but a stay-at-home Scotchman [*sic* – although McCrie worked in London] could have conceived and written bulky pamphlets to establish the extraordinary notion that Mr Macaulay has, in his "History", done wilful injustice to Scotland?' With perhaps too much confidence that the matter was settled, the writer suggested that Macaulay was no more condemnatory of Scottish bigotry than he was of any other kind, and added that 'we are glad to find that this last attack has provoked a reply from another Scotchman, and that an able pamphlet by Mr Gordon has at least settled the question of fact as to the conduct of the clergy'.[16] Clearly the perception of a tolerant, enlightened England in contrast to a narrow-minded Scottish theocracy still held sway in some quarters.

Anyone who has read newspapers or followed other media in recent years has probably noticed that, while the Aikenhead case seems nearly forgotten, blasphemy has resurfaced as an issue with global repercussions. In May 1989, a group of United States senators, led by Alphonse D'Amato of New York and Jesse Helms of North Carolina, protested that financial support from the National Endowment of the Arts had aided the artist Andres Serrano in the display of 'Piss Christ', a photograph of a crucifix submerged in Serrano's urine. Despite the fact that taxpayer funding for the work was indirect (the work won an award from an NEA-supported regional arts competition), Helms took to the Senate floor to denounce 'the blasphemy of the so-called artwork', and warned 'do not dishonor our Lord. I resent it and I think the vast majority of the American people do'.[17] The stakes here were much lower than they were for Thomas Aikenhead, though; the result was increased scrutiny for the NEA. Much more dangerous was the predicament of the Indian-born British author Salman Rushdie, whose novel *The Satanic Verses*, while winning the Whitbread Prize in 1988, earned its author the execration of Muslim authorities worldwide, who condemned him for blasphemously presenting words attributed to God in the Qur'ān as actually being those of the Prophet Muhammad or even Satan instead. Rushdie went into hiding after the Iranian government put a price on his head, but the global furor cost an estimated twenty-two deaths from rioting and other acts. While Christian religious leaders, including the Archbishop of Canterbury, condemned the book for its disrespect to Islam, the British government, then under the leadership of Margaret Thatcher and the Conservative Party, resisted efforts to ban sales of the book or to revive the law of blasphemy and extend it to cover offences against non-Christian religions.[18]

The governments holding jurisdiction in the Serrano and Rushdie cases (the United States and the United Kingdom, respectively) took no punitive actions against the artists or their works. Similarly, the publication of cartoons that allegedly denigrated the Prophet Muhammad by the Danish newspaper *Jyllands-Posten* in September 2005 aroused a storm of protest in the Islamic world, leading to many deaths and attacks on the Norwegian and Danish embassies in Syria. While many Muslim groups denounced the cartoons as blasphemous, Danish authorities concluded that their publication was not a criminal offence, and the ensuing controversy highlighted the divide between the claims of free expression versus those insisting that religious views not be offended. On the other hand, governments in Muslim countries have seen it as part of their duty to ensure that certain forms of Islam, as well as its symbols, be protected by the laws

Conclusion 161

of blasphemy. Thus Iranian judges sentenced Hashem Aghajari to death for blasphemy in 2002 (for claiming that the Qur'ān should be subject to modern interpretation), a sentence later commuted to imprisonment. In that case, the Iranian government, like Scottish authorities in 1696–7, sought to affirm its legitimacy by the harshest enforcement of orthodoxy. A government that views its duty as the maintenance of a revolutionary religious legacy will do such things, particularly if it feels threatened.

But blasphemy can also be the result of severe cultural misunderstanding; as this conclusion was being written, crowds in Khartoum demanded that a British teacher in a school there, Gillian Gibbons, be put to death for allowing her seven-year-old students to name a teddy bear 'Muhammad'. A Sudanese court had sentenced her to fifteen days' imprisonment for the offence, but rioters demanded harsher retribution. In the end, she was returned to the United Kingdom, shaken but unharmed. Aikenhead, Serrano, Rushdie, and Aghajari all came of age within the religious cultures they were accused of offending, and all doubtless knew that their views or works would be controversial, at least. This was not so in the Sudanese case, in which news reports portrayed Gillian Gibbons as honestly shocked by the uproar her action had caused. Muslim leaders in Britain also questioned the harshness of the sentence, suggesting that she had simply made a mistake. Surely all would be better off in a world of faiths that see God as strong enough to withstand insult, whether intentional or not, without humans (or their governments) taking up arms to help out.

NOTES

1. For Spinoza, I have relied heavily on Steven Nadler, *Spinoza's Heresy: Immortality and the Jewish Mind* (Oxford: Clarendon Press, 2001). The quoted passages are on pp. 2–3.
2. Ibid. p. 32.
3. James Webster accused Picairne of atheism, to no avail, in 1712. See Wodrow, *Analecta*, iii, p. 307.
4. Sara T. Nalle, *Mad for God: Bartolomé Sánchez, the Secret Messiah of Cardenete* (Charlottesville: University Press of Virginia, 2001).
5. Ginzburg, *The Cheese and the Worms*.
6. Macaulay, *History of England*, iii, pp. 507–10.
7. [Revd Dr McCrie], *Macaulay on Scotland*, from *The Witness* (13 February 1856), pp. 5–11, 21.
8. John Gordon, *Thomas Aikenhead: An Historical Review* (London: Edward Whitfield, 1856), p. 1.
9. Ibid. pp. 6, 21–3, 32, citing Lorimer, *Two Discourses*, p. 75.

10. Gordon, *Thomas Aikenhead*, pp. 24, 28–30.
11. Christopher Hill, *The World Turned Upside Down: Radical Ideas during the English Revolution* (London: Maurice Temple Smith, 1972), p. 249.
12. 'Mr Macaulay and the Case of Thomas Aikenhead', *The Witness*, 5 April 1856.
13. *Scotsman*, undated clipping included in NLS copy of Gordon, *Thomas Aikenhead*.
14. *Scotsman*, 5 April 1856.
15. *Scotsman*, 9 April 1856.
16. *Saturday Review*, undated clipping, probably 1856, from NLS copy of Gordon, *Thomas Aikenhead*.
17. *Congressional Record: Senate*, 18 May 1989.
18. Levy, *Blasphemy*, pp. 558–64.

Bibliography of Works Cited

MANUSCRIPT SOURCES

Edinburgh

Edinburgh City Archives
Burgh Court Register of Decreets, vol. 48 (2 January–31 December 1696)
Moses Bundle 93
Moses Bundle 108
SL1/1/34 – Burgh Council Minute Book, 1 January 1692–27 April 1694
SL1/1/35 – Burgh Council Minute Book, 2 May 1694–5 October 1697

Edinburgh University Library
Da.1.18 – Catalogus Bibliothecae Publicae Academiae Jacobi Regis Edinburgenae
Da.1.30/5 – Deed of Gift of James Wallace, Baxter in Edinburgh, of 200 vols
Da.1.32 – Magistrand Graduation Receipts and Disbursements, 1627–96
Da.1.33 – Matriculation Receipts and Disbursements, 1653–95
Da.1.34 – Library Accessions Book, 1693–1719
Matriculation Roll Transcripts: Arts, Law, Divinity, 1623–1751

National Archives of Scotland, Register House and West Register House
CC8/2/93 – Commissariat of Edinburgh, Register of Acts and Decreets, January 1696–April 1697
CC8/8/77 – Edinburgh Register of Testaments, 1681–5
CH1/2/2a – Minutes of Old and New Kirks, Edinburgh
CH2/131/1 – Minutes, Edinburgh General Kirk Session, 1657–99
CH2/140/2 – Tolbooth Kirk Session Register, 1689–1863
CH2/141/5 – Trinity College Kirk Session Register, 1685–1700
CH12/16/25 – 'The Assemblie, or the Scottish Reformation, A Comedie'
E70/4/7 – Poll Tax Register for Tron Parish, 1694
GD26/13/99 – Letters from Sir James Ogilvy to the Earl of Melville, 1696–8
GD103/2/3/17/1 – Robert Wylie Letter (Society of Antiquaries Collection)
GD18/2090 – Notebook of Sir John Clerk, 1676–1722
GD18/2092/1 – Sir John Clerk of Penicuik's Spiritual Journal, 1692–8
GD18/2093 – Clerk of Penicuik's Covenant with God

GD158/560 – Lord Jedburgh's Vision of Angels, Including Gabriel
GD158/964 – Letter Book of Patrick Hume, Lord Polwarth, 1696–8
GD158/1097 – Letters from Robert Pringle to Sir Patrick Hume of Polwarth
GD158/1103 – Letters from the Earl of Tullibardine to Sir Patrick Hume of Polwarth
GD158/1570 – Religious Meditations of Patrick Hume, Lord Polwarth
GD18/3994 – Clerk of Penicuik's Notes on Sermons and Religious Meditations
GD406/1/4204 – David Crawford to the Earl of Arran, 9 January 1697
JC2/15 – Justiciary Court Book of Adjournal, 3 June 1678–4 July 1682
JC6/10 – Justiciary Court Minute Book, 27 November 1677–10 April 1682
JC6/14 – Justiciary Court Minute Book, 3 July 1693–25 July 1701
JC26/78/1/1–14 – Justiciary Court Process Papers, Aikenhead Case
PA7/15 – Minutes of Parliament's Security Committee, May–June 1695
PA10/2 – Parliamentary Visitation of Universities, 1690–1702
PA10/4 – Parliamentary Visitation of Edinburgh University, 1690–9
PC1/50 – Privy Council Register of Acts, 4 September 1694–3 September 1696
PC1/51 – Privy Council Register of Acts, 4 September 1696–11 July 1699
PC2/26 – Privy Council Register of Decreets, 6 August 1695–6 July 1697
PC4/2 – Privy Council Minute Book, 2 January 1696–28 December 1699
PC12/16 – Miscellaneous Privy Council Papers, 1696
PC13/2 – Privy Council Proclamations, 1690–6
RD4/82–83 – Register of Deeds, 1698
SP3/1 – James Johnston's Letter Book, 1692–4
SP4/18 – Warrant Book of the Scottish Secretary, 1695–8

National Library of Scotland
1393 – Delvine Papers
7018 – Letters to John, First Marquess of Tweeddale, January–August 1695
7019 – Letters to John, First Marquess of Tweeddale, September–December 1695
7020 – Letters to John, First Marquess of Tweeddale, 1696–9
7029 – Letters of John, First Marquess of Tweeddale, November 1694–December 1695
7030 – Letters of John, First Marquess of Tweeddale, December 1695–May 1696
14408 – Letters of James Johnston to the First Marquess of Tweeddale, 1690–6
14410 – Miscellaneous Tweeddale Papers
14413 – Family Correspondence, Yester Manuscripts
14593 – Marquis of Tweeddale's Register Book, January 1677–December 1695
20492 – 'Account of the Four Generall Religions in the World …'
H.23.a.16 – 'Pitcairne Collection'
Wodrow Folio XXXIX
Wodrow Quarto XXX

Registrar General's Office, New Register House
OPR 685.1/6 – Edinburgh Baptisms, 1657–68
OPR 685.1/7 – Edinburgh Baptisms, 1669–75
OPR 685.1/8 – Edinburgh Baptisms, 1675–80
OPR 685.1/44 – Edinburgh Marriages, 1649–94

London

British Library
Harleian MS 6846

Oxford

Bodleian Library
Ballard V
Locke b.4
Locke f.10 – John Locke's Journal, 1689–1704

NEWSPAPERS

Flying Post (London)
Post Boy (London)
Post Man (London)
Protestant Mercury (London)
Scotsman (Edinburgh)
Votes of the House of Commons (London)

OTHER PRINTED PRIMARY SOURCES

Acts of the Parliaments of Scotland, 1124–1707, 12 vols (London: HMSO, 1814–75).

Aldis, H. G., *A List of Books Printed in Scotland to 1700*, 2nd edn (Edinburgh: National Library of Scotland, 1970).

An Account of the Last Words of Christian Kerr (Edinburgh, 1702).

An Almanack and New Prognistication for the Year of Our Lord, 1696 ... Exactly Calculated for the Famous City of Edinburgh, by G.C., Mathema[ticus] (Edinburgh: Heirs of Andrew Anderson, 1696).

Anstruther, Sir William, *Essays Moral and Divine* (Edinburgh, 1701).

Arnot, Hugo, *A Collection and Abridgement of Celebrated Criminal Trials in Scotland, 1536–1784* (Glasgow: Napier, [1785] 1812).

Balfour-Melville, E. W. M. (ed.), *An Account of the Proceedings of the Estates of Scotland, 1689–90*, 2 vols (Edinburgh: Scottish History Society, 1954–5).

Bibliotheca Balfouriana, sive Catalogus Librorum, In quavis Lingua & Facultate Insignium Illustris Viri D. Andreae Balfourii M.D. & Equitis Aurati (Edinburgh: Heirs of A. Anderson, 1695).

Blount, Charles, *The Miscellaneous Works of Charles Blount, esq.* ([London?], 1695).

Boston, Thomas, *Memoirs of the Life, Time and Writings of the Reverend and Learned Thomas Boston* (Edinburgh: Murray & Cochrane, 1776).

Brown, Peter, *A Letter in Answer to a Book Entitled Christianity not Mysterious* (Dublin, 1697).

Burnet, Gilbert, *History of his own Time*, 2 vols (London: Thomas Ward, 1724–34).

Burton, John (ed.), *The Darien Papers* (Edinburgh: Bannatyne Club, 1849).

Calendar of State Papers Domestic Series, of the Reign of William and Mary, 11 vols (London: HMSO, 1895–1937).

[Carstares, William], *The Scottish Toleration Argued* (London, 1712).

A Catalogue of the Graduates of the Faculties of Arts, Divinity, and Law, of the University of Edinburgh (Edinburgh: Neill & Co., 1858).

Catalogus Librorum Bibliothecae Iuris Utriusque, tam Civilis quam Canonici, Publici quam Privati ... A Facultate Advocatorum (Edinburgh: Mosman, 1692).

Cobbett, William and Howell, T. B. (eds), *A Complete Collection of State Trials*, 34 vols (London: Hansard, 1809–26).

Cowan, William (ed.), *A Journey to Edinburgh in Scotland by Joseph Taylor, Late of the Inner Temple* (Edinburgh: William Brown, 1903).

Cowan, William and Watson, Charles, *The Maps of Edinburgh: 1544–1929* (Edinburgh: Edinburgh Public Libraries, 1932).

Craig, Mungo, *A Lye Is No Scandal, Or a Vindication of Mr Mungo Craig from a Ridiculous Calumny Cast upon Him by T. A. Who was Executed for Apostacy at Edinburgh, the 8 of January, 1697* (Edinburgh[?], 1697).

Craig, Mungo, *A Satyr against Atheistical Deism, with the Genuine Character of a Deist* (Edinburgh: Robert Hutchison, 1696).

De Beer, E. S. (ed.), *The Correspondence of John Locke*, 8 vols (Oxford: Clarendon Press, 1976–89).

Dickson, William K. (ed.), 'Letters to John MacKenzie of Delvine from the Rev. Alexander Monro, 1690–1698', *Scottish History Society Miscellany V* (Edinburgh: Scottish History Society, 1933), pp. 193–290.

Donaldson, Gordon (ed.), *Scottish Historical Documents* (Edinburgh: Scottish Academic Press, 1970).

Dunton, John, *The Life and Errors of John Dunton, Citizen of London*, 2 vols (London: J. Nichols, 1818).

Earbery, Matthias, *Deism Examined and Confuted, In an Answer to a Book intitled Tractatus Theologico Politicus* (London, 1697).

Early Views and Maps of Edinburgh, 1544–1852 (Edinburgh: Royal Scottish Geographical Society, 1919).

Edwards, John, *The Socinian Creed: Or, a Brief Account of the Professed Tenets and Doctrines of the Foreign and English Socinians* ... (London, 1697).

[Erskine, James, Lord Grange], *Extracts from the Diary of a Senator of the College of Justice* (Edinburgh: Thomas Stevenson, 1843).

Fairly, John A. (ed.), 'The Old Tolbooth: Extracts from the Original Records', *Book of the Old Edinburgh Club*, 11 (1922), pp. 21–73.

Forbes, William, *The Institutes of the Laws of Scotland*, 2 vols (Edinburgh, 1722–30).

Gailhard, Jean, *The Blasphemous Socinian Heresie Disproved and Confuted* (London, 1697).

[Grant, Sir Francis], *A Letter from a Magistrate in the Countrey to his Friend* (Edinburgh, 1701).

[Grant, Sir Francis], *A True Narrative of the Sufferings and Relief of a Young Girle Strangely Molested, by Evil Spirits and their Intsruments* [sic] *in the West* (Edinburgh, 1698).

[Grant, Sir Francis], *Sadducismus Debellatus, or, A True Narrative of the Sorceries and Witchcrafts Exercis'd by the Devil and his Instruments upon Mrs Christian Shaw* (London, 1698).

Grant, James (ed.), *Seafield Correspondence, 1685–1708* (Edinburgh: Scottish History Society, 1912).

Halyburton, Thomas, *Natural Religion Insufficient and Reveal'd Necessary to Man's Happiness In His Present State* (Edinburgh: Heirs of Andrew Anderson, 1714).

Hamilton, Alexander, *The History of the Ancient and Honorable Tuesday Club*, ed. Robert Micklus, 3 vols (Chapel Hill: University of North Carolina Press, 1990).

Historical Manuscripts Commission, Fourteenth Report, Appendix, Part III, Manuscripts of the Duke of Roxburghe (London: HMSO, 1894).

Historical Manuscripts Commission, Fifteenth Report, Appendix, Part IX: The Manuscripts of J. J. Hope Johnstone, esq. Of Annandale (London: HMSO, 1897).

Historical Manuscripts Commission, Supplementary Report on the Manuscripts of the Duke of Hamilton (London: HMSO, 1932).

The Humble Representation of the Ministers from the Synods and Presbytries of this Church, Met at Edinburgh, May 30 1695 Years (Edinburgh, 1695).

Hume, David, *Commentaries on the Law of Scotland Respecting the Description and Punishment of Crimes*, 2 vols (Edinburgh, 1797).

Johnston, W. T. (ed.), *The Best of Our Owne: Letters of Archibald Pitcairne, 1652–1713* (Edinburgh: Saorsa, 1979).

Journals of the House of Commons.

Journals of the House of Lords.

Kelsall, Helen and Kelsall, Keith (eds), *An Album of Scottish Families 1694–96, Being the First Installment of George Home's Diary* (Aberdeen: Aberdeen University Press, 1990).

Laing, David (ed.), *Historical Notices of Scottish Affairs Selected from the Manuscripts of Sir John Lauder of Fountainhall*, 2 vols (Edinburgh Bannatyne Club, 1848).
[Leslie, Charles], *The Charge of Socinianism against Dr Tillotson Considered* (Edinburgh, 1695).
Lidgould, Charles, *A Sermon Preach'd in the Cathedral-church at Ely ... on occasion of His Majesty's Proclamation against Atheism, and Profaneness, etc.* (London, 1699).
Lorimer, William, *Two Discourses: The One Setting forth The True and only way of Attaining Salvation. The Other shewing why and How all ought to Reverence Jesus Christ, the Son of God and Saviour of Men* (London: John Lawrence, 1713).
MacKenzie, George, *The Laws and Customs of Scotland in Matters Criminal* (Edinburgh: Thomas Brown, 1678).
McCormick, Joseph (ed.), *State Papers and Letters Addressed to William Carstares* (Edinburgh: John Balfour, 1774).
Memoirs of the Life of the Reverend Mr Thomas Halyburton, 2nd edn (Edinburgh: Heirs of Andrew Anderson, 1715).
Memoirs of the Public Life of Mr James Hogg (Edinburgh, 1798).
Memoirs of the Secret Services of John Macky, esq. (London, 1733).
Memoirs, or Spiritual Exercises of Elisabeth West (Edinburgh: Ogle & Aikman, 1807).
Memoirs or Spiritual Exercises of Mistress Ross (Edinburgh, 1735).
[Morer, Thomas], *A Short Account of Scotland* (London, 1702).
Paton, Henry (ed.), *Register of Interments in the Greyfriars Burying Ground, Edinburgh, 1658–1700* (Edinburgh: Scottish Record Society, 1902.
Paton, Henry (ed.), *Register of Marriages for the Parish of Edinburgh, 1595–1700* (Edinburgh: Scottish Record Society, 1905).
Paul, Robert (ed.), 'The Diary of George Turnbull, Minister of Alloa and Tyningham, 1657–1704', *Scottish History Society Miscellany*, 1 (Edinburgh: Scottish History Society, 1893), pp. 295–445.
Pickering, Danby (ed.), *The Statutes at Large, from Magna Charta to 1761*, 24 vols (London, 1762–9).
Pinkerton, John M. (ed.), *The Minute Book of the Faculty of Advocates, 1661–1712* (Edinburgh: Stair Society, 1976).
[Pitcairne, Archibald], *A Modest Examination of a Late Pamphlet Entituled Apollo Mathematicus* ([Edinburgh?]: [Watson?], 1696).
Pitcairn, Thomas (ed.), *Acts of the General Assembly of the Church of Scotland, 1638–1842*, 2 vols (Edinburgh: Ritchie, 1843).
Register of the Privy Council of Scotland, third series, 16 vols (Edinburgh: HM General Register House, 1908–).
Remarks on the Life of Mr Milton, as Published by J.T. (London, 1699).
[Ridpath, George], *The Scots Episcopal Innocence* (London, 1694).

Scott, Hew (ed.), *Fasti Ecclesiae Scoticanae*, 9 vols (Edinburgh: Oliver & Boyd, 1915–51).
Scott-Moncrieff, Robert (ed.), *The Household Book of Lady Grisell Baillie, 1692–1733* (Edinburgh: Scottish History Society, 1911).
Scott-Moncrieff, W. G., (ed.), *Narrative of Mr James Nimmo, 1654–1709* (Edinburgh: Scottish History Society, 1889).
Selections from the Family Papers Preserved at Caldwell, 3 vols (Glasgow: Maitland Club, 1854).
Simon, Richard, *Critical Enquiries into the Various Editions of the Bible* (London, 1684).
Telfair, Alexander, *A True Relation of an Apparition, Expressions and Actings of a Spirit, Which Infested the House of Andrew MacKie in Ring-croft of Stocking* (Edinburgh: George Mosman, 1696).
[Tindal, Matthew], *An Essay Concerning the Power of the Magistrate, and the Rights of Mankind, in Matters of Religion* (London, 1697).
To the Memory of the very Reverend and Truly Pious Mr George Meldrum (Edinburgh, 1709).
Toland, John, *Christianity Not Mysterious: Or, a Treatise Showing that There is Nothing in the Gospel Contrary to Reason nor Above it, and that No Christian Doctrine Can Properly be Called a Mystery* (London, 1696).
Toland, John, *A Collection of Several Pieces of Mr John Toland*, 2 vols (London: J. Peele, 1726).
Townley, Maureen (ed.), *The Best and Fynest Lawers and Other Raire Bookes: A Facsimile of the Earliest List of Books in the Advocates' Library, Edinburgh* (Edinburgh: Edinburgh Bibliographical Society, 1990).
Tweedie, W. K. (ed.), *Select Biographies*, 2 vols (Edinburgh: Wodrow Society, 1845–7).
A Vindication of Our Blessed Saviours Genealogy from the Cavils of Antiscripturalists and the accounts that two Evangelists give of it; set in so clear a Light, as may at once satisfy the well meaning Seeker, and Silence the Irreligious Disputant (Edinburgh: Heirs of Andrew Anderson, 1696).
Watson, Charles B. (ed.), *Roll of Edinburgh Burgesses and Guild Brethren, 1406–1700* (Edinburgh: Scottish Record Society, 1929).
Webster, James, *An Essay upon Toleration* (Edinburgh, 1703).
Weitzman, Arthur, (ed.), *Letters Writ by a Turkish Spy* (New York: Columbia University Press, 1970).
Williamson, David, *A Sermon Preached in the High Church of Edinburgh, June 9th 1695* (Edinburgh: George Mosman, 1696).
Wodrow, Robert, *Analecta: Or Materials for a History of Remarkable Providences*, 4 vols (Edinburgh: Maitland Club, 1842–3).
Wood, Marguerite (ed.), *Edinburgh Poll Tax Returns for 1694* (Edinburgh: Scottish Record Society, 1951).

SECONDARY SOURCES

Allan, David, *Scotland in the Eighteenth Century: Union and Enlightenment* (Harlow: Longman, 2002).

Anderson, Robert, Lynch, Michael and Phillipson, Nicholas, *The University of Edinburgh: An Illustrated History* (Edinburgh: Edinburgh University Press, 2003).

Berry, Helen, *Gender, Society and Print Culture in Late-Stuart England: The Cultural World of the Athenian Mercury* (Aldershot: Ashgate, 2003).

Bevan, Jonquil, 'Seventeenth Century Students and their Books', in Gordon Donaldson (ed.), *Four Centuries: Edinburgh University Life, 1583–1983* (Edinburgh: Edinburgh University Press, 1983), pp. 16–27.

Bostridge, Ian, *Witchcraft and its Transformations, c. 1650–c. 1750* (Oxford: Clarendon Press, 1997).

Bowie, Karin, *Scottish Public Opinion and the Anglo-Scottish Union, 1699–1707* (Woodbridge: Boydell Press, 2007).

Broadie, Alexander, *The Scottish Enlightenment* (Edinburgh: Birlinn, 2001).

Brown, Henry L., 'The Old Scots Law of Blasphemy', *Juridical Review*, 30 (1918), pp. 56–68.

Brown, Keith, *Kingdom or Province? Scotland and the Regal Union, 1603–1715* (London: Macmillan, 1992).

Brunton, George, and Haig, David, *The Senators of the College of Justice* (Edinburgh: Clark, 1832).

Cameron, James, 'Scottish Calvinism and the Principle of Intolerance', in B. A. Gerrish and Robert Benedetto (eds), *Reformatio Perennis* (Pittsburgh: Pickwick Press, 1981), pp. 113–28.

Cameron, James, 'Theological Controversy: A Factor in the Origins of the Scottish Enlightenment', in R. H. Campbell and Andrew S. Skinner (eds), *The Origins and Nature of the Scottish Enlightenment* (Edinburgh: John Donald, 1982), pp. 116–30.

Cant, Ronald G., 'Origins of Enlightenment in Scotland: The Universities', in R. H. Campbell and Andrew S. Skinner (eds), *The Origins and Nature of the Scottish Enlightenment* (Edinburgh: John Donald, 1982), pp. 42–64.

Champion, Justin, *Republican Learning: John Toland and the Crisis of Christian Culture, 1696–1722* (Manchester: Manchester University Press, 2003).

Claydon, Tony, *William III and the Godly Reformation* (Cambridge: Cambridge University Press, 1996).

Cowan, Brian, *The Social Life of Coffee: The Emergence of the British Coffeehouse* (New Haven: Yale University Press, 2005).

Cowan, Ian, *The Scottish Covenanters, 1660–1688* (London: Gollancz, 1976).

Dalzel, Andrew, *History of the University of Edinburgh from its Foundation*, 2 vols (Edinburgh: Edmonston & Douglas, 1862).

Davidson, Neil, *Discovering the Scottish Revolution, 1692–1746* (London: Pluto Press, 2003).

Davie, George, *The Scottish Enlightenment* (London: Historical Association, 1981).
Davis, Natalie Zemon, *The Return of Martin Guerre* (Cambridge, MA: Harvard University Press, 1983).
De Beer, E. S., 'The English Newspapers from 1695 to 1702', in Ragnhild Hatton and J. S. Bromley (eds), *William III and Louis XIV* (Liverpool: Liverpool University Press, 1968), pp. 117–29.
Dingwall, Helen, *Late Seventeenth-Century Edinburgh: A Demographic Study* (Aldershot: Scholar, 1994).
Drummond, Andrew and Bulloch, James, *The Scottish Church 1688–1843: The Age of the Moderates* (Edinburgh: Saint Andrew Press, 1973).
Duncan, Douglas, *Thomas Ruddiman: A Study in Scottish Scholarship of the Early Eighteenth Century* (Edinburgh: Oliver & Boyd, 1965).
Dunlop, A. Ian, *William Carstares and the Kirk by Law Established* (Edinburgh: Saint Andrew Press, 1967).
Dunlop, A. Ian, *The Kirks of Edinburgh* (Edinburgh: Scottish Record Society, 1988).
Ellenzweig, Sarah, 'The Faith of Unbelief: Rochester's "Satyre", Deism, and Religious Freethinking in Seventeenth-Century England', *Journal of British Studies*, 44 (2005), pp. 27–45.
Fairley, John, 'The Old Tolbooth: With Extracts from the Original Records', *Book of the Old Edinburgh Club*, 4 (1911), pp. 75–144.
Ferguson, William, *Scotland: 1689 to the Present* (Edinburgh: Oliver & Boyd, 1968).
Foster, Walter R., *The Church before the Covenants: The Church of Scotland, 1596–1638* (Edinburgh: Scottish Academic Press, 1975).
Gatrell, V. A. C., *The Hanging Tree: Execution and the English People, 1770–1868* (Oxford: Oxford University Press, 1994).
Ginzburg, Carlo, *The Cheese and the Worms* (Baltimore: Johns Hopkins University Press, 1979).
Gordon, John, *Thomas Aikenhead: An Historical Review* (London: Edward Whitfield, 1856).
Graham, Michael F., 'The Civil Sword and the Scottish Kirk, 1560–1600', in W. Fred Graham (ed.), *Later Calvinism: An International Perspective* (Kirksville, MO: Thomas Jefferson University Press, 1994), pp. 237–48.
Graham, Michael F., *The Uses of Reform: 'Godly Discipline' and Popular Behavior in Scotland and Beyond, 1560–1610* (Leiden and New York: E. J. Brill, 1996).
Grant, James, *Old and New Edinburgh*, 3 vols (London: Cassell's, 1883).
Habermas, Jürgen, *The Structural Transformation of the Public Sphere* (Cambridge, MA: MIT Press, 1989).
Hannay, R. K., 'The Visitation of the College of Edinburgh in 1690', *Book of the Old Edinburgh Club*, 8 (1915), pp. 79–100.
Hayton, David, 'Moral Reform and Country Politics in the Late Seventeenth-

Century House of Commons', *Past and Present*, 128 (August 1990), pp. 48–91.

Herman, Arthur, *The Scottish Enlightenment: The Scots' Invention of the Modern World* (London: Fourth Estate, 2002).

Herrup, Cynthia, *A House in Gross Disorder: Sex, Law and the 2nd Earl of Castlehaven* (Oxford: Oxford University Press, 1999).

Hill, Christopher, *The World Turned Upside Down: Radical Ideas during the English Revolution* (London: Maurice Temple Smith, 1972).

Hopkins, Paul, *Glencoe and the End of the Highland War* (Edinburgh: John Donald, 1986).

Houston, R. A., *Social Change in the Age of the Enlightenment: Edinburgh, 1660–1760* (Oxford: Clarendon Press, 1994).

Hunter, Michael, 'The Problem of "Atheism" in Early Modern England', *Transactions of the Royal Historical Society* (5th series), 35 (1985), pp. 135–57.

Hunter, Michael, ' "Aikenhead the Atheist": The Context and Consequences of Articulate Irreligion in the Late Seventeenth Century', in Michael Hunter, *Science and the Shape of Orthodoxy: Intellectual Change in Late Seventeenth-Century Britain* (Woodbridge and Rochester, NY: Boydell, 1995), pp. 308–32.

Kerr, Henry, 'The Old Tolbooth of Edinburgh', *Book of the Old Edinburgh Club*, 14 (1925), pp. 7–24.

Levack, Brian, *The Witch-Hunt in Early Modern Europe*, 2nd edn (London: Longman, 1995).

Levy, Leonard, *Blasphemy: Verbal Offense against the Sacred from Moses to Salman Rushdie* (New York: Knopf, 1993).

Lund, Roger, 'Irony as Subversion: Thomas Woolston and the Crime of Wit', in Roger Lund (ed.), *The Margins of Orthodoxy: Heterodox Writing and Cultural Response, 1660–1750* (Cambridge: Cambridge University Press, 1995), pp. 170–94.

Lynch, Michael, *Edinburgh and the Reformation* (Edinburgh: John Donald, 1981).

Lynch, Michael, *Scotland: A New History* (London: Pimlico, 1992).

Macaulay, Thomas Babington, *The History of England from the Accession of James II*, 3 vols [1849–55] (London: J. M. Dent, 1905).

MacDonald, Alan, *The Jacobean Kirk, 1567–1625: Sovereignty, Polity, and Liturgy* (Aldershot: Ashgate, 1998).

MacDonald, Michael, '*The Fearefull Estate of Francis Spira*: Narrative, Identity and Emotion in Early Modern England', *Journal of British Studies*, 31 (1992), pp. 32–61.

MacInnes, Allan, *The British Revolution, 1629–1660* (New York: Palgrave Macmillan, 2005).

Makey, Walter, 'Edinburgh in Mid-Seventeenth Century', in Michael Lynch (ed.), *The Early Modern Town in Scotland* (London: Croom Helm, 1987), pp. 192–218.

Malcolm, Noel, *Aspects of Hobbes* (Oxford: Clarendon Press, 2002).

Mann, Alastair, *The Scottish Book Trade, 1500–1720: Print Commerce and Print Control in Early Modern Scotland* (East Linton: Tuckwell, 2000).

Marshall, John, *John Locke, Toleration and Early Enlightenment Culture* (Cambridge: Cambridge University Press, 2006).

Mitchison, Rosalind, *Lordship to Patronage: Scotland, 1603–1745* (Edinburgh: Edinburgh University Press, 1990).

Mullan, David, *Scottish Puritanism, 1590–1638* (Oxford: Oxford University Press, 2000).

Nadler, Steven, *Spinoza's Heresy: Immortality and the Jewish Mind* (Oxford: Clarendon Press, 2001).

Nalle, Sara T., *Mad for God: Bartolomé Sánchez, the Secret Messiah of Cardenete* (Charlottesville: University Press of Virginia, 2001).

Nash, David, *Blasphemy in the Christian World: A History* (Oxford: Oxford University Press, 2007).

Omond, George, *The Lord Advocates of Scotland*, 2 vols (Edinburgh: David Douglas, 1883).

Overell, M. A., 'The Exploitation of Francesco Spiera', *Sixteenth Century Journal*, 26 (1995), pp. 619–37.

Patrick, Derek, 'Unconventional Procedure: Scottish Electoral Politics after the Revolution', in Keith Brown and Alastair Mann (eds), *Parliament and Politics in Scotland, 1567–1707* (Edinburgh: Edinburgh University Press, 2005), pp. 208–44.

Riley, P. W. J., *King William and the Scottish Politicians* (Edinburgh: John Donald, 1979).

Rose, Craig, *England in the 1690s: Revolution, Religion and War* (Oxford: Blackwell, 1999).

Scally, John J., 'The Rise and Fall of the Covenanter Parliaments, 1639–51', in Keith M. Brown and Alastair J. Mann (eds), *Parliament and Politics in Scotland, 1567–1707* (Edinburgh: Edinburgh University Press, 2005), pp. 138–62.

Shepherd, Christine, 'Newtonianism in Scottish Universities in the Seventeenth Century', in R. H. Campbell and Andrew S. Skinner (eds), *The Origins and Nature of the Scottish Enlightenment* (Edinburgh: John Donald, 1982), pp. 65–85.

Shepherd, Christine, 'University Life in the Seventeenth Century', in Gordon Donaldson (ed.), *Four Centuries: Edinburgh University Life, 1583–1983* (Edinburgh: Edinburgh University Press, 1983), pp. 1–15.

Sher, Richard, *Church and University in the Scottish Enlightenment* (Princeton: Princeton University Press, 1985).

Smout, T. C., *A History of the Scottish People, 1560–1830* (Glasgow: William Collins, 1969).

Stevenson, David, *The Scottish Revolution, 1637–1644: The Triumph of the Covenanters* (Newton Abbot: David & Charles, 1973).

Stevenson, David, *Revolution and Counter-Revolution in Scotland, 1644–1651* (London: Royal Historical Society, 1977).
Stevenson, David, *The Origins of Freemasonry: Scotland's Century, 1590–1710* (Cambridge: Cambridge University Press, 1988).
Sullivan, Robert E., *John Toland and the Deist Controversy* (Cambridge, MA: Harvard University Press, 1982).
Todd, Margo, *The Culture of Protestantism in Early Modern Scotland* (New Haven: Yale University Press, 2002).
Treadwell, Michael, 'The Stationers and the Printing Acts at the End of the Seventeenth Century', in John Barnard and D. F. McKenzie (eds), *The Cambridge History of the Book in Britain*, vol. 4 (Cambridge: Cambridge University Press, 2002), pp. 755–76.
Warrick, John, *The Moderators of the Church of Scotland, 1690–1740* (Edinburgh: Oliphant, Anderson & Ferrer, 1913).
Wasser, Michael, 'The Western Witch-Hunt of 1697–1700: The Last Major Witch-Hunt in Scotland', in Julian Goodare (ed.), *The Scottish Witch-Hunt in Context* (Manchester: Manchester University Press, 2002), pp. 146–65.
Whatley, Christopher, *Scottish Society, 1707–1830: Beyond Jacobitism, towards Industrialisation* (Manchester: Manchester University Press, 2000).
Whyte, Ian D., *Scotland before the Industrial Revolution: An Economic and Social History, c. 1050–c. 1750* (New York: Longman, 1995).
Williamson, Arthur, *Scottish National Consciousness in the Age of James VI* (Edinburgh: John Donald, 1979).
Wooton, David, 'New Histories of Atheism', in Michael Hunter and David Wooton (eds), *Atheism from the Reformation to the Enlightenment* (Oxford: Oxford University Press, 1992), pp. 13–53.
Wrightson, Keith, *Earthly Necessities: Economic Lives in Early Modern Britain* (New Haven: Yale University Press, 2000).
Yeoman, Louise, 'Archie's Invisible Worlds Discovered: Spirituality, Madness and Johnston of Wariston's Family', *Records of the Scottish Church History Society*, 27 (1997), pp. 156–86.
Yeoman, Louise, 'The Devil as Doctor: Witchcraft, Wodrow and the Wider World', *Scottish Archives*, 1 (1995), pp. 93–105.

UNPUBLISHED THESES

Beisner, E. Calvin, 'His Majesty's Advocate: Sir James Stewart of Goodtrees (1635–1713) and Covenanter Resistance Theory under the Restoration Monarchy' (Ph.D. thesis, University of St Andrews, 2002).
Patrick, Derek J., 'People and Parliament in Scotland, 1689–1702' (Ph.D. thesis, University of St Andrews, 2002).
Shepherd, Christine, 'Philosophy in the Arts Curriculum of the Scottish Universities in the 17th Century' (Ph.D. thesis, University of Edinburgh, 1975).

Index

Aberdeen, 11, 16, 28
Aghajari, Hashem, 5, 161
Aikenhead, Alexander, 84, 87
Aikenhead, Anna, 84, 86, 101, 123
Aikenhead, James (father of
    Thomas), 83–5, 123
Aikenhead, James, commissary of
    Edinburgh, 84
Aikenhead, Jonet, 83–4
Aikenhead Katharine, 83–4, 86, 123
Aikenhead, Margaret, 83–4
Aikenhead, Sir Patrick, 86–7, 96, 101,
    123
Aikenhead, Thomas, 5, 14, 16, 22,
    25, 28, 34, 42, 47, 48, 54, 55,
    64, 69, 72–4, 80, 113–17, 122–3,
    126–44, 146–50, 155–61
  alleged beliefs, 81–2, 93–6, 103–6,
    108–11, 117–20
  education, 87–92
  execution, 1–4, 121–2
  family background, 83–7
  trial, 82, 92, 96, 100–13
Aikenhead, Thomas (grandfather of
    Thomas), 83
Aikenhead, Thomas (uncle of
    Thomas), 84, 86, 87
Amsterdam, 22, 69, 155
Anne, queen, 146
Anstruther, Sir William, 64, 114–15,
    132–3
Apollonius of Tyana, 69
Arian heresy, 46, 63
Aristotle, 87, 94, 147
Argyll, ninth Duke of, 22, 34

Argyll, tenth Duke of, 23
Arnauld, Antoine, 87
Arnot, Hugo, 150, 158
Arran, Earl of, 55, 122

Bacon, Nathaniel, 80
Baillie of Jerviswood, Robert, 21
Baldwin, Richard, 136
Balfour, Sir Andrew, 67–8
Biddle, John, 158
Blackness Castle, 22
Blair, David, 43
Blair, Hugh, 6
Blasphemy Act, England (1698), 143–6
Blasphemy Acts, Scotland (1649,
    1661, 1695), 36, 41–3, 46, 48,
    60–1, 63–4, 102, 106–7, 110–11,
    130, 137, 143, 146
Blount, Charles, 46, 61–3, 66–72, 90,
    91, 94, 118–19, 147
Borthwick, Francis, 36–7, 48
Borthwick, George, 85
Bostridge, Ian, 130
Bothwell, Bridge, Battle of (1679), 20
Boyle, Robert, 89
Brown, Adam, 112–13
Brown, Peter, 67, 140–1
Buchanan, George, 15, 89
Bunyan, John, 81
Burnet, Gilbert, bishop of Salisbury,
    40–1, 55, 59, 71
Burnet, Thomas, 68, 91

Calvin, John, 15, 89
Cameron, James, 47

Cameronians, 23
Campbell, Agnes (widow of Andrew Anderson), 89, 147–8
Campbell of Aberuchil, Colin, 100–1, 123
Canongate, 2, 12, 15, 24, 53, 58, 72, 74, 88
Carmichael, John, lord, 45
Carstares, William, 21–2, 35, 37, 38, 43–4, 57, 115, 146
Catholicism, 21, 24, 33, 38, 45, 65, 67, 76–7, 87–9, 157, 159
Charles I, 18–19
Charles II, 19–22, 24, 33, 89, 157
Clerk, George, 112–13
Clerk of Penicuik, Sir John, 2–3, 74, 121–2
Cockburn of Ormiston, Adam, 34, 38, 45, 56, 64, 73, 100–1, 116, 117
Compton, Henry, bishop of London, 145–6
Covenanters, 19–21, 23–5, 27–8, 33, 35–6, 38, 40, 64, 73, 100, 116, 148, 158
Craig, Mungo, 92–6, 104–8, 110–11, 113, 120, 122, 126–8, 133, 137, 142, 156
Crawford, David, 122
Crawford, Earl of, 14
Crawford, Hugh, 107
Crichton, William, 39, 116
Cromdale, Battle of (1690), 23
Cromwell, Oliver, 19, 158
Cunningham, Alexander, 26, 87–92, 107, 148
Cyrus, Emperor of Persia, 109

Dalkeith, 57
Dalrymple, Hew, 51
Dalrymple of Stair, James, 45
Dalrymple, Sir John, master of Stair, 35, 41, 44
D'Amato, Alphonse, 160
Darien project, 37, 41, 44, 54, 64, 73

Davis, Natalie Zemon, 5
De Fonvive, J., 136
deism, 6, 40, 46–8, 59, 62, 90, 92–3, 103, 116, 119, 131, 140, 142, 143, 147, 156
Descartes, René, 26, 68, 89, 91, 94, 142
Dickson, George, 96, 99, 107
Dublin, 26, 140
Dunton, John, 136–7

Earbery, Matthias, 142
Eckford, William, 107
Edinburgh, 10–17, 20, 22, 24, 25–8, 36, 53–5, 57–8, 61, 65, 67, 69, 95, 123, 127, 147, 149–50, 158–9
  burgh council, 11, 14, 15–17, 26, 55, 58, 89, 107, 128
  Castle, 2, 10, 11, 25
  College Kirk, 58
  Cowgate, 11, 107
  Faculty of Advocates library, 14, 68, 70, 91
  Grassmarket, 2, 11
  Greyfriars Parish and Kirk, 11, 15, 20, 84, 86
  New Kirk Parish, 15
  Old Kirk Parish, 15, 53
  population, 12, 14
  presbytery, 24, 64, 73
  St Giles' Kirk, 10, 14, 15–16, 26, 53, 82, 101, 114
  Tolbooth Parish and Kirk, 1, 15–16, 65, 101, 107, 112, 114, 133, 135
  tolbooth, 1, 4, 10, 64–5, 73, 74, 82–3, 86, 92, 95–6, 100, 108, 112, 113–14, 127, 129, 132, 149
  town college/university, 11–12, 14–15, 21, 25–7, 47, 48, 69, 71, 87–92, 127
  Tron Parish and Kirk, 1–2, 10–11, 14, 15–16, 26, 28, 47, 64, 84, 86, 109, 111
  West Kirk Parish, 39, 70
  West Port, 24

Edmonston, James, 84
Edmonstone, Elizabeth, 85
Edwards, John, 92, 140, 142
Elder, Jonet, 107
England, 4, 11, 18–19, 21–4, 27, 33–5, 45, 48, 54–6, 58, 66–7, 71–2, 75, 126, 130, 134–47, 158–9
Epicurus, 94
Episcopal Church (Scotland), 19–21, 23–4, 28, 33, 35, 37, 39–43, 56–7, 134, 157
Ezra, 6, 68, 81, 103, 108–9, 111

Ferguson, Robert, 65
Findlater, Alexander, 122
Flying Post, the, 14, 42, 71, 135, 136–7
Forbes, William, 132
France, 24, 34, 37, 54–6, 89, 130
Fraser, John, 60–5, 66, 68, 69, 70, 72–4, 81, 86, 90, 95, 100, 105, 106, 107, 113, 115, 118, 131, 135
Fraser, Robert, 64
Freemasonry, 27

Gailhard, Jean, 143
Gallowlee, 2–3, 113, 121, 123
Gassendus, Pierre, 142
Gibbons, Gillian, 161
Gibson, Edmund, 27
Gildon, Charles, 68
Ginzburg, Carlo, 5
Glasgow, 20, 66, 74
Glasgow Synod, 132
Glencoe massacre, 35, 40–2, 44
Gordon, Duke of, 25, 75
Gordon of Earlston, Alexander, 22
Gordon, John, 157–9
Graham, James, 111
Graham of Claverhouse, John, viscount Dundee, 23
Grant, Sir Francis, 131–3, 136, 143
Gray, Robert, 67

Gregory, David, 26, 27, 88–9, 90
Grierson, John, 112
Grotius, Hugo, 62, 70, 90, 95, 127

Halyburton, Thomas, 47, 79–81, 87, 88–9, 90, 92, 117, 147–8
Hamilton, Alexander, 149–50
Hamilton, George, 39
Hamilton of Pencaitland, James, 55
Hamilton, Janet, 22, 24–5
Hamilton of Halcraig, Sir John, 64
Harley, Sir Robert, earl of Oxford, 140, 153n
Harvie, James, 84
Helms, Jesse, 160
Henderson, Robert, 89, 107
Henry, Robert, 61–2
  wife of, 61–2
Hepburn of Blackcastle, Patrick, 84–6, 101
Hepburn, a 'hill preacher', 95
Herbert, Edward, baron of Cherbury, 62, 90
Heriot, George, 27
Herrup, Cynthia, 82
Hezekiah, 39
Hobbes, Thomas, 63, 68, 90–1, 94, 109, 142, 147–8
Hogg, James, 25, 91
Home, George, 12–13, 38, 40–1, 44–5, 53, 68–9
Hope of Rankeillor, Archibald, 73, 100–1, 114
Hume, David (philosopher), 6, 70
Hume, David (jurist), 150
Hume of Crossrig, David, 100–1
Hume of Polwarth, Sir Patrick, earl of Marchmont, 21–2, 25, 26, 45, 59, 64, 72, 74, 88, 102, 115–17, 130, 134–8, 149, 156
Hume, Patrick (solicitor), 72, 102, 106–7, 110, 136
Hunter, Michael, 4–5, 9, 32
Hutchison, Robert, 92–3, 95, 107, 127

Innes, Alexander, 60, 64–5, 68
Iran, 5, 161
Ireland, 18, 23, 55, 66, 105, 141
Irving, Dr, 85
Isaiah, 39
Islam, 68, 160–1

Jacobites, 23, 40, 56
James VI (Scotland) and I (England), 18
James VII (Scotland) and II (England), previously duke of York, 20–5, 28, 33, 34–5, 56, 88
Jesus, 6, 27, 36, 63, 69, 81, 103, 108–11, 113, 114, 117, 129, 136, 140, 149–50, 156
Johnston of Wariston, Archibald, 35, 138
Johnston, James, 35, 37–41, 43–5, 56, 59, 71, 101, 115, 137–9, 150, 152–3
Judaism, 36, 48
Jyllands-Posten, 160

Kennedy, Herbert, 26–7, 88–9
Khartoum, 161
Killecrankie, Battle of (1689), 23
Kinninmont of Kinninmont, Patrick, 129–30
Kirkton, James, 81
Knox, John, 10, 157

Laud, William, archbishop of Canterbury, 18
Lauder of Fountainhall, Sir John, 16, 64, 73, 100–1, 114–15
Lawson, George, 84
Leiden, University of, 26, 47
Leith, 2–3, 11, 54, 57, 113
Leslie, Charles, 71–2
Licensing Act (England), 66, 135, 144
Lidgould, Charles, 144–5
Little, Clement, 15

Locke, John, 45, 117, 137–8, 140, 147, 152n, 158
London, 6, 12, 14, 21, 42, 44, 46, 58, 66, 67, 69, 73, 91, 96, 105, 112, 114, 132, 134–9, 144, 157–9
London Gazette, the, 42, 135
Lorimer, William, 46–7, 73, 95–6, 104, 115, 122, 148–9, 158
Louis XIV, 24, 34
Lucretius, 62, 68
Luther, Martin, 15, 89

Macaulay, Thomas Babington, 4–5, 130, 157–9
MacDonalds of Glencoe, 35, 40–1
MacKenzie of Rosehaugh, Sir George, 36
Macky, John, 101, 152–3
McLean, William, 17
McCrie, Thomas, 157, 159
Malcolm, Noel, 6
Mann, Alastair, 69
Mary II, 23, 26, 33–4, 40
Maryland, 149
Melanchthon, Philip, 15, 89
Meldrum, George, minister of the Tron, 1, 16, 28, 39, 81, 115, 116, 121, 131, 132, 149, 158
Melville, Andrew, 157
Melville, Earl of, 34, 43, 74–5
Mennochio (Domenico Scandella), 5, 157
Menzies, William, 111
Mercer, Thomas, 96
Middleton, Patrick, 95, 108–10
Mitchell, Adam, 107–9
Moncrief, John, 58
Monmouth, Duke of, 20
Monro, Alexander, 25–6, 27, 88, 139
More, Henry, 95, 127
Morer, Thomas, 11–12
Moses, 6, 62, 81, 90, 98, 103, 108–9, 111, 143, 144, 155–6

Mosman, George, printer and bookseller, 14, 16, 70, 91–2, 112, 132
Muhammad, 81, 103, 109, 139, 160
Murray of Blackbarrony, Archibald, 64
Murray of Philiphaugh, Sir James, 64
Mylne, Robert, 11, 112

Nash, David, 36
National Endowment for the Arts (USA), 160
Naylor, James, 158
Netherlands, 21–2, 26, 34–5, 89, 101, 122
Newton, Isaac, 26, 89
Nicea, Council of, 63
Neilson, John, 108–10
Nimmo, James, 55

Ogilvy, Sir James, 45, 60, 74–5, 116, 134–7
Oswald, Alison, 107
Oswald of Eastbarns, David, 84
Oxford, 26, 27, 88, 135

Paisley, 54, 130, 138
Parliament, English, 19, 44, 56, 143–6, 158
Parliament, Irish, 66
Parliament, Scottish, 3, 5, 12, 16, 23–4, 25, 34, 36–44, 48, 58–60, 70, 72, 86, 102, 129, 143, 146, 157
Parliament, British (1707 and after), 146
Paterson, William, 84
Pentland Rising (1666), 35
Philipps, Sir John, 145
Pitcairne, Dr Archibald, 26–8, 47, 64, 67–8, 70, 84, 86, 88, 156
Portland, Willem de Bentinck, earl of, 34, 44
Post Boy, the, 42, 135–6

Post Man, the, 122, 135–6
Potter, John, 15, 107–8, 110
Pringle, John, 111
Pringle, Robert, 41
Privy Council (Scotland), 12, 16, 20, 22, 28, 34, 54–66, 68, 70, 72–5, 82, 85, 88, 90, 95, 96, 100, 101, 105, 113–17, 120, 129, 130, 131, 135–7
Protestant Mercury, the, 57, 66, 114, 135

Quakers, 21, 24, 33, 45, 158
Queensberry, Duke of, 43, 60, 64
Qur'ān, 5, 69, 90, 160, 161

Ramsey, Helen (mother of Thomas Aikenhead), 83–6, 96, 123
Ramsey, Thomas (uncle of Thomas Aikenhead), 85
Reformed Kirk (Scotland), 4, 16, 17–19, 28, 33, 35, 39, 48, 58, 70, 112, 139
  General Assembly of, 12, 16, 28, 35–8, 43, 45–6, 48, 57, 59, 60, 115, 116, 128
Ridpath, George, 42, 136–7
Roper, Abel, 136
Rosicrucianism, 27
Ross, Katherine, 20
Row, John, 89
Ruddiman, Thomas, 70
Rule, Gilbert, 12, 26, 65, 67, 74, 87, 89, 95, 104, 146
Rullion Green, Battle of (1666), 20
Rushdie, Salman, 160–1
Russell, William, lord, 21
Rye House Plot (1683), 21, 35, 116

St Andrews, 11, 20, 47, 79, 149
Sánchez, Bartholomé, 156
Scotsman, the, 159
Scott, James, 84
Scottish National Covenant (1638), 6, 18–19, 21, 22

Serrano, Andres, 160–1
Sharp, James, archbishop of St Andrews, 20
Shaw, Kristen, 130–2
Sidney, Algernon, 21
Simon, Richard, 68, 77, 90–1, 142
societies for the reformation of manners, 58, 132, 143–4, 145
Society for Promoting Christian Knowledge, 145
Solemn League and Covenant (1643), 24
Spanish Inquisition, 156–7
Spinoza, Baruch, 68, 90–1, 94, 109, 142, 147–8, 155–6
Spira, Francis, 80–1, 97n, 142
Stevenson, Dr Archibald, 84
Stevenson, David, 19
Stevenson, Elizabeth, 84
Stewart of Goodtrees, James, 22, 28, 34, 44–5, 64, 68, 72–3, 82, 101–2, 106–7, 110, 113, 115, 117, 129–30, 156, 159
Stewart, Jonet, 85
Stirling, James, minister in Glasgow, 16
Stirling Castle, 95
Strachan, John, 26, 27

Taylor, Joseph, 15–16, 17, 30
Telfair, Alexander, 47, 70–1
Tenison, Thomas, archbishop of Canterbury, 37, 71
Thatcher, Margaret, 160
Tilh, Arnaud du, 5
Tillotson, John, archbishop of Canterbury, 66, 71–2
Tindal, Matthew, 140
Toland, John, 27–8, 66–7, 70, 71, 91, 119, 136, 140–2, 143, 146
Toleration Act (1712), 146–7
Tranent, 57

Trinity, doctrine of the, 1, 6, 36, 46, 63, 66, 81, 90, 96, 102–4, 108–9, 111, 113, 119, 121, 134, 136, 141, 144–6, 156, 158
Tullibardine, John Murray, earl of (later marquis of Athol), 43, 45, 55–6, 59–60, 116, 134–7
Turnbull, George, 122
Tweeddale, John Hay, marquis of, 34, 37–45, 55, 59, 70, 86

Vanini, J. C., 67
Virginia, 57

Wallace, James, baxter, 15
Wasser, Michael, 130
Wardlaw, James, 112
Webster, James, minister of the Tolbooth, 1, 16, 17, 65, 67, 114–15, 121, 132, 133–4, 144
Weir, Thomas, 115
West, Elisabeth, 58, 80–1, 97, 121
Westminster Confession, 24
William I of Orange, 56
William II (Scotland) and III (England), also Dutch Stadholder, 21, 22–4, 26, 33–5, 37–8, 40–1, 53–4, 55–6, 86, 101, 144, 146, 158
Williamson, David, minister of West Kirk, 39–40, 70
Wilson, Thomas, 84
Witchcraft, 5, 9, 54, 128, 130–2, 138, 139, 157, 159
Witness, the, 157–9
Wodrow, Robert, 16, 26, 47, 121
Wolseley, Charles, 95, 127
Worcester, Battle of (1651), 19
Wylie, Robert, 4, 122, 139, 141

Yeoman, Louise, 79, 138

Zwingli, Ulrich, 15, 89

EU representative:
Easy Access System Europe
Mustamäe tee 50, 10621 Tallinn, Estonia
Gpsr.requests@easproject.com

www.ingramcontent.com/pod-product-compliance
Lightning Source LLC
Chambersburg PA
CBHW051645230426
43669CB00013B/2448